Encounters with Kenneth Burke

Encounters with
Kenneth Burke

• • •

William H. Rueckert

University of Illinois Press
Urbana and Chicago

Manufactured in the United States of America
1 2 3 4 5 C P 6 5 4 3 2

This book is printed on acid-free paper.

Library of Congress Cataloging-in-Publication Data

Rueckert, William H. (William Howe), 19260
Encounters with Kenneth Burke / William H. Rueckert.
p. cm.
Includes index.
ISBN 10: 0-252-02054-5 (cloth : acid-free paper). —
ISBN 10: 0-252-06350-3 (pbk. : acid-free paper)
ISBN 13: 978-0-252-02054-4 (cloth : acid-free paper). —
ISBN 13: 978-0-252-06350-3 (pbk. : acid-free paper)
1. Burke, Kenneth, 1897—Criticism and interpretation.
I. Title.
PS3503.U6134Z85 1994
818'.5209—dc20 93-15560
CIP

For Kenneth Burke

1897–1993

A monument of unaging intellect

Contents

Prefacc

. . .

My written encounters with Kenneth Burke can be divided into three stages: 1951–56, 1958–69, and 1977–91. Most of the material collected here is from stage 3, but a brief account of stages 1 and 2 will help to clarify the changes that have occurred in my encounters with Kenneth Burke since 1977 and will help to point out the coherence of the various pieces collected here.

My first serious encounter with Kenneth Burke took place in a graduate seminar in literary criticism at the University of Michigan. For reasons best known to himself, Norman Nelson suggested that I do my seminar paper on Kenneth Burke's literary theory and critical practice. *A Rhetoric of Motives* was just off the press. Burke was beginning to publish some of the major essays that would make up his dramatistic poetics, "A Symbolic of Motives." *A Grammar of Motives* had hardly been around long enough for critics to begin to figure out what it was all about. Undaunted by all of this, I took on Burke and did write my seminar paper on his literary criticism. It was the only essay I ever got an A+ on. All of the subsequent work I did was powerfully influenced by this initial emphasis on his literary criticism and critical practice.

I finished my doctoral dissertation on Kenneth Burke at the University of Michigan in the spring of 1956. Entitled "The Rhetoric of Rebirth: Kenneth Burke's Literary Theory and Critical Practice," its primary focus was Burke's theory of symbolic action as the key to his literary theory and critical practice. After the defense, I never looked at it again, though everything I did in stage 2 was a direct result of what I discovered in stage 1.

After three years (1954–57) of full-time apprentice teaching at Russell Sage College and Oberlin, I began my "serious" professional life at the University of Illinois at Urbana-Champaign in the fall of 1957. In the spring of 1958, I decided I would write my first book on Kenneth Burke. My dissertation was a hopeless stylistic embarrassment and I knew I could not go back to it except in a substantive way. So I began all over again, rereading everything, reading whatever I had not covered in the dissertation and whatever Burke had published since 1955. I conceived and wrote a completely "new" work. I meant to be thorough and intended to place the literary theory and critical practice within the context of dramatism and Burke's overall development up to the point when I was writing—that is, before logology. *Kenneth Burke and the Drama of Human Relations* was finally published in 1963, but it was finished and off seeking a publisher before *The Rhetoric of Religion* was published in 1961. Burke had pretty much finished his dramatistic poetics by the time I was writing and had worked out all of the main coordinates of dramatism as a system. It was clear by the time I wrote that Burke was not primarily a literary critic but a thinker who had a completely worked-out poetics to go along with his grammar and rhetoric as part of the larger, more comprehensive dramatistic theory of language that lay behind and encompassed all of his theorizing from 1941 on about the human and natural scenes and the drama of human relations. My emphasis was on his poetics and the place of literature and literary criticism in his development and upon the formidable methodology Burke had developed over the years for the analysis of language and verbal actions in general.

I suppose it was inevitable that having written what was essentially an expository study that lays out Burke's various positions and traces his development from *Counter-Statement* on without, however, either evaluating his work or trying to place it in any kind of context, I would next do a book like *Critical Responses to Kenneth Burke: 1924–1966,* which in fact does try to place him in terms of the intellectual history of his own time and does offer evaluations of his work by many different critics and scholars in a lot of different fields. The publication of *Critical Responses* in 1969 brought stage 2 to an end. It also marked a critical turning point in Burke's life, since it is the year Burke's second wife, Libbie, to whom the book is dedicated, died.

I gave two public talks about Burke during the last years of stage 2, both of which are included in this volume. The first, in 1965, was an application of Burke's basic critical methodology ("indexing") to President Kennedy's inaugural address and the second, in 1967, was a brief comparison between Burke's dramatistic literary theory and the Geneva School of criticism. Neither of these strays very far from the primary emphasis on Burke's poetics and critical methodology, which characterized all of my work on Burke from 1951 to 1969.

I did not write anything else about Burke until the fall of 1977, though I did keep up with what he was publishing and carried on a regular correspondence with him. I also taught him and directed dissertations at the University of Rochester that made use of him. Mostly what I did during these years was try to use some of what I had learned from Burke, both in the classroom and in the writing I was then doing on prose fiction. Burke in the classroom was always a great success; the same was not always true of the writing. I began and wrote hundreds of pages of a later abandoned study entitled "The Disguises of Fiction," which was an attempt to apply Burke's theory of literature as symbolic action to the works of Glenway Wescott, Katherine Anne Porter, James Gould Cozzens, and William Faulkner. My intention was to develop and apply a theory of symbolic autobiography. I abandoned this study for a variety of reasons: I kept encountering insoluble theoretical problems in my attempts to move back and forth from fiction to reality; I kept getting mired down in the detailed Burkean analyses of individual texts—e.g., Cozzens's *Castaway;* and, once I began to write about Faulkner, I realized that he was so much greater than these other fiction writers that I was probably wasting my time writing about them. So I began a book on Faulkner, which I did finish 550 pages later, and during the writing I learned a lot about how to apply Burke to the analysis of novels.

By 1969, so far as I was concerned, I was done writing about Burke, having been at him for eighteen years, and was ready to move on to other things. The book on Faulkner preoccupied me for many years because it underwent so many revisions in its futile search for a publisher. I also began writing essays, which I had not done before, in which I made use of Burke, without ever really dealing with him in a central way. Then two things happened that got me going on Burke again. Bob Zachary, who was largely responsible for making the University of California Press Burke's primary publisher, asked me to do a second edition of *Kenneth Burke and the Drama of Human Relations,* which, by the midseventies, was both out of print and out of date. After a certain amount of haggling, we agreed that I would bring the book up to date by writing an additional chapter, while the original book would be reprinted just as it was. I began work on this new chapter in 1977, which meant reading, rereading, and sorting out all that Burke had written and done since 1960. I wrote what is now chapter 6 of the second edition in the spring of 1978. The second edition was finally published by the University of California Press in 1982, twenty years after the first edition. By then, Burke had pretty much finished writing and publishing all of his major late essays and it was possible to interpret and evaluate his works in ways that were quite impossible back in 1960, when he was just finishing up the writing of *The Rhetoric of Religion.*

The second thing that happened that caused me to reimmerse myself in Burke was that someone asked me to give a talk on Burke at the 1977 meeting of the Modern Language Association in Chicago. A special session on Burke had been arranged and a book of essays was being planned. Ten years earlier I had spoken on Kenneth Burke and structuralism at another MLA meeting in Chicago. In 1985, I was to give my last MLA talk on Burke—also in Chicago—entitled "Criticism as a Way of Life." To prepare for this second MLA talk, I wrote "Some of the Many Kenneth Burkes" in the fall of 1977, part of which I read at the meeting. Burke was present at the meeting, sitting, as usual, in the front row. He had also been in Chicago earlier in the year, as a visitor at the National Humanities Institute at the University of Chicago, where I was spending the year as a fellow. He returned to Chicago in the spring of 1978 to give a series of talks at Northwestern University, which were arranged by his longtime admirer Leland Griffin. (It was Lee Griffin who arranged for me to give my first public talk on Burke in 1965, again in Chicago, where I did a Burkean reading of the rhetoric of President Kennedy's inaugural address.)

The year 1977–78 was Burkean and started me off on the third stage of my long series of encounters with Kenneth Burke. By 1978 I had been studying and writing about Burke for twenty-seven years. Burke was eighty-one years old and was completing his "summing up" essays. We had met many times and exchanged hundreds of letters. It was quite clear to me that I still had a lot to learn about and from Burke. What I began to do in 1977–78, and what I have continued to do in all the work undertaken since that time, was to reread and rethink Burke as a whole, getting away from—or perhaps beyond—the emphasis on his poetics and literary criticism that had characterized all of my earlier work on him and trying to discover what the larger, global, and universal aims of his work were. Burke has not written any literary criticism as such since 1966. By 1985, when he was eighty-eight, Burke had finished publishing significant new pieces of work and one got the sense that, though he always had "new" work in progress, his major works were all available to us and could be studied and evaluated with a certain amount of finality.

As some of the pieces in this collection will indicate, it was during the eighties that Burke was finally recognized and celebrated in a way that was commensurate with his achievements. This was in part due to his "discovery" by people in speech communications and by their widespread use of Burke to reinvigorate their discipline. They arranged two important national conferences on Burke and his work (in 1984 and 1990) and they were largely responsible for starting and sustaining the Kenneth Burke Society. The various regional chapters of the Speech Communications Association regularly feature sessions on Burke and usually manage to have him in attendance. Scholars in the discipline have published widely on Burke. One new book, *The Legacy of Kenneth Burke,* which came out of the 1984 conference of the same name, has been published and a second, *Extensions of the Burkeian System,* which came out of the 1990 conference, was published in 1993. A second national meeting of the Kenneth Burke Society was held in 1993.

But that was not all. Though Burke has not published a new book since 1969, when his *Collected Poems* came out, the University of California Press has republished or published new editions of his books so that, by 1984, when third editions, with long new afterwords, of *Permanence and Change* and *Attitudes toward History* came out, all of Burke's books were and have remained in print. In addition, new books (besides mine, in 1963, and those of Hugh Duncan and Armin Paul Frank in 1969) finally began to appear on Burke in the eighties. There was the second edition of my book in 1982; *Representing Kenneth Burke,* edited by Hayden White and Margaret Brose, in 1982; Frank Lentricchia's *Criticism and Social Change* in 1983; Robert Heath's *Realism and Relativism: A Perspective on Kenneth Burke* in 1986; Samuel B. Southwell's *Kenneth Burke and Martin Heideigger* in 1987; Greig Henderson's *Kenneth Burke: Literature and Language as Symbolic Action* in 1988; *The Legacy of Kenneth Burke,* edited by Trevor

Melia and Herbert W. Simons, in 1989. There was a special issue of *Pre/Text* (1985) devoted to Burke, and there was the wonderful selection from the Burke-Cowley letters, edited by Paul Jay (1988).

In addition to the two national conferences mentioned above, there was a third in the fall of 1986 at Seton Hall University, which was arranged by John Harrington and at which, in addition to myself, the following people spoke: J. Hillis Miller, Paul Jay, Howard Nemerov, Harold Bloom, Denis Donoghue, and Ralph Ellison. Unlike the two conferences arranged by the people in speech communications, the Seton Hall conference was devoted entirely to Burke the poet, novelist, and critic. In one way or another, I have been part of, and much of the work that I have done in stage 3 has been inspired by, this great upsurge of interest in Burke in the late seventies and beyond.

The notes for the pieces included in this collection provide brief explanations of how each came to be written and what I tried to accomplish in them. Most were written because someone asked me to give a talk or contribute an essay to a book on Burke, but some were done because there were things in Burke I wanted to write about before I was done with him—notably, "Kenneth Burke's Encounters with Walt Whitman" and "Symbolic Action in Kenneth Burke's Novel, *Towards a Better Life*."

I was always conscious when writing the different talks and essays collected here of not wanting to repeat what I had accomplished in my first book and, with each subsequent later encounter, of not wanting to repeat what I had accomplished in an earlier one. A certain amount of repetition was inevitable since I was covering and recovering the same body of material over and over again, but, as was always my practice, only after rereading the major texts. For example, "Some of the Many Kenneth Burkes" (1977), chapter 6 of the second edition of *Kenneth Burke and the Drama of Human Relations* (1982), "Rereading Kenneth Burke" (1984), and "A Field Guide to Kenneth Burke" (1990) represent successive attempts to rethink Burke's overall development and achievement. "Field Guide" is the culmination of this effort and represents what is probably my final view after forty years of reading, thinking, and writing about Burke. Other talks and essays have attempted different things: turning Burke on Burke through an analysis of his novel as symbolic action; examining his relationship to and his use of Walt Whitman, including his own Whitmanian poetry; his long involvement with technology, culminating in his view that our entelechy is technology;

his commitment to criticism as a way of life; some of the influences on him; his always fundamental ironic and optimistic practice of comic criticism; his late or post-1970 essays; and, recurrently, his refusal to collect and publish as a coherent book the essays from the fifties that make up his dramatistic poetics and his refusal (or failure) to collect and publish as a book the many fine and important essays written after 1969 so that the final phase of his long development could be readily studied and assessed.

I have never regretted my long involvement with Burke. His mind is much larger than mine and I have never returned to his works nor written about him another time without learning something new and valuable, either about him or for my own use. And, so far as I can tell, after all these years and all these encounters, there is always more to be learned.

Acknowledgments

Grateful acknowledgment is made to the University of California Press for permission to quote from the following works of Kenneth Burke: *Attitudes toward History,* third edition with a new afterword © 1984 The Regents of the University of California. *Collected Poems, 1915–1967* © 1968 Kenneth Burke. *Counter-Statement* © 1968 The Regents of the University of California. *A Grammar of Motives* © 1969 The Regents of the University of California. *Language as Symbolic Action: Essays on Life, Literature, and Method* © 1966 The Regents of the University of California. *Permanence and Change: An Anatomy of Purpose,* third edition with a new afterword © 1984 The Regents of the University of California. *The Philosophy of Literary Form,* third edition, revised © 1973 The Regents of the University of California. *A Rhetoric of Motives* © 1969 The Regents of the University of California. *The Rhetoric of Religion: Studies in Logology* © 1970 The Regents of the University of California. *Towards a Better Life,* second edition © 1966 The Regents of the University of California. The text of the Appendix is from *Inaugural Addresses of the Presidents of the United States from George Washington 1786 to John F. Kennedy 1961,* 87th Congress, 1st sess., H. Doc. 218 (Washington, D.C.: GPO, 1961), 267–70.

Some of the pieces in this book would never have been written if various people had not asked me to do them. I want to thank the following motivators: Lee Griffin, who was the first to ask me to give a talk on Burke in 1965; John Simon, who asked me to give the first of many talks on Burke at the annual meeting of the Modern Language Association; Mike Stugrin, Bob Garlitz, and Bob Wess, who facilitated many of the Modern Language Association sessions on Burke; Herb Simons and Trevor Melia, who organized and ran the Legacy of Kenneth Burke conference in Philadelphia in 1984; John Harrington, who arranged the Seton Hall University conference on Burke in 1986; and Jim Chesebro and Sheron Dailey, who organized the splendid first national meeting of the Kenneth Burke Society in May 1990 at New Harmony, Indiana.

Dick Martin, of the University of Illinois Press, and Harold Fromm had a lot to do with this book coming into being. Greig Henderson and Cary Nelson, who read the manuscript for the press, are largely responsible for the present arrangement of the material and for helping in important ways with revisions of some of the essays. Bob Zachary helped get me started writing on Burke again when he asked me to do a second edition of *Kenneth Burke and the Drama of Human Relations* for the University of California Press. All Burke scholars have to be grateful to him and to the University of California Press for getting and keeping all of Burke's books in print.

Like many writers, my debt to my wife Barbara is extensive, complex, and hard to express. I may have written this book on my trusty old manual Hermes 3000, but Barbara input it on her Mac Plus, revised it (many times), printed the final copy, and prepared the disk that went to the copy editor. I can say to Barbara what Burke said to Libbie: "Without Whom Not."

Part 1

Three Summarizing Essays

Chapter 1

• • •

Some of the Many Kenneth Burkes

Working Proposition: There are as many Burkes as there are books and essays by him and probably more Burkes than there are books because there are often many Burkes in one book—as for example, in *The Philosophy of Literary Form, Language as Symbolic Action, The Rhetoric of Religion,* or *A Grammar of Motives.* And there are Burkes not in the books yet, the Burkes of the letters or all those Burkes since 1966. The Burke we experience now, live, in 1977 is not the same one we experienced five years ago or ten years ago. None of the Burkes contradicts any of the others.

I have had a long and complex association with Kenneth Burke, in and out of print, going back now more than twenty-five years. Without exception, for me anyway, it has been a generative relationship. When I began to think about this essay under its original title, "The Uses of Kenneth Burke," the task of reducing all these generative uses of Burke to a manageable number seemed hopeless. I was confronted by what seemed to be mind-breaking alternatives: What uses? Which Burke—the early, middle, mature, or late Burke? Which of the many Burkes: the methodological genius, the ironic intelligence, the system-builder, the "dramatist," the logologer, the counter-stater, the poet, the aphorist, the rhetorician, the dialectician, the literary critic, or the tropist? Should I choose? Did I have a right to choose, subordinating one part of this magical man, this remarkable intelligence and achievement, to another?

However, to go on, I would clearly have to choose at least some place to begin, since choice, as Burke reminds us, is intrinsic to the movement from motives to symbolic action. So I chose: I would begin with Burke the aphorist, as we find him in his "Flowerishes"—collections of sayings arranged every which way on the page so that one has to keep turning the book to read and to earn all of the sayings in any one "Flowerish."

Burke the Aphorist

Here is a sampling of aphorisms from the Flowerishes.[1] A huge collection could be compiled from Burke's works as a whole.

> His friends said he could see around corners, his enemies said he had crooked vision.
>
> One must learn to be just morbid enough.
>
> In a world full of problems, he sat doing puzzles.
>
> By saying no to himself he gave form to his life.
>
> After fifty, one further thing to learn: how to ripen without rotting.
>
> Why leave of your own accord when you can contrive to be thrown out?
>
> Why does a chicken cross the road to get to the other side?
>
> Having nothing to tempt thieves, he was robbed by a kleptomaniac.
>
> Art turns liabilities into assets, guilt into solace, weakness into strength; it transforms the onus of owing into the honor of ownership.
>
> When you tried to make him feel good, he thought it was a plot; if you said hello, he accused you of lying.
>
> Always say grace before kicking about the food.
>
> When the mice are away the cats will play.
>
> Things aren't so bad. Buck up! Put on your pants, put in your teeth, and go for a walk.

The cure for digging in the dirt is an idea; the cure for any idea is more ideas; the cure for all ideas is digging in the dirt.

Though he despised mankind he dearly loved an audience.

He held that poets are made for critics, just as sick people are made for doctors.

They got themselves good berths by policies that would sink a ship.

Pity the weeds in your garden all trying to make an honest living.

He resolved always to wait two weeks before committing suicide.

God his goal and goad.

For exercise, he read the sports column.

Burke the aphorist is most obviously Burke the ironist and humorist. Burke has always been something of a comedian, and these aphorisms show that part of him, but of course there is more contained here than mere humor. The aphorisms are often built on ironies, reversals, and deviated cynicism. *Always say grace before kicking about the food*—just in case God is really up there, listening—even though, we realize, nothing so simple-minded and childlike as this is going to fool an omniscient god. The aphorisms bear a lot of analysis and they tell us a lot about Burke. They all contain a form of perspectival wisdom. They are cautionary. They reflect a mind that cannot help but perceive ironically, seeing around corners to crooked vision, seeing through to the ends of things where they reverse and become something else (God as goal and goad), perceiving that, whether we like it or not, our ideas perfect themselves and we are "rotten with perfection." This ironic reversing, often incongruous, end-of-the-line thinking is very characteristic of Burke, in person and in print. Irony, reversal, laughter, end-of-the-lining, seeing around corners, seeing the backsides and insides of things while looking at the surfaces and outsides, and thinking of the low (say the urinary, fecal, and sexual Demonic Trinity) as one looks at and contemplates the high (say the Father, Son, and Holy Ghost of the Divine Trinity)—this double, triple, multiple penetrating vision is one of the central characteristics of Burke from the beginning. It is intrinsic to all the books and is stated as an operative principle in the title of his first work of criticism—*Counter-Statement*.

The aphorisms often work by effecting a change of perspective, by making you look at something from a sudden new angle of vision—for example, "When the mice are away the cats will play" or "He held that poets are made for critics just as sick people are made for doctors." They work by adding unexpected motives ("He resolved always to wait two weeks before committing suicide"), by circling and cycling things back on themselves, or returning to the point of departure but with a difference (as with the one about the cure for ideas being digging in the dirt), by pointing out ambiguities of motivation or situation ("He hated mankind but loved an audience") or absurdities ("For exercise, he read the sports column"), and by working out ambivalent transformations (as in the most complex of the aphorisms about art, where negatives are transformed into positives by means of the creative process—liabilities into assets, guilt into solace, weakness into strength, onus into honor). At every point, these aphorisms keep us from single-minded vision, from seeing things in only one way, from settling for simple-minded answers to complex or even simple questions, from looking at things from only one perspective, from staying on the surface. They refuse us the satisfactions of a single doctrine, and they won't let us deny the complexity and variety of the world, the irony, ambiguity, and paradoxical and foible-ridden nature of language, human motives, and actions. These are all antidoctrinal aphorisms; they tend to deflate or defeat (not debunk, for Burke has never been a debunker) doctrine in favor of fluidity, of the mind in action, of rationality and reasonableness, and of the mind's ability to turn itself on itself and the world and perceive itself ironically, comically.

Whenever and however you encounter Kenneth Burke, you are liable to see this aphoristic mind-set at work and at play in what he is doing. One is especially conscious of this when he comes into your presence as a human resource, as his own text, talking, lecturing, teaching, and commenting. Then you see him as a living perceptual apparatus, moving through time and human experience, working from inside a complete and enormously complex vision and methodology, a kind of Charlie Chaplin of dialectics and the word, performing with the same consummate, breathtaking (truly) skill, using the mind and words in the same way that Chaplin used his body and gestures—often to some of the same ends.

By one of those strange conjunctions of life, I recently saw both Burke (at eighty) and Charlie Chaplin (in *Modern Times*) within a week of each other and was struck not only by how much they looked like each other back in 1936 but by how each was a truly magical presence in his own field. I might not even have made a connection between them beyond the physical resemblance except that at one point during his visit to the National Humanities Institute at the University of Chicago, Burke referred to himself as a comedian. The accuracy of this self-naming struck me very forcefully then, after two days of watching him in action, and later, while I watched Chaplin in *Modern Times*—especially in the department-store scene, where he roller-skates with such exquisite grace and marvelous threat-tinged humor at the edge of the dark "abyss." This is precisely what Burke has been doing in some of his many roles for the past fifty years.

Burke the Comedian

Comedy has always been central to Burke, so long as one realizes that by comedy Burke means the whole range of possibilities intrinsic to this term, from the joke, through social comedy and the stage play, to *The Divine Comedy*—and beyond, if that is possible, right to the end of the line, to some galactic or cosmic comedy, conceived, perhaps in the manner of Vonnegut's *Slaughterhouse Five*. In many ways, Burke's vision is more comic than anything else, if one takes the trouble to find out what he means by this term. Only a comedian in Burke's sense would indicate, in his most formidable book, *A Grammar of Motives*, which was published in 1945 and written during World War II, right on the title page that its larger purpose was "toward the purification of war." "War," Burke has said, "is a disease of cooperation." He dedicated his first book of poems to "my sparring partners" saying, punningly, "and long may we spar without parting." If you purify war you do not get peace, but dialectics—that is, verbal sparring instead of physical killing, a war of words, which, so far as Burke is concerned, is where the great *secular* comedy takes place. If war is a disease of cooperation, then you should be able to cure it by removing the malign elements and retaining the benign. Health, then, is cooperation, and cooperation is promoted and maintained by the work of dialectics and by efforts to purify war. If war is recognized as a disease, rather than as inevitable, then it is susceptible to cure. If you dedicate your most creative and peaceful verbal acts to your sparring partners—and Burke has had plenty of them—and hope that you can keep sparring without parting (becoming out-and-out enemies), you indicate in this way a faith in the creative, cooperative, and restorative powers of the word, a belief in the power of dialectics to purify war and to reduce it to, or keep it at, the level of verbal sparring. These beliefs are all intrinsic to a comic vision.

In *Attitudes toward History* (1937), Burke made a series of statements about comedy (as a frame of reference, a frame of acceptance, an attitude toward history) that it is still useful to keep in mind when trying to think about what he has been trying to do and to tell us all these years. "Like tragedy, comedy warns against the dangers of pride, but its emphasis shifts from *crime to stupidity.*"[2] The shift in locus here is from the ethical and moral (law and sin) to the rational, stupidity being a function (or dysfunction) of mind, and curable by means of education, enlightenment, or knowledge, or by any of the means by which these can be promoted—say dialectics. In a now-famous passage (for Burkeans, anyway) Burke says:

> The progress of human enlightenment can go no further than in picturing people not as *vicious,* but as *mistaken.* When you add that people are *necessarily* mistaken, that *all* people are exposed to situations in which they must act as fools, that *every* insight contains its own special kind of blindness, you complete the comic circle, returning again to the lesson of humility which underlies great tragedy. The audience, from its vantage point, sees the operation of errors that the characters of the play cannot see; thus seeing from two angles at once, it is chastened by dramatic irony; it is admonished to remember that when intelligence means *wisdom* (in contrast to the modern tendency to look upon intelligence as merely a *coefficient of power* for heightening our ability to get things, be they good things or bad), it requires fear, resignation, the sense of limits, as an important ingredient.[3]

Clearly, Burke has been a comedian in this sense since he began the line of books that comes to us from *Counter-Statement.* He has, in fact, been writing comedy all along, even as he has observed it, written about it, been involved in it, and acted in it. Typical of Burke is the fact that he would write a four-part book, *The Rhetoric of Religion,* in which the first three parts are among the most complex and implicationally far-reaching things he ever wrote, and then follow these with a comic parody in dramatic form, entitled "Epilogue: Prologue in Heaven." The two speakers are TL (The Lord) and S (Satan), who discuss the eschatological subject matter of the three preceding essays. The burden of this subject matter is the logological transformation of theology into logology (words about God into words about words) and the derivation of the divine comedy (that is, Christian Creation and human history) from secular and naturalistic (rather than divine) grounds. The result is a secular comedy of words entirely accessible to the dialectician or logologer. It is this secular comedy of words ("man is the symbol-using animal," Burke finally said in the fifties) that has always been Burke's principal concern and it is to the completion of the "comic circle" (as described above) that so much of his work has been devoted.

Burke admonishes us that if we want to see something accurately, we should at least try to see it whole; therefore, I have taken his version of the essential secular human comedy from the end of his line of thinking about it so that I can present it in its quintessential nature. Burke's comedy is, first of all, entirely secular—it is the great comedy of language, words—and it is not necessarily moral at all, as it is in Dante, but derives its essential nature from humankind the symbol-user. This comedy can be studied anywhere humans are, have been, or will be. It is a vast ironic drama in which humans are their own victimizers, having invented words, and having perfected them, and in their perfection created problems they can't solve. It is a tragicomic drama in which, according to Burke's principles of entitlement and entelechy, everything human is being driven toward the perfection of itself, to the end of its line. Burke says, for example, that machines are the perfection of human rationality, or that humankind's own entelechy is technology (the perfection of symbol-systems). Pursue these for a while and you come on comic ironies that are indeed very sobering; or apply the principle of entelechy, which Burke says is intrinsic to language (symbol-systems), to recombinant DNA research and you again come on comic ironies of such a nature that you do not know whether to laugh or to cry or both.

Burke the comedian is also Burke the tragedian, whose model is the Greek tetralogy in which three tragedies are followed by a satyr play, as in *The Rhetoric of Religion*. The logic of Burke's own methodology and vision tells us that, pursued far enough, comedy reverses and becomes ironic, or that if we apply the aphoristic perspective to comedy we see that tragedy is hovering around in there—both at the edges and in the center—and vice versa, of course. Now I don't want to put Burke on a wheel and just spin him (or run him around in a circle, as if he were a dray horse going round and round forever). I only want to indicate that if, as I have suggested elsewhere, tragedy is Burke's representative anecdote, all tragedies are followed by satyr plays, and that, as he gets older, more and more (as with so many other great minds and imaginations) his vision becomes more purely, perhaps resignedly, comic. What does it mean to say that the vision is comic in the end? For one thing, it means that this extraordinary mind has avoided the sadomasochistic double-binding ironies of a Derrida and that it has not yet lost its faith in reason (even as it acknowledges the irrational), in dialectic, and in the capacity of the human mind and language to purify war and to move humankind toward some form of enlightenment. This mind has not lost its capacity to believe in a future, and it refuses, stubbornly, to succumb to despair, cynicism, and the dubious resonances of doomsdayism. Even if humankind's entelechy is technology, maybe it is still not too late: maybe technology can be taught how to save humankind from itself. This may be the perfection of the comic vision itself.

Burke the Dialectician

Dialectics, Burke has said, is the use of symbol-systems to check on symbol-systems. It would be a mistake to assume that Burke thinks that humans are nothing but an aggregate of symbol-systems. *Humans are the symbol-using animals,* in Burke's definition, and the animal part is as important as the symbol-using part, except that, according to Burke, and from our own experience, we know that probably every part of the animal in humans, and much of the physical world (even the moon), now has a symbolic ingredient added to it. Burke has even made the marvelous statement that words create things and that symbols create humans. Of course, properly understood, both of these ideas are true and tell us, in part, why it is important to become a practicing dialectician and to come to as full an understanding as possible of symbol-systems and how they effect and affect our lives. This may not save us from symbol-systems; perhaps it may do no more than bring us to a perception of our dilemmas as symbol-using animals. However, ignorance has never been bliss for Burke: if he has preached or promoted anything throughout all of his writing and teaching life it has been the value of knowledge and thoroughness, especially about language and symbol-systems generally.

Nobody but Burke provides us with such a formidable set of dialectical tools for the analysis of verbal symbol-systems and symbolic

Table 1.1. Pentad Matrix

scene	act	agent	agency	purpose	scene
act	agent	agency	purpose	scene	act
agent	agency	purpose	scene	act	agent
agency	purpose	scene	act	agent	agency
purpose	scene	act	agent	agency	purpose

action—and this includes the structuralist and poststructuralist critics. I have no interest in setting these people against each other; we have too much to learn from them all. I only want to make a statement about the quality and quantity of dialectical and rhetorical resources Burke makes available to us, both in his specifically dialectical book *A Grammar of Motives* and elsewhere, say in *A Rhetoric of Motives, The Rhetoric of Religion,* and in some of the brilliant later essays collected in *Language as Symbolic Action.*

All terminologies and methodologies are also ideologies, as Burke has brilliantly demonstrated in his essay "Terministic Screens."[4] A given terminology and methodology both enable you to see and to do certain things and prevent you from seeing and doing others. What Burke says of others is also true of his terminologies and methodologies, going all the way back to *Counter-Statement* and coming as far forward as *Language as Symbolic Action.* Even the most inclusive terminologies and methodologies are limiting and determining, if only because they limit you to inclusiveness. This might be said of Burke's pentad and ratios or relationships between these five apparently inclusive factors. In the first place, the five terms of the pentad are themselves a selection of terms from a possible range of terms too vast to enumerate, and the nature of the terms themselves implies either the metaphor or the analogy of the theater and lays a heavy stress upon the primacy of act or action. The five terms impose a pentadal, relational mode of thought on the mind, as is made clear by the pentad matrix (see Table 1.1). A complete set of ratios is gotten by reading across, through the reflexive ratios (scene-scene, act-act, and so forth). A reflexive ratio simply indicates the extent to which any one of the five operates as the locus of its own motivation, or, to change terminologies, generates its own motives out of itself. This is most obvious with agent, but it is true of the other four terms. You can begin anywhere in the matrix but you cannot stop until you have worked through the pentad and considered the reflexive ratio. Wherever you begin, you shift the locus and move the primary values into that term. That is, scene or environment can be primary and determining, act (whether verbal or physical) can be primary, agent (person, self) can be primary, agency or means can be primary, and purpose (end, teleology) can be primary. I do not want to say here what it took Burke 450 pages to say in *A Grammar of Motives*. I merely want to suggest some of the ways in which the pentad is resourceful as a dialectical tool.

What you cannot do with the pentad and the ratios is also instructive. There is no way to discuss natural things except as scenic material, unless you treat them as agents; but an agent in Burke's terms can't act without language, and animals do not act in the human sense. A tree, for example, has to be scenic, or in an agency function as means (that is, lumber or firewood). There is no term for "thing" in the pentad. The only "thing" term is scene, in which things are part of the scene or instrumentalities or are involved in the purpose or are acted upon by the agent. Much of the *Grammar* is concerned with nonverbal substances (that is, things), but you have to get out of the terminology of the pentad to discuss them, because the stress in the pentad is so heavily upon the act/action, agent/action set.

There are an enormous number of variables here, as Burke well knows, and the apparently neutral terminology of naming, placing, and relating is hardly neutral at all. It imposes a pentadal mode of thought on the mind; it forces the mind into acts of naming, differentiating, placing. It makes it impossible not to think relationally. It celebrates the almost infinite variety of possible acts, agents, agencies, scenes, and purposes—even as it affirms certain universals or constants present and operative in the midst of this mighty plethora. It provides a way of placing and understanding without necessarily judging, although Burke himself says that he favors the term *act*. He does not say you can't favor some other term—say the pragmatic agency, the romantic agent, the religious purpose, or the environmental scene. Set up as a pentadal matrix, as I have done it, so that all possible ratios are present, including the reflexive ratio of, say, act-act, or pure act, the pentad and ratios become a mighty dialectical tool—enough, one would think, for one mind to work with, but only one among many in Burke's department store of terms and methodologies.

One wonders why he must have so many terms and methodologies, since Burke has gone on inventing, borrowing, stealing, perfecting, and proliferating them for fifty years now. Furthermore, even as he has adjusted them to the needs of his own mind and system, he has made them available for others to use differently—as the many users of Burke have shown. (As Burke once said in defending himself from some attack or other: "Well, you don't have to use a term the way the Pope does.") I have picked the pentad and ratios as an example. I might have picked the "Lexicon Rhetoricae" from *Counter-Statement* or "Perspective by Incongruity" from *Permanence and Change* or the "Dictionary of Pivotal Terms" from *Attitudes toward History* or dream, prayer, chart from *The Philosophy of Literary Form.* Or I might have chosen the marvelously resourceful triad of formulas also from *The Philosophy of Literary Form:* what goes with what (clusters), what versus what (agon), and what becomes what (transformations). Or I could have picked the theory of entitlement, the principle of entelechy, the temporizing of essence, the four master tropes (irony, metaphor, metonymy, and synecdoche), cyclic and rectilinear form, or terministic screens, etc. One could fill pages just listing the hundreds of terms and methods available for use in Burke's books from *Counter-Statement* on. Burke is a truly formidable terminological and methodological resource for the analysis of language and symbolic action and symbol-systems and, by extension, for the analysis of humans and human actions generally.

What does the dialectician do with all this stuff? Why does he need such a variety of tools, such a formidable symbol-system to check on other symbol-systems? For one thing, if the humanistic intellectual endeavors of the last seventy years have taught us anything, if they have converged upon a primary truth, it has been about the centrality of language to humans and human history. There is not a single branch of humanistic study that is not now language-centered, and if not specifically language-centered, as in some kinds of ecology, then systems-centered, which is, after all, a variation of the symbol-system intrinsic to language. Our most sophisticated bodies of knowledge are now all language-centered, and language analysis, at a level of abstraction and theoretical and methodological complexity no one could have imagined twenty-five years ago, has become the central tool of almost all humanistic studies. Burke has always been ahead of his time. In the thirties he was saying things about the importance of language and symbol-systems that we have just now begun to appreciate. Since then, all of his work has been part of one of the most intensive and extensive studies of language carried out by anyone in our time.

For Burke, the capacity for language is prior to the capacity for thought, and thought is really a function of language. Hence, humans are not rational animals or even tool-using animals, but symbol-using animals. For Burke, then, it is language that one needs access to, because all of the most basic and fundamental human truths can be got at by way of language. For Burke, access to language is by way of dialectics, or, as he was later to rename it, logologic—not the logic of thought but the logic of words. Dialectics is really a branch of what Burke was later to call *logology*—the study of words, of language, of symbol-systems. Logology is really larger and more inclusive than dialectics or logologic, and if we are to answer the question posed above (Why does the dialectician or logologician need such a variety of tools, such a formidable symbol-system to check on other symbol-systems?) we must consider Burke the logologer.

Burke the Logologer

The subtitle of *The Rhetoric of Religion* (1961) is *Studies in Logology.* Logology, Burke says, is words about words, but that does not tell us much. As soon as there were written words, and no doubt before, there were words about words—or various forms of criticism and commentary. Burke as logologer is not just using words to study words. Logology is really what gives dialectics its controlling purpose. *The Rhetoric of Religion* is the book in which the work on language that Burke began to systematize in *A Grammar of Motives* comes to some kind of culmination. (Students of Burke were expecting "A Symbolic of Motives" when this book came out. That work, in fact, is essentially complete and exists in published form in different essays never yet brought together in a single book of that title. It is the culmination of Burke's study of poetics, which goes back to *Counter-Statement,* and insofar as poetry is for Burke [and for many others] one of the most perfect uses of language, it would also represent some part of the culmination of Burke's work on language and the imagination.) However, there is, for Burke, a use of language more ultimate than poetry, and that is theology—or words about God—and the central tenets of logology are developed by Burke out of this four-part logological study of theology—or words about words about God.

The table of contents of *The Rhetoric of Religion* is very instructive. There is a little introduction, "On *Theology* and *Logology*," a chapter called "On Words and the Word," a chapter entitled "Verbal Action in St. Augustine's *Confessions*," a chapter called "The First Three Chapters of *Genesis*," and an epilogue entitled "Epilogue: Prologue in Heaven." *The Rhetoric of Religion* is one of Burke's most difficult, brilliant, and original works. Its range of uses alone is considerable because it takes us right to the end of the line of Burke's systematic thought on language and gives us both conceptual and methodological paradigms for much of his work, from *A Grammar of Motives* (1945) on up to the present. One of Burke's most recent (1977) summarizing essays, for example, is entitled "Theology and Logology" and returns to take up the basic postulates of *The Rhetoric of Religion* after twenty years of further mediation upon them. The attraction of this pairing for Burke is worth thinking about. "Theological doctrine," Burke says, "is a body of spoken or written *words*."[5] Whatever else it may be, and wholly regardless of whether it is true or false, theology is preeminently *verbal*. It is "*words* about 'God.'"

> In being words about so "ultimate" or "radical" a subject it almost necessarily becomes an example of words used with thoroughness. Since words about god would be as far reaching as words can be, the rhetoric of religion furnishes a good instance of terministic enterprise in general. Thus it is our logological thesis that, since the theological use of language is thorough, the close student of theology and its forms will provide us with good insight into the nature of language itself as a motive. Such an approach involves the tentative belief that, even when men use language trivially, the motives inherent in its possible thorough use are acting somewhat as goads, however vague.[6]

There is a lot of Burke in the above quotation, and the dense, continuous brilliance with which Burke carries out his logological enterprise in the book itself is dumbfounding. Since the forties Burke's primary interest has been in the nature of language, whether written or spoken, in the nature of language itself as a basic human motive, in the ways in which the paradigms of language (language in its most perfect or thorough uses) are present and operative in all verbal actions, and in the ways in which the top (the god term, the abstraction, the idea) is always present and operative at the bottom (the empirical, descriptive terms). Much of Burke's work consists of tracking the upward and downward transformations that language makes possible. For Burke, words, like theological discourse, go upward and come to a head, in God or in ultimate, perfect god terms. This is what Burke means by entelechy, the motive toward perfection that is intrinsic to language. The genius of so much of Burke's work has always been his capacity to perceive the whole in the part, which is a function of thoroughness, and to read the whole back into the part, either by analogy, metonymy, synecdoche, paradigmatic modes of thought, or dense symbolic readings that discover the hidden secret motives and meanings in something. Burke has always been a marvelous cryptologist.

What we need to recognize here is, to use one of Burke's own phrases, "the astounding thoroughness" with which Burke has worked out the analogies between theology, in particular Christian theology, and logology, *and then* made clear that logology is to be our secular theology in the twentieth century. This is certainly the burden of the essay "The First Three Chapters of *Genesis*," in which Burke works out and then substitutes a logological account of the Creation for the Christian one presented in Genesis, and so grounds himself, and anyone who wants to follow him, in an essentially secular, naturalistic, and linguistic account of human history. He derives human *history* from language, or humans as the symbol-using animals. If logology has an animating proposition, it is that logology can say as much about what is fundamentally human as Christian theology, and it does this by deriving God (god) from our capacities as symbol-using animals, rather than deriving humans, and the whole physical universe, from God's powers of creation. In this way, humans are grounded in words and God (whether real or not) becomes a function of words. In fact, one of the arguments of *The Rhetoric of Religion* is that there is nothing that theology can say about humans, the world in which we live, and the worlds God creates that logology can't say, working empirically with language.

Burke's brilliant essay on the first three chapters of Genesis confronts this issue right at its source, where human history is given its sacred origins and is thus tied to the Father, the Son, and the Holy Ghost through all of its long unfolding until it—human history—ends with the Apocalypse. We are at the highest, furthest reaches of Burke here, where he addresses first and last questions and tries to account for them with his own system. Burke has never been anything if not thorough, and to follow him, to use him, is to come on most of the basic and ultimate questions implicit in one's own condition and in the things one is studying. This is one thing that is always disturbing about Burke. If you send him an essay to read, he will say that, yes, there is some good stuff here, but you have not worked it all out. If you begin a Burkean analysis, and do it carefully, it takes you to those often unanswerable questions. Put Burke on someone's methodology and he inevitably turns up the partialities of that methodology. Logology does not just insist on the priority and primacy of language, it also insists upon a conceptual and methodological end-of-the-line thoroughness. Who else would think of taking on Christian theology with logology, trying to demystify it yet still retain the grandeur of its moral-ethical conception of the drama of human relations? Burke calls this not throwing out the baby with the bath.

Recently (November 1977) Eliade spoke, in a brilliant reversal, of the need to demystify the profane and secular in order to recover, or rediscover, the sacred—the universal world of spirit that humans have in common. It is worth pointing out here that Burke has tried to keep both worlds in his scheme. He does not want to say God is dead, God does not exist; he wants to say God can never be dead, God—perfection—is intrinsic to language—in fact, many gods are intrinsic to language, as many as you could possibly need. "God" is the true confirmation to the generative powers of language. What other resource available to humans has the power in it to conceive gods, and hence to provide humans with a continuous source of generation and regeneration if they but learn how to use it? If we are looking for an energy source, we certainly have found it here, in a system that locates and concentrates the powers of the Word in words and makes it possible to start out in the body, from an empirical base, in humans the symbol-using animals, and to proceed upward by means of a series of analogical linguistic transformations until we arrive at the idea of, or words for, highest or most perfect authority and power (the Word), and then to bring all that high power back down with us and infuse it into the empirical base from which we began. To put it in Burke's terms, we can find the powers of the Word in words everywhere. As Burke is fond of pointing out, this is both a good and a goad. We can even infuse this power into nonverbal things so that, in one of those marvelous Burkean reversals, things become the signs of words.

It is characteristic of Burke both to use this power to develop his own symbol-system and then to use the symbol-system to study the genius of itself in other symbol-systems, to demystifying, ironic, cautionary ends, so that even as he does it he is undoing it, and one wonders what the end result could (should) be. There is no system that cannot be desystematized, there are no holy terms that cannot be shown to have their demonic counterparts. We could say here that the aphoristic mind-set writ much larger is the genius of logology. If you do not believe this, you should read the "Epilogue: Prologue in Heaven," which is introduced by a Charlie Chaplin–like "Impresario" whose upper half is dressed in formal attire and whose lower half is dressed in ragged pants and worn-out shoes. The Impresario's introductory remarks consist of a series of swirling paradoxes about cyclical and rectilinear, logical and chronological, high and low, language and not language, human purpose, humans the symbol-using animals, and bodily motives and linguistic motives working for and against each other—to name a few. The "Prologue in Heaven" is offered to us as a "Parable of Purpose." It consists of a conversation between The Lord (TL), a bearded Blakean patriarch, and Satan (S), "an agile youth," in a "fool's cap with devils' horns and a harlequin costume of two colors, dividing him down the middle," who greatly admires TL. The dialogue, with much good humor and irony, swirls through Burkean paradox after Burkean paradox as TL and S discuss humans the symbol-using animals *before the Creation*. The dialogue is primarily about the "Word-People" and the "life of words." It begins *before* words and the Word-People, moves *through* the life of words created by the Word-People, and *ends after* words. It ends thus, to give us one of the great acts of ironic closure in Burke:

> S (pensively): In some ways they will be dismal, in some ways they will have a feeling for the grandeurs of form. But when these Word-People are gone, won't the life of words be gone?
>
> TL: Unfortunately, yes.
>
> S: Then, what of us, the two voices in this dialogue? When words go, won't we, too, be gone?
>
> TL: Unfortunately, yes.
>
> S: Then of this there will be nothing?
>
> TL: Yes . . . nothing . . . but it's more complica—.[7]

Yes, to use the refrain of this dialogue in heaven, it is always "more complicated than that." Burke has been telling us this and showing us why it is true since the twenties. Burke the logologer is the Word-Man of Word-People, nowhere more brilliantly represented than in *The Rhetoric of Religion*. The major resource of the Word-Man is the creative word. If this creative word cannot redeem us in the old sense, it can at least purify us in a new sense by bringing us to curative knowledge about the divine comedy of words. One cannot believe too much in or know too much about the creative word, the logologer tells us, even though it has great destructive powers. There is no other resource. When the conversation ends, the war begins. Conversations, dialogues (between TL [high] and S [low]) keep us in the middle realm of comedy as much as possible and away from the tragic abyss. The amazing thing about Burke the logologer is that he has kept on talking and skating at the edge of this abyss for sixty years now, strong as ever. To take him as a model is to commit oneself to the principle of, the value of, dialogue and dialectics, which means that we must keep talking and writing even as we stare down into the abyss itself or dream upon the heavenly illusions of perfection. Remember the logologer's perfectly ironic cautionary remark: "Man is rotten with perfection."

Burke the Dramatist

Aphorist, comedian, dialectician, logologer, and now dramatist. Burke will forgive me this pun. Burke the system-builder is a dramatist because dramatism is the name he gave to his own system. In this system human relations are viewed as a drama. More accurately, Burke has taken drama as his model for human behavior and has accounted for the nature of the drama of human relations by means of his definition of humans as the symbol-using animals. There are two kinds of drama that are never really completely separable: there is the actual real drama of human relations involving *physical and verbal actions* and there is the drama that consists purely of *symbolic actions*. The first is not possible without the second (or language), but the second (the realm of potential freedom in Burke) is possible without the first and is in fact the main resource we have for studying the first. The drama of human relations begins and ends with language, symbol-using. The brilliance of Burke's system is that it makes so much available to us through the study of language and symbol-systems because it acknowledges the power and resourcefulness of this other reality (beyond nature) that humans have created for themselves, and it acknowledges all of those other things that language and symbol-systems have made possible, which are, according to Burke, everything humans have added to nature, or all of human culture and technology, all the principles of governance and economics, the whole vast monetary system, and moral/ethical conceptions of *law* and *love,* or, in short, whatever is not part of nature before humans and words. Dramatism is a complete and complex system. (This is not the place to recapitulate it. Burke has done it elsewhere, and so have I.) It offers a complete view of the drama of human relations. It is a powerful humanistic vision, centered on the primacy of moral action and ethical purpose, language, creativity, and the paradoxical human drive toward perfection, a drive that Burke says is intrinsic to the very nature of language itself. The point to be made here is that since the forties, Burke has always worked from within this dramatistic system, and, even before that, in the thirties and twenties, he was building the beginnings of the system. There is a remarkable consistency to Burke's work, especially to the basic, fundamental humanistic vision that is at the center of it. Over the last thirty years, Burke has seldom spoken from outside this system, and one has the sense in reading or listening to him that he is always somewhere inside it when he is writing or speaking about anything. This system has a complete theory of language (spoken and written), a complete grammar or dialectics and logic, a complete rhetoric, a complete poetics, and, I think, a complete ethics. At the center of it there is a vision of man/woman, complete with a basic definition of humans as the symbol-using animals and a set of interlocked concepts from which everything else can be generated. It has a set of theoretical postulates that are common to all the parts of it—for example, the theory of entitlement, the concept of entelechy, the logological postulates discussed above, and the theory of the negative, to name a few among the many operative concepts found in his work from *A Grammar of Motives* on. It is a powerful, resourceful, and persuasive system. It is sane and humane. It is, when properly understood, a major contribution to human ecology.

I stress all of this because the system is, in fact, one of the major uses one can make of Burke. Most of the Burkes are in it, and it is so great a resource that few of us have yet begun to take out even a fragment of what is actually in there. We all tend to use bits and pieces of Burke, who must certainly have one of the most generative minds of our time. Some, like the late Hugh Duncan, have tried to use great chunks of Burke, in the sense that Duncan tried to develop a complete Burkean sociology and set it in among the other major sociological theories of his time.

This is not the place to recapitulate the many uses to which Burke has been put by literary critics, historians, anthropologists, sociologists, rhetoricians, linguists, political scientists, speech theorists, and others.

The range of his uses is as great as the inclusiveness of his system. One does not have to lock into the system to use some part of it, one of its concepts, or one of its methodologies. Even Burke himself uses his own system with great flexibility, often working almost entirely with one of his own most generative concepts—the principle of entelechy, which is the drive of everything human, including language, to perfect itself—or with his theory of entitlement, the central idea of which is that language is not primarily descriptive but gives titles for things. These titles then become charged with symbolic content and eventually you get that reversal whereby things become the signs for words; or, to put it somewhat differently, where words become capable of creating another reality—say the whole, vast, technological realm, beyond nature, which, in Burkean and ecological terms, threatens to destroy the very nature from which it came and out of which it is made, because technology, like everything else, is striving to perfect itself and, in a classic Burkean paradox, the perfection of itself would be the destruction of its resources and itself. There is a suicidal motive built into, intrinsic to, everything human in Burke, and it functions as a cautionary device when you think along Burkean lines.

Not many people have taken the trouble or have been inclined to internalize Burke's system or vision and to use it as a major conceptual resource for thinking about and dealing with the contemporary world. However, certainly there is a whole, coherent vision in this man's work of the last thirty years that would make it possible to use him in just this way. Burke the system-builder is as usable as Burke the aphorist or Burke the comedian or Burke the dialectician or Burke the logologer. In fact, as system-builder he probably includes all the other Burkes and constitutes a formidable resource. Even as one begins to master him to use him in this way, the central ironic postulates of the system begin speaking to you: "Empirically," he says, "I sanction dialectic, which giveth and taketh away" and "any terminology is suspect to the extent that it does not allow the progressive criticism of itself."[8] What can one say in response to this? Attend, as always, to the cautionary aphoristic voice in Burke: to criticize yourself is to move beyond yourself so that the dialectic can go on, the dialogue can continue. It is always more complicated than that, as TL says and Burke knows. No system is complete, and what one thinker has built up the next one will build upon. There is an archeology of systems just as there is an archeology of cities.

Burke the Poet

Burke has been a poet longer than he has been anything else—since at least 1915, or for more than sixty years now. He was also a creator of prose-fictions during his early years and published a book of stories, *The White Oxen,* in 1924 and a novel, *Towards a Better Life,* in 1932. Later, in 1957, he made his last appearance (to date) as a fiction writer with a marvelous story entitled "The Anesthetic Revelation of Herone Liddell," a dense symbolic account of the fundamental nonverbal grounds of his being. However, he has been a poet off and on continuously since 1915 and with great regularity since the midfifties. The bulk of his poetry has been published since 1955 (when *Book of Moments,* the first collection, came out); and there has been some important poetry written or published but not yet collected since the appearance in 1968 of *Collected Poems.* The poetic voice of Burke has spoken most insistently in his later years, really from his late fifties on. One would not want to say that at the end he was primarily a poet, only that during the last years of his long and amazing career (and who can say how long, since he is still going strong at eighty) he wrote a lot of poetry on a range of subjects and in a variety of styles and modes too great to enumerate here. Say only that as in his discursive and theoretical books, his range is great and his voices are many. His talents were always myriad, as Faulkner's were, and he is, like Whitman (to whom he returns so often in his own work), one of our fabulous Word-Men.

Burke the poet is a voice that keeps singing, stronger and stronger as it gets older and realizes that the system-building days are over and that the time for singing and summation is upon him. Burke the poet is closest to Burke the aphorist and Burke the comedian, although it is misleading to run them all together this way. Some of Burke's poems resemble the aphorisms of the "Flowerishes" (which were published with the poems), and in some of the poems, as in the "Epilogue: Prologue in Heaven," Burke is clearly being a comedian. He has a great gift for the epigrammatic phrase and for irony of all kinds, especially ironies of reversal. He has the comedian's gift of timing and phrasing and the artist's gift for playing and joking with the medium itself (here, words and the conventions of poetry). There is the kind of creative gaiety to Burke's poems that Yeats speaks of in his marvelous poem "Lapis Lazuli." Just as Burke the dialectician and Burke the logologer are voices that keep talking and analyzing, keep deconstructing (to use the current fad word for the process Burke has been engaged in for more than forty years—he was one of our first great deconstructors, dazzling in his ability to take a poem, play, prose-fiction, any verbal structure, really, apart, right down to the bare bones and then into the marrow bone and back to the genes from which it all came), and just as Burke the system-builder is the voice that keeps putting things back together, so Burke the poet is the voice that keeps singing and creating. What is it singing about and why should we listen? (What do we hear?) Well, for one thing, we hear the playful, inventive voice of this genius. The poems are full of high and low jinks; they are often very whimsical, often scatological, often very funny. Yet many of them are very serious, even somber, and it is a mistake to think that Burke the poet is all laughs. If we have all of the many discursive and theoretical Burkes in the dramatistic system, then we have all of the bits and pieces of the many Burkes in these poems. We have the profound thinker in his odd personal moments. Actually, we find some other Burkes here that it is worth paying attention to, and I will quit playing around with phrases and get on to what (who) they are.

"Our moods do not believe in each other," Burke says by way of Emerson on the title page of *Book of Moments*. "Lyrics are 'moments'" he says, "insofar as they pause to sum up a motive." "In one's moments, one is absolute." "Day after day, year after year" Burke says, a man "may have a fairly fixed attitude towards something, and may in fact build the whole logic of his life in accordance with this attitude—yet of a sudden, for a spell, he may be invaded by some quite different attitude and this irruption may be the element that, for him, falls into the pattern of a momentary poem."[9] These poems or past moments are "records of dead selves" Burke says, and in them, he implies, he has ranged freely among many moods that do not necessarily believe in each other because "only by a maximum of such free ranging" can "poetry best help to keep us free."[10] In another place in *Collected Poems*,[11] again discussing himself as lyric poet, Burke offers a random list of subheads under which he might have arranged some of the poems collected in this book:

nostalgia
stock taking
tinkering
impatient
on the last time
frisky

thrashing about
bellyaching
anecdotage
editorializing
good clean fun (that is mildly doity)
towards stentorianism (blustering)
self-pity for others
paranoid
running scared
petulant
dwindling
enigmatizing
being complimentary
on the Zeitgeist
feeling mean
apprehensive
epistolating
pious.[12]

At best, this comical twenty-four-item list is but a partial index of the many moods, attitudes, motives, and styles of the Kenneth Burkes expressed in the 166 poems (plus "Flowerishes") of this three-hundred-page book. Here, among the millions of words Burke has written and published in his lifetime, we see him at his most personal. As he said of Whitman, so we might say of him—that in his poems we see his policies made personal, and we discover the personality of the poet glowing in the words of the poems. The mighty thinker who can work out the fiendishly ingenious analogies between theology and logology, the monumental symmetries of dramatism, the dazzling dialectical resources of *A Grammar of Motives*—this mighty thinker feeds birds from his hands, fights dandelions, stares into the black beady eye of the chickadee and sees into an essentially different realm, admires his outhouse, and writes a nursery rhyme, a "Jingle for Mother Goosey," that goes:

Young Mrs. Snooks was sick of sex
But Mr. Snooks was soaked in it
Whenever he beheld a hole
He took a stick and poked in it.

He even tried to frig a frog
But fell in the pond and croaked in it.[13]

Or he writes a poem addressed to "Alky, My love," which begins:

Spirit of Alchohol
Bejeez,
One by one we have failed you.

Jack's liver, Tom's kidneys
Bill's pump, Howard's bean
(they took him off in a wagon)

Always there was something or other
Just couldn't stand it.[14]

Or he ends a poem entitled "Lines out of My Scatterhood" thus:

Oh, lead me
to the dew
at dawn
in
First-
Land.[15]

And he writes a lovely, somber, highly formal poem, "The Scene behind the Scene—Mystique of a Drunken Word-Man."

How can men help but misconceive
When hearts are worn upon the sleeve
Yet outward senses, duplicate within,
Are but a passage to their nether twin?

In the attempt to get things true
Poets confess to things they did not do,
And reproduce the dutiful
In clamoring for the beautiful.

The worm of living death,
Digestive tract with trimmings,
Expends it evolutionary breath
In exhortations, oaths, and hymnings.

How far from where men daily dwell
To that rare realm within the body's shell,
The scene-behind-the-scene's unseen frontier
And sounds like touch beyond the inner ear?

Up from the depths of secret utterance
(The innerness beneath each vital thing)
Into a trance of dance and chance
Standing on tiptoe in a tide's upswing

Words rise unbidden
Calling to and from the hidden
The verbal engine throbs ahead full throttle
While sick old age returns to nurse the bottle.

Already will-less as the dead
Except to swill while words get said,
Merging of east and west and north and south
The serpent-circle joining tail and mouth—

The sea sinks into oneness with its ships
And universal Love would kiss its own orating lips.[16]

The temptation is to go on quoting, for the pleasure and fun of it, but that will not hasten the conclusion of this essay. So I will try another strategy: In the depths of his imagery, Burke said, long ago, the poet cannot lie. I take this as axiomatic, in spite of stanza two of the above poem, and it applies to Burke the poet as well as to any other poet. What do we hear and discover in Burke the poet, then? The scene behind the scene? Surely not, even if we take the title and that poem as pure metaphor, for that would imply that the true inner Burke is in the poems and nowhere else. The agent within the scene, then? Surely not, again, for the other works cannot possibly be conceived as accidental or the scene for the poetic acts. All the works are symbolic actions. The man within the critic? Well, that is closer, but the critic is a man, a human, all along, just as the poet is. At the very least, Burke is a "batch of selves," and, as he has admonished us from the beginning of his own career, in what at first seemed to be a somewhat perverse assertion, he is a counter-stater. What his imagery tells us is that Burke the poet is always counter-stating, counter-singing against the solemnities of his system, parodying the self that built the system, picking away at the overly serious dialectician, reducing the logologer to jingles, pushing the divine comedy on over into farce, and returning again and again to the ironic, often comic voice of aphorist and the small, often trivial concerns of daily life. The most serious truths can be coached into jokes. The system-builder, the maker of monuments is finally to be seen as a little old man, with piercing blue eyes and white beard, standing at the base of his monument, looking up, dwarfed by the size of his own creation, realizing as he looks at it that thieves will rob its inner secret chambers (which may be empty anyway), that time will alter its configurations, that even a great man—and surely Burke is that—must, can, write these cautionary lines about himself (in a poem entitled "Know Thyself"):

> When I itch It's not from fleas
> But from a bad case
> Of Burke's disease.[17]

I used to have a dachshund named Burke, and Kenneth Burke used to punningly refer to himself as Kennel Bark. Sometimes, visiting Burke the man, when I was accompanied by Burke the dog, I would yell at the dog and the man would answer. This marvelous self-irony is similar to Burke's capacity to say that war is the disease of cooperation or that any system must provide the instruments for its own criticism. And that is what Burke the poet tells us—that he is not one, but many: that he is aphorist, comedian, dialectician, logologer, dramatist, *and* poet; that we must remember that the man who built the system is also the man who fought dandelions—fair and square.

If I could design a dust jacket for another book on Burke I would not have it display only a single picture or an abstract design, but many pictures, arranged on the principle of the collage or surrealist painting, without regard to age, time sequence, or development, without borders, and in some ingenious arrangement that eliminated the center, or principle of centering, so that no one picture would have temporal or spatial priority. I would try to produce the visual equivalent, for Burke himself, of Burke's own logological concept of the timeless cycle of terms implicit in the idea of order. I would like to minimize Burke's own rectilinear development and try to suggest the timeless cycle of Burkes implicit in all the Kenneth Burkes (and Kennel Barks) one finds in all the books, essays, and appearances of Kenneth Burke over these many years. As he says in *A Grammar of Motives,* the substance of anything is equal to the sum of its attributes. The uses of Burke, then, are as many as there are Burkes. He is truly one of our most protean figures, and it would seem that we have, at last, just begun to discover him.

Notes

This essay was originally written in the fall of 1977 for a session on Kenneth Burke at the 1977 meeting of the Modern Language Association in Chicago and for inclusion in a projected book of essays on Burke—which never came into being. Now slightly revised, it was originally published in *Representing Kenneth Burke,* edited by Hayden White and Margaret Brose (Baltimore: Johns Hopkins University Press, 1982), 1–30. Reprinted with permission.

1. Kenneth Burke, *Collected Poems, 1915–1967* (Berkeley: University of California Press, 1968), 88–92, 297–300.
2. Kenneth Burke, *Attitudes toward History,* 2d ed., rev. (Los Altos, Calif.: Hermes Publications, 1959), 41.
3. Ibid., 41–42.
4. Kenneth Burke, "Terministic Screens," in *Language as Symbolic Action* (Berkeley: University of California Press, 1966), 44–62.
5. Kenneth Burke, *The Rhetoric of Religion* (Boston: Beacon Press, 1961), vi.
6. Ibid.
7. Ibid., 315.
8. Ibid., 303.
9. Burke, *Collected Poems,* vii, viii.
10. Ibid., viii.
11. Ibid., 268–70.
12. Ibid., 206–7.
13. Ibid., 14.
14. Ibid., 16.
15. Ibid., 296.
16. Ibid., 189–90.
17. Ibid., 208.

Chapter 2

. . .

Rereading Kenneth Burke: Doctrine without Dogma, Action with Passion

Epilogue as Prologue

Every career has its own logic and integrity. At one point—in the fifties and sixties—it seemed as if Burke's career was going to reach or achieve its culmination in the building of his dramatistic system. But, from a later vantage point in the late seventies and early eighties, it became clear that this was but a stage in, rather than the culmination of, his career. Criticism as a way of life, rather than system-building, is what accounts for the logic and integrity of Burke's career. That was the discovery I made while conceiving and writing this essay. Its double purpose is to characterize the role of critics and to characterize more overtly the nature of Burke's enduring legacy to us. If I have used myself in this essay it is not because I wanted to intrude myself upon the reader, but because I am one of Burke's primary legatees, and I have tried throughout to think of Burke in history—mine as well as his. Critics, as Burke well knows, are historical counteragents, or counteragents to history, taking what their own time provides them with and subjecting it to the scrutiny of the critical intelligence. Critics do not deny history but accede to it by asserting through their actions as critics the role of the critical intelligence in history. Critics cannot escape their own time, but they can, as Burke most clearly has done, transcend it, rising above it to provide us, their legatees, with a critical doctrine free of destructive dogma and to show us, by the passion of their repeated critical actions, what it means to be a true critic.

A Beginning—Dialogue with Myself

"Legacy: anything received from or passed on by an ancestor, predecessor, or earlier era." Well, at least Burke is not yet an earlier era, so we can ignore that part of the definition. Ancestor and predecessor: Yes, by all means. What, exactly, has he left us, passed on to us? To be literal minded about it, he has left us his verbal symbolic acts, and they are what will survive and endure. But, of course, others have left us their symbolic acts and though many have survived, few have endured. Burke's will endure. Why? Because in these verbal symbolic acts he has left us so much of such great value that we do not really know what to do with it all and have only now begun to understand some of it. How reduce this plenitude, this abundance to something manageable? Try to sum up what Burke *says?* But his symbolic *acts do* as well as *say*—as he has so often reminded us. Try to sum up what they *do?* No. Burke, the dualist, says and does, does and says, and any such reduction to one or the other would be false to the reality of his legacy. Try to combine the two and write about such essential doings and sayings as symbolic action, the centrality of language, dialectic, dualism, words as facts, the centrality of texts, the intrinsic, the power of knowledge, the astounding creativity and resourcefulness of this body that learned language, the reductionism of scientism, the threat of technology, the ironic nature of the human species—hopeless under the circumstances. We would become an era before we finished that task. Learn from Burke and seek a better way.

Fusion, In-, Con-, Re-

When I first began getting ready to do this essay, I subjected myself to a huge new infusion of Burke: I read as much of the new criticism as I could, I talked and corresponded with Burkeans, and I reread many of the sacred texts. This huge new infusion caused a massive confusion in my head and a condition that Burke has described as "counter-gridlock."[1] Gridlock is when, in monumental traffic jams, you can't go any way at all: counter-gridlock is when, confused out of your mind, you go every which way. Anxious for some way to end my counter-gridlock—because the more I read, the worse I got—I decided on refusion. If we joyce this term a bit, we get *re*fuse, re*fuse,* and refuse (as trash or garbage), a pun that should delight Burke. To bring about *re*fusion, you have to re*fuse* and try to get rid of the refuse. You have to say NO to some of those seductive YESES. So that is what I did. I refused exposition in any sustained form, since I think we are beyond that in our work on Burke and ready for synthesis, placement, application, and evaluation. I refused the powerful temptation to dissolve Burke in particular into an elaborate discussion of genius in general, especially American genius. I refused synecdoche, or the detailed treatment of Burke in terms of one representative text—which is his own favorite way of doing things; and I refused the exploitation of my knowledge of a Burke few others seem to know—the Burke of the unpublished "Symbolic." I decided instead that I would shoot the moon and attempt refusion. I would try to put Burke together for myself in a new way and then characterize his legacy to us by spinning out an essay strung on the titles of his major symbolic acts. What better way to break a counter-gridlock than to lock onto the relentless irreversible rectilinear forward movement of Burke's titles; what better way to arrive at the tautological cycle of terms implicit in the idea of Kenneth Burke.

Counteragent

For my purposes, Burke's first significant symbolic act is *Counter-Statement* (1931). I prefer to leave *The White Oxen* lowing contentedly in the fictional world Burke created for them. *Counter-Statement* is another matter. It identifies an essential ingredient of everything that Burke has done and said as a critic from the twenties to the present. From the very beginning, Burke conceived of the critic—not just the literary critic but the critic at large—as a counteragent, and of his writing as counter-statements and counteractions. To be a counteragent is always to be in a dialectical relationship to one's culture. Twenty years after most people retire, Burke, tireless as ever, is still on the road as a counteragent, admonishing us, educating anyone who will listen. His ferocious energy has fueled him, and his driving, corrective ironic goal (to counter and correct what is wrong, mistaken, destructive) has motivated him throughout. This has been very clear from the thirties on, and is perfectly embodied in the title of his only novel, *Towards a Better Life.*

Realistic Idealist

The *towards* in this title is as essential as *a better life,* for Burke has always moved, and tried to move others, toward some nondogmatic conception of a better life. Burke has spent a lifetime fighting the tyranny of dogma—as can be studied in his efforts to secularize God and turn God into a linguistic marvel. (I'm not being entirely facetious here: Burke, a great pluralist in his own way, has always wanted to have his divinities and secularize them too. An inveterate empiricist, he will die with his words on.)

But let's not lose track of the better life; let's not stray back toward counter-gridlock. Whatever *Towards a Better Life* (1932) is about (and Burke has said many times that of all his symbolic acts this one most perfectly names his number), it is quite clear that writing this novel enabled Burke, at a time of great personal difficulty and anguish, to move himself toward both the conception and the reality of a better life. If we must search for a motive as to why critics, following out their own entelechy, keep writing, I think we can find it here. If critics are counteragents working for the good of society—the noblest of all human motives, we are told—then they must work against the factional disputes that keep humans at war, with themselves and others, and thus prevent them from moving, progressing toward a better life. In some essential way, the work of Burke the critic—as was true of Burke the novelist and will later be true of Burke the poet—is purgative-redemptive. Catharsis is absolutely essential to any understanding of Burke's legacy to us.

We may tend to discount Burke's many rhetorically elegant statements about the overall purpose of his work because we find them overly idealistic and perhaps a bit naive, but in doing this we forget that behind Burke the idealist is Burke the realist, and ever and always Burke the dualist. The motto for *A Grammar of Motives*—"Towards the Purification of War"—should be understood in the most literal way. Millions were killed while Burke was writing this book. Such a brute reality might make thoughtful critics wonder about what their words should do.

Burke has never defined the better life, nor is he likely to. He has, however, often described the worser life and written about those ideas and forces that distract us from and, worse, corrupt our view of the better life. What is important is that we have some idea of the better life that does not contradict our nature as symbol-using animals and keep striving to move toward it. Stasis is as antithetical to Burke as dogmatism; and process, the great Whitmanian and pragmatic good, is probably more important than any final truth. Almost every major Burkean proposition is a process/towards one. He has had a lifelong concern with moving on, with purification, with dialectic, with locating and taking on new antagonists. Even his latest definition of human beings as bodies that *learn* language is a process definition. We should remember that Burke ends his wonderful "Epilogue: Prologue in Heaven" with an unfinished word-in-progress. And we should recall the many *towards* titles in Burke: *Towards a Better Life,* "Towards the Purification of War," *Attitudes toward History,* "Towards Looking Back," "Towards Helhaven." I cannot think of a single point in Burke's development where he is not moving on toward something new, some more perfect way of saying or doing it. If we have to identify the salient characteristics of his genius, this application of energy and creativity to a single sense of mission and purpose is certainly one of them.

Knight of the Stethoscope

Burke's next title, one that belongs to an unpublished manuscript he wrote between *Towards a Better Life* and *Permanence and Change,* is almost too perfect: "Auscultation, Creation, and Revision." Auscultation, for those of you who, like me, did not know this term until I met it in Burke, is what doctors do when they listen to your insides with a stethoscope. Once we understand Burke's metaphor, can we not see how this title perfectly describes what critics like Burke do with their instruments—their minds, knowledge, dialectical and verbal abilities, the language itself and the technology of the printed word—when they study society. They put on their critical stethoscope to find out if things are normal or abnormal, sick or well with the heart and lungs of society. Then, assuming that they find something is not well, not OK, as Burke and many others did during the early days of the Great Depression, they begin, as Burke did, the creative-critical work of revision and cure. Burke the critic has been doing social auscultation since the early thirties. Diagnosis and cure have always been what Burke was concerned with, whether it was a sick self, his own sickly selph, a sick society, or a sick world. Perhaps society is always sick; it seems sicker today than ever before, sometimes fatally so. But Burke keeps right on reminding us—often quite ironically—that we are not powerless, that we can fight back in our minds and our words, and that even if we must sicken and die with our society, at least we can do it knowingly, and with style.

Poetic Anatomist

Burke's turn toward social criticism (and far beyond that) occurred in the early thirties. It was a turn he never turned back from. Burke's next title is *Permanence and Change* (1935). There are probably more terms for this opposed pair than there are for any of the many other dualities we find in Burke. Just to list some of these oppositions would take one a long way toward understanding the always dualistic, always dialectical nature of Burke's thought.

Like many Americans, Burke is divided between a conservative body and a radical mind. There are some things he does not want to change. Though Burke has been everywhere in his head and, of late, thanks to modern technology, practically everywhere in the United States, his "sickly selph" has spent most of its life in rural New Jersey. While he was conceiving and writing his most radical books, he lived in Andover without running water, flush toilet, or electricity, and modernized his house there only when necessity forced his hand. Burke is profoundly conservative in the way he thinks about our biological, technological, and ecological needs. His dazzling learning makes us forget his homely life-style and simple country ways. All of his thought is deeply grounded in nature and the body.[2]

But let us not forget the subtitle of this book: *An Anatomy of Purpose*. Having studied and diagnosed the sickly body of society, Burke is now going to do us a detailed anatomy of human purpose so that he can suggest a cure. Burke was never one to shy away from the big questions. In this subtitle we have the first of many similar kinds of tropes Burke is going to use to describe his own purpose. Other obvious ones are philosophy, calculus, grammar, and dramatism. These figures give us variations of the same drive in Burke and also reveal a rather interesting progression (from body to mind to mathematics to drama to language.)[3] Every major title from the *Grammar* on has language in it, and all bring language and human purpose together in some way. From the thirties on, Burke was to keep on trying to define, in the most Occamistic way possible, just exactly what human purpose is. *Purpose* is but another term for *motives,* and the whole enterprise begun in *Permanence and Change* was brought to a systematic completion in the *Motives* books.

Permanence and Change is a radical book devoted to intense social analysis and organized around the ways in which we inherit, establish, and create our individual and collective identities. It is most appropriately dedicated to Burke's parents. Burke said he put the book together to keep himself from falling apart. He clearly also did this in *Towards a Better Life,* but there he seems much more personal because he is intent on killing off an old self and an old relationship so that a new one may be born. In *Permanence and Change,* we have a conjunction of individual and social, critic and society: Burke acts out in symbolic form a permanent individual human motive or purpose—the need to define the individual self and to have a larger sense of social purpose—in the midst of chaotic historical change. The larger purpose is reflected in the diagnostic and corrective intent of the book, which goes far beyond whatever therapeutic function the book may have had for Burke. It is the critics' way of turning their personal problems into policy, and so partially transcending them.

Burke defined the major overriding purpose of all his subsequent work in this book. If Burke defined the literary critic's function in *Counter-Statement,* he defines and enacts the function of the social critic in this book. Critics must study human beings first to discover what their permanent psychophysical needs are, then they must try to determine if these needs are being met in the kingdom of necessity—that is, society at the critic's own point in history. If critics find that these permanent human needs are not being met, then they must undertake corrective action, both for themselves and for such others as they can reach by means of the printed word. It seems almost inevitable, after the fact, that Burke's next book would be about attitudes toward history, history being the kingdom of necessity.

Comic Historian

We are up to 1937 now. Europe is killing itself in Spain in a trial run for the great slaughter of World War II—an event that is to have a profound effect on Burke. America is still working its way out of the Great Depression. The Russian communists are purging themselves.

The Nazis are gathering strength. Burke is forty years old. I am eleven years old. My father has recently been killed in a stupid car accident. I have entered history. Ten years later I will first encounter Burke in print. Burke will later become one of my spiritual fathers. Later still, I will name one of my sons after him. Burke is studying history and making it. He has begun an amazing period of productivity that will last thirty years, on through the publication of *Language as Symbolic Action* in 1966. He will write and publish millions of words during this period in a sustained action of the critical intelligence that is unmatched (and as yet poorly understood and appreciated) by any other critic writing in America during this time. I will study and write about Burke during this period. Our histories will converge. I will become one of his legatees. He will remake my mind. I will carry on his work in my own way.

Part of Burke's legacy to us is the comic/ironic attitude toward history as he first worked it out in this wonderfully playful and intellectually resilient book. Many have adopted this comic/ironic perspective as part of their own equipment for living. Burke's true genius is perhaps first evident in *Attitudes toward History.* One characteristic of that genius—perhaps a characteristic of every genius—is its essentializing, entelechial, to-the-end-of-the-line nature: ask the essential questions; construct a dictionary of *pivotal* terms; identify the most *fundamental* psychological responses; determine the *basic, brute* realities; offer a corrective, a way of diagnosing and coping with our problems; give us ways of developing our own attitudes toward history so that we may move, knowingly, toward a better life. Vitality, variety, energy, boundary breaking, and creativity—all essential characteristics of Burke's mind—everywhere abound in this most Emersonian book.[4] Though this book was clearly an action of the critical mind upon a historical scene, it seems as fresh and relevant today as ever because there has never been a time, nor is it likely there will ever be one, in which we do not need and cannot use the comic frame and comic correctives Burke provides us within this book.

Philosopher of Symbolic Action

Strictly speaking, Burke probably cannot be considered a systematic philosopher.[5] In general, philosophers have negative reactions to him because they find his logic suspect and his methods much too unorthodox. Their loss, I think, is our gain, and Burke's great originality of mind will probably win out in the end. If Burke is not a systematic philosopher, he is certainly very philosophically inclined, because he asks so many essential, fundamental questions, and clearly has one of the great questing, questioning minds of our time. Looking up at the high peaks, he has not been one to fall backward into a faint, nor has he ever hesitated to enter and explore any labyrinthian text that he came upon. He began asking hard questions about literary form in the twenties. He kept asking them long after *The Philosophy of Literary Form* (1941) was published. He did not really get answers that satisfied him until he wrote his "Symbolic of Motives" in the fifties. In a culture dominated and almost suffocated by trivia, and in a discipline (the study of literature) devoted to trivia in a kind of monumental way, Burke, true to his idiosyncratic and philosophical bent, went his own way and went after first principles. In developing his theory of symbolic action and the methodology to apply it, he bewildered and offended many of his fellow workers in this most conservative of professions.[6] In an age of science, he asserted that all poems are highly subjective and deeply personal and that this subjective content could be got at by objective methods. In an era of the well-wrought urn—of the poem as dead artifact—he asserted that all poems are acts, the dancing of an attitude, and that, furthermore, poems are an essential part of our equipment for living. Here, as elsewhere, he continued his role as counteragent, reminding us that we should take literature at least as seriously as do those who write it.

Consider these titles: *The PHILOSOPHY of Literary Form, ATTITUDES toward History, ANATOMY of Purpose,* and *A GRAMMAR of Motives*. Do we not have here the powerful, fearless Aristotelian drive of Burke's mind, the impossible desire of the Sage of Andover to do for his time what Aristotle did for his? One could say that Burke has spent a lifetime trying to formulate first principles and the first principle of first principles—a new definition of humans that would replace the Aristotelian one.[7]

What of the subtitle *Studies in Symbolic Action?* Symbolic action is a concept Burke introduced into the language and thence into our heads and critical terminology. Burke has added many terms to our language and critical vocabulary, but symbolic action is among the most potent. Everything that he wrote could be considered, as I have been doing here, as *his* symbolic actions. Let's favor one of these two terms as the foremost among equals: let's favor and talk about action for a bit.

One of Burke's major contributions to the way in which we think about ourselves, the texts we have inherited, and the way we interact with the world into which we were born has been his insistence upon the fact that in speaking and writing, especially in writing, we are engaging in authentic, essential human actions, and that in the written word, especially, the action remains active and can be reenacted by the reader—or the actors and spectators, if it is a play. There is a symbolic transfer from the agent into the act so that the symbolic action contains in itself not just its linguistic ingredients but its human, personal ingredients. This most fundamental Burkean conception has had a profound effect upon the ways in which we approach speaking, writing, literature, language, and all verbal symbolic acts. Burke gave us a theory of the text long before the current obsession with this question began proliferating supposedly "new" theories of the text.[8] Everything that Burke writes from this point on will be tied to his theories of language, symbolic action, and texts. By 1941, he has discovered his main subject, which is not literature, but language. Everything that he does from here on will be language-centered. Like every other genius I have ever studied, Burke eventually found and then concentrated on his own special field. Faulkner wrote novels; Stevens wrote poems; Burke, the critic, studied and wrote about language and humans as the symbol-using animals.

Grammarian/Antinomist/Dialectician

This is Burke's big book—all 517 pages of it. It is so big that most of us do not even know or fully understand what is in it. The *Grammar* (1945) represents a quantum leap forward from the previous book where Burke tried to work out a philosophy of literary form. To go from literature to language is to go from the part to the whole, from one kind of human symbolic action and its motives to human symbolic action in general with its enormous variety and complexity of motives. Any lingering confusions that Burke was merely a literary critic were removed by this monument to human energy, adventuresomeness, ingenuity, and intelligence. As our teenagers say, this book is awesome. It is a true critical cornucopia and represents Burke the critic at his very best as grammarian, working out the grammars of many different systems; as antinomist, attacking reductionism wherever he finds it in terminological networks; and as dialectician, lining up the terms, pounding the paradoxes, revealing the ambiguities lurking in the apparently simple explanations of human motives. We can say of this book what Burke said of Freud: reading it, or rereading it, is suggestive to the point of bewilderment.

This book, after all, is the home of dramatism as a concept and method, of the pentad and ratios, of the paradox of substance, the representative anecdote, the paradox of purity, antinomies of definition, the noble critical motive of *ad bellum purificandum,* the Demonic Trinity, the temporizing of essence, tropes as a mode of perception, the concepts of act and substance so essential to dramatism, ambiguity as a necessary part of the human condition, admonition as a critical function, language as the essential human trait, reductionism and oversimplification as curable, correctable habits of mind (language), neo-stoicism and linguistic skepticism as critical ideals, the dazzling analysis of Keats's "Ode on a Grecian Urn"—and more. No other book of Burke's tells us so much about language and, if we take the metaphor of his title seriously, so much about the relation between language, terminological networks, motives, actions, and nonverbal realities. And no other book of his gives us so many different ways to deal with language as an action and texts as symbolic acts.

Burke says of this book and the dramatistic project in general that it should help "toward the purification of war" through "encouraging tolerance by speculation." The book is addressed, he says, "to a speculative portion of the mind," and the work it does helps us to "transcend" our problems by teaching us to "appreciate them," by teaching us something about "the ways in which we are victims of our own and one another's magic."[9] This should remind us that Burke is a critic, not a politician, and that knowledge, not action, is his business. We may well act differently after reading this book; we are certainly liable to think differently after taking it into our heads and making it part of our equipment for living as critics in our own right.

Passionate Persuader

A Rhetoric of Motives (1950) is Burke's second big book. It, too, has proved to be awesome and almost seems more persuasive now in the time of terrorism and resurgent fanatical fundamentalism than when it was first published. If we ever had any doubts about the passionate ethical-social motives behind Burke's rhetoric—that is, his conception of the social function of the critic—we need only refresh our memories from this socially conscious book with its relentless emphasis upon the hierarchic, especially the social hierarchy, and upon the way in which motives, especially destructive social motives, may be manipulated by means of rhetoric.

> Order, the Secret, and Kill. To study the nature of rhetoric, the relations between rhetoric and dialectic, and the application of both to human relations in general, is to circulate about these three motives. . . . Starting from any one of them, you find a vast network of dialectical possibilities in the offing, whereupon you may tend to see the whole of the dialectic itself in terms of the starting point, thereby being conservatively slavish to Order, morbidly fascinated by the Secret, militantly envenomed for the Kill. We must consider how the fullness of dialectic ("reality") is continually being concealed behind the mists of one or the other of these rhetorical overemphases. Here would be the outer reaches of a Rhetoric of Motives.[10]

Without worrying too much about the syntactically ambiguous title —an ambiguity that is uncharacteristic of Burke and persists into his next title, *A Symbolic of Motives*—let's explore what Burke is doing here, since he seldom does the same thing twice or anything in exactly the same way in any two books. This methodological and conceptual originality and variety are an essential part of his legacy to us. His mind has pushed forward with great American restlessness from book to book, and every book has taken him, and us, into new territory. He has a great westering mind and has, like Whitman, always been in search of his own passage to India.[11]

It is 1950 and cold war time. The superpowers are squaring off. We have entered the nuclear age. It seems somehow appropriate that Burke would write a book about dialectic during the terrible years of World War II, committing it to the purification of war, and that he would write a book about persuasion during the rancorous years following the war, committing it to "tolerance and contemplation." Every book of Burke's is tied in some way to the events of his own time—a fact we often forget when considering his work. *The Rhetoric of Religion*, for example, is filled with topical allusions and comments that cast quite another light on the apparently rather remote essays in that book.

A Rhetoric of Motives (1950) is too well known for me to offer what could only be a quick, foolish summary. I want to use it to make three points about the way in which Burke works. The *Rhetoric* is probably our purest sustained example of the action of Burke's mind. It is his most coherent and tidy book, written almost entirely without footnotes and appendages. Very little of it was published separately ahead of the book and almost none of it, so far as I know, is occasional or "on request" work. The book seems to have been conceived and written all of a piece. It is arranged in Burke's characteristic triadic structure, as is *A Grammar of Motives.*[12] Burke likes to begin with concrete examples—usually texts—which allow him to introduce the key terms for a given book and illustrate them and their relationships at the same time. Here, in part 1, "The Range of Rhetoric," Burke begins with examples of identification (what goes with what, what equals what) and different kinds of persuasions that are affected by various kinds of identifications. Ranging is one of the most characteristic actions of Burke's mind and is always related to his concept of scope (thoroughness) and his belief that one must always have an adequate (rather than reductionist, oversimplified) range of terms as well as examples, a truly representative anecdote. This is Burke's "way into" the subject of the book. The middle part of this book—"Traditional Principles of Rhetoric"—is, as is part 2 of the *Grammar,* Burke's attempt to ground himself in history. At least, that is what it begins as. Having established his own terms and the relationships between them, as he does in the *Grammar* with the pentad and the ratios, he begins to look at other similar endeavors in relation to his own terms. Somewhere around the middle of the book—say in the "Act" section of the *Grammar,* and pretty much dead center here—Burke introduces the concepts that constitute the Burkean conceptual center of the book. Burke is not a historian of ideas but an originator of ideas. As Burke says near the end of part 2: "We do not pretend that our foregoing pages have been a comprehensive survey of works on rhetoric. We have attempted to consider only those writers who, by one device or the other, could be brought to 'cooperate' in building this particular 'philosophy of rhetoric,' and whose presence might prevent it from becoming too 'Idiosyncratic' " (RM 169). By the end of part 2, this "philosophy of rhetoric" with its sociolinguistic and psychological coordinates is well laid out, and we have been made aware of the essential sociopolitical concerns of the book.

Part 3, "Order," is a detailed working out of Burke's concept of hierarchy, in a series of characteristically text-centered analyses. Hierarchy is one of the most important concepts in all of Burke: it is linguistic (positive, dialectical, and ultimate terms), sociopolitical (socioanagogic), and theological (rhetorical radiance of the divine). The importance of this concept to Burke's way of thinking about language and the drama of human relations cannot be overestimated. Within this hierarchic concept Burke works out most of his dramatistic moral-ethical concepts: guilt, mortification, hierarchic awe, hierarchic psychosis, catharsis, social courtship, and the like. This book about rhetoric turns out to be considerably more than just a study of the linguistic or literary or even the psychological devices used in various forms of persuasion. According to this book, our very existence is essentially rhetorical, a kind of continuous drama of identification, persuasion, and transformation. This idea, of course, is the basis of Burke's other great book on rhetoric, *The Rhetoric of Religion* (1961).

One point of this structural summary—which seems to me to be an essential point about almost all of Burke—is that he always gives you at least triple value for your reading: universal formulas and methods, such as the identification-persuasion one, which one can use to one's own ends; his own dramatistic theory, as we get it in parts 2 and 3, which you can accept or reject, as you choose; and, overall, the sustained action of his mind as it works its way into, over, and out of a subject.

All three of these have proven to be valuable legacies. There are probably more usable formulas in Burke than in any other modern critic. Many—such as the late Hugh Duncan—have found Burke's dramatistic theory a powerful and persuasive conceptual frame and have applied it at great length in their own disciplines; and many of us have found the text-centered ranging action of Burke's mind a useful antidote to the constraints of conventional logic and have adapted it to our own uses.

Symbolicist and His Sinbolix

"A Symbolic of Motives" is Burke's most enigmatic title and nonbook. The title is enigmatic because, unlike all of Burke's other titles, this one is not comprehensible apart from Burke's dramatistic system. Reading this title, no one could possible know that it describes a book about poetics, the original title of which was, rather more prosaically, "Poetics, Dramatistically Considered." The nonbook is enigmatic because

Burke apparently intends it to be his secret posthumous legacy to us. He calls it his "Sinbolix" because he feels guilty about having bolixed this nonbook for all these years.

All this aside, let's examine the title: "A Symbolic of Motives." Grammar, Rhetoric, Symbolic: we all know what grammar and rhetoric are because they conform to their lexical definitions. However, nothing but confusion can result from trying to apply a lexical meaning to *symbolic* as it is used here by Burke in this syntactically incorrect and confusing title. What, we ask ourselves, does Burke mean by *symbolic* here and why would you entitle your poetics "A Symbolic of Motives"? Here is what Burke says about the "Symbolic" in *A Rhetoric of Motives:*

> The *Grammar* was at peace insofar as it contemplated the paradoxes common to all men, the universal resource of verbal placement. The *Symbolic* should be at peace, in that the individual substances, or entities, or constituted acts are there considered in their uniqueness, hence, outside the realm of conflict. For individual universes, as such, do not compete. Each merely *is,* being its own self-sufficient realm of discourse. And the *Symbolic* thus considers each thing as a set of interrelated terms all conspiring to round out their identity as participants in a common substance of meaning. An individual does in actuality compete with other individuals. But within the rules of the Symbolic, the individual is treated merely as a self-subsistent unit proclaiming its peculiar nature. It is "at peace" in that its terms *cooperate* in modifying one another. But insofar as the individual is involved in conflict with other individuals or groups, the study of this same individual would fall under the head of RHETORIC. (RM 22–23)

Burke has said that in going from dramatism to logology he went from ontology to epistemology. Yes and no. The epistemological emphasis in the *Grammar* is very strong. But there is a lot of truth to what he says, and one way to understand "A Symbolic of Motives" is to see it as the culmination of the ontological concerns of dramatism with its emphasis on substance and act. We should remember that as Burke was finishing the "Symbolic" he was beginning *The Rhetoric of Religion*—the first of his logological works. The "Symbolic" completes or perfects dramatism, taking it to the end of the line, working out its entelechy by treating literary *works* or forms—that is, whole literary works—as ontological paradigms, as perfections of being and language for their own sake. Using Burke's terms, we can speak of literary forms—that is, completed symbolic acts—as the perfection of the ontological motive intrinsic to language and symbolic acts. Just as pure persuasion is persuasion undertaken for its own sake, to persuade itself, as it were, so a literary work would represent pure verbal being, or verbal being interested only in being itself. As Burke has argued most eloquently, poetry is the realm in which we can be most completely free.

Conceptually, the "Symbolic" is exceptionally interesting, not just because of what it says about poetics, the poetic motive, and specific texts, but because it completes the dramatistic system as Burke originally conceived it in the midforties. And, whether we like systems or not, dramatism, as we get it in the trilogy of *Motives* books, is certainly one of Burke's major legacies to us, and a monumental achievement in its own right.

Godsaken Logologer

It is 1961 and a new term enters our vocabularies just as dramatism and the pentad did in 1945. That term is *logology* and gives *The Rhetoric of Religion* its subtitle: *Studies in Logology.* This new term indicates that as usual Burke is moving on again, moving on down the open road, exhorting us as Whitman did in "Song of the Open Road" to join him, to travel with him, because traveling with him we will find what never tires. One could keep quoting from this wonderful poem, and much of it would be true of Burke. "Listen, I will be honest with you," Burke-Whitman says, "I do not offer the old smooth prizes, but the rough new prizes." Isn't Burke the critic like Whitman the poet, trying out the road ahead so that we may follow him? If Whitman is our great democratic poet, then Burke is surely one of our great democratic critics, in the American grain, right from the start, calling us to intellectual battle, telling us to join him, follow him in the search for knowledge, taking such risks as are necessary.[13]

Logology, where is logology going to take us? It initially took Burke through a series of analogical permutations on the relation of words to the Word, and, by that route, right on up to the top of his range of mountings; it took him deep into the verbal action of Saint Augustine's *Confessions* and back to the narrative of the Creation itself and to a long mediation on the tautological cycle of terms implicit in the idea of order; it took him on up to heaven and a dialogue with God;

and later, it took him beyond heaven to Helhaven and counter-nature to what may be the furthest reaches of where Burke's kind of knowledge can take us, to the very end of his line of thought. If theology takes us to God in heaven, then logology, in its relentless examination of the ways of humans, the symbol-using species, takes us to humans in Helhaven, which is the ultimate ironic creation of the symbol-using genius of human beings. If there are profound similarities between Burke and Whitman, there are equally profound differences, as Burke pointed out in his Helhaven satire. At the end, Whitman the poet finds his passage to India, sailing forth on the winds of his own ecstatic rhetoric in search of the secrets of the cosmos. At the end, or, at least, near the end, Burke the logologist, following the epistemological logologic of his lifelong calling—he was sometimes a poet but always a critic—finds what? Not his passage to India certainly, and not the secrets of the cosmos: he finds the secret, ironic, and paradoxical human species knowledge he has always been after. Knowledge is Burke's religion, empirical/theoretical secular knowledge. Burke is one of our truly great rhetoricians of knowledge. In studying the rhetoric of religion, Burke demonstrates the rhetoric of logology for us. If dramatism comes to its culmination in the study of ontological paradigms, in the study of words persuading themselves to perfect themselves in autonomous symbolic forms, then logology comes to its culmination in the study and contemplation of humans' entelechy as the symbol-using animals, of humans persuading themselves to perfect themselves in accordance with the entelechy of a symbol-using genius. This takes us beyond poetry, beyond theology, beyond words, to technology. As you may remember, Burke's ironic motto for logology is that humans' entelechy is technology.

Dramatism and logology do not contradict each other; rather, they complement each other by showing us two of the main ways of humans, the symbol-using species. Are not poetry and technology two of the highest manifestations of our creative genius? What could be more closely connected than being and knowing?

Omnivorous Critic at Large

Burke brings twenty-five years of productivity and creative thinking to an end with the publication of his omnibus collection *Language as Symbolic Action* (1966). This book should remind us of *The Philosophy of*

Literary Form, not only because both are omnibus collections, or because the subtitle of one is generalized into the main title of the other, but because both show us Burke as the omnivorous critic at large. The *Motives* books show us Burke the systematizer.[14] This book shows us again the first Burke we ever met in *Counter-Statement;* the Burke who worked and wrote for a variety of journals all through the twenties and thirties; the Burke who has written hundreds of reviews over the past fifty years; the Burke who took to the road in the late sixties and has stayed on the road ever since, lecturing, talking, reading, thinking on his feet—the critic at large in the most literal and Emersonian sense of this phrase, which is the thinker let loose in our midst.

In some ways, this is the most representative of Burke's books, and the many readers who know him through it have here met the essential Burke. Headnotes precede the sections of the book, and many of the essays are followed by comments or addenda. Many of the essays and comments contain poems by Burke, which are also commented on. He includes and analyzes his own dreams in some of the essays. The comments elaborately cross-reference Burke's other works. There are, as usual, numerous footnotes. In sum, he follows an old habit of his, which is to return after the fact to comment on his own work, trying to make sure he has got everything straight. Burke's mind is almost compulsively self-reflective. The epitome of this is his later long Helhaven essay in which he writes a satire, examines his reasons for wanting to write one, and analyzes the satire as he is writing it.[15]

A lifelong tendency of Burke's mind has been to make repeated attempts to understand the same thing. In a way, we could say that Burke has been writing the same book over and over again since the midthirties, but the subject matter of this book is so vast that one can never finish it. Burke has kept at this task with remarkable determination, intelligence, ingenuity, and energy. His mind has seldom faltered: it wants to be understood; it wants to come to real knowledge; it wants to talk things out, to share knowledge, to set the record straight. Burke really believes that this is important, and by his actions he constantly renews our often-faltering belief in the power of mind, the powers of the critical word, the ability of the intellectual to affect the course of human events.

Nowhere, I think, is this clearer than in *Language as Symbolic Action* where Burke takes on so many different topics, covers such a wide variety of subject matter, comments on himself, corrects himself (and others), doubles back on himself, quotes his own poems, explores the most minute details of his seemingly trivial dreams, discusses his own insomnia and bladder functions, and in many other ways tries to bring mind and language to bear upon events in a series of "methodical meditations" and in this way counteract the high-speed, high-tech, fast-knowledge journalistic culture of his native land.

Logo-philos at Play in the Field of Words

No major critical book by Burke has been published since 1966, but all of his earlier works have been republished by the University of California Press. Though he has written and published numerous essays and reviews during this period, there are only two new books: *Collected Poems* (1968) and *Dramatism and Development* (1972), which contains the two splendid lectures he gave at Clark University. *Collected Poems* brings together the poems Burke wrote between 1915 and 1954, which were originally published under the title *Book of Moments* and dedicated to his sparring partners; and the many poems he wrote between 1955 and 1967, which are collected under the title *Introduction to What*. It is always tempting to quote at length from these poems because Burke not only is a pretty good poet but has a wonderful sense of the comic, ironic, absurd, and satiric. What I want to do here is pause long enough to acknowledge Burke's legacy to us as poet, letter writer, and performer—performer because Burke does not just stand up and lecture, he enacts a discourse. Though it may not be immediately obvious, there are remarkable similarities between Burke the poet, the letter writer, and the performer. Since I have known Burke in all three of these roles, I'll draw upon my own experience here.

"Dear Billions," his letters to me begin. If he is at home in Andover, his letters will usually have something above the address, like "Back at Clutcher's Gulch, 154 Amity Road, And/Or 07821; or, more simply, "Groove 154." His letters are usually written in a combination of standard orthography and Burke-orthography, which is a phonetic manipulation that allows him to exploit every pun he can think of as he writes. If he writes you when he's a bit tanked, or the mood is on him, the whole letter may be in Burkese. Here is a typical opening: "Dear Billions, by heck your new stuffo in your book anent my Sickly Selph, and your friendly exercising in the REPRESENTING volume do make look as though somethinks is going on. Thanks slavishly." The letters vary, of course, but always attentive to formal proprieties, Burke closes his letters as deliberately as he opens them. Here is one random example: "But I must hobble-cobble back to my last, while I last, Bestest to thee and thine, K.B." Sometimes Burke will end his letters rather more startlingly, as in this short one about some troubles he was having with the University of California Press: "Love, love, love, love—Killkillkillkill Holla! K.B." If I were the only person Burke was writing letters like this to, that would be one thing; but I am one among a great many who have gotten the attention of this most generous great man. His letters are like a visit to Burke in the old days when you shared his outhouse, with its pyramidal dung heap, with him, helped him draw water from his wonderful dug well by the side of the house, sat in the kitchen while his wife fixed dinner, haggled with him in the deck chairs in the yard, or walked the country roads with him in the middle of the night, while he talked on and on. This is part of the legacy of the living man that many of us have been lucky enough to enjoy.

Burke the poet is the critic at play in the field of words. Of course, we also encounter this playful, ironic, pun-loving Burke elsewhere: in his early satiric piece "Waste: The Future of Prosperity"; with the intellectual playfulness of his perspective by incongruity and of his presentation of Western history as a five-act drama; in the wittiness of "Anthony in Behalf of the Play"; in the marvelous "Epilogue: Prologue in Heaven," which brings *The Rhetoric of Religion* to closure; and in the more recent Helhaven satire. But it is in the poetry that we experience the perfection of these playful, ironic, comic, satiric motives in Burke. Let me quote a single representative poem, and then move on.

A Huge Tribute

He had mighty bulges
This poet
With vigor of movement

His output was substantial

When he swished
By god he swished—
And better keep your distance.

Magnitude?

Solemnity

Poise?

Calm self affirmation?

This one had them all—

And curvature.

I mean
He was a horse's ass.[16]

Burke is a logo-philos—a lover of words. He is also a great believer in logo-power. Words are for play and power, for knowledge and purification, for edification and delight, for mediation and meditation. Burke has used them to all of these ends—and more. If variety and thoroughness are marks of genius, then Burke is a genius in his relationship to words. Anyone who has experienced a Burke performance is well aware of this. In one of these performances we move from the written word to the spoken word; we experience the overwhelming presence of the man himself; we come face to face with Burke on behalf of himself, dramatism, and logology. It would certainly be a mistake to think that his legacy to us consisted entirely of ideas. Some of us hardly touch our times and do little more than ripple the water as it flows by. But Burke—to use a phrase from William Carlos Williams—has been a great toucher of others, as Whitman was, using both words and himself to promote tolerance and contemplation, laughter and irony, a comic perspective, the free play of the mind, self-awareness, language awareness, earth awareness, global awareness.

Beginning and End in One: The Now Forever New

The legacy that I have just been discussing is the legacy of the living man. Some of us are lucky because we have experienced, enjoyed, and learned from his living presence. But it is the written word that lives on and carries the legacy into the future. And that is what I want to end with.

Burke's tentative title for a collection of the work he has done since 1966 is "On Human Nature, a Gathering, While Everything Flows." Readers with good memories will recognize part of this as a rejected title for *The Philosophy of Literary Form*. And readers with better memories will recall that this same phrase appears in a long complicated poem by Burke entitled "Introduction to What," in the following context:

> It's a wrangle
> It's a tangle
> It's a Jingle-jungle
>   JANGLE
> This world of Mr. Seat-Up and Miss Seat-Down
> And their Ultimate Interminglings
> While everything flows
> (panta rhei to you).

Let's break this title down into its three parts and take them up separately:

"On Human Nature"—this has been Burke's subject since the thirties. If he has seemed to concentrate exclusively on language, it is because language provides him with his access to the study of human nature. Let us remember, as we move toward closure, Burke's latest definition of human beings as bodies that learn language. You could spin a lot of books out of this dualistic definition that grounds language in the body and never allows us to talk for long about one apart from the other or the whole human being apart from nature. "On Human Nature" recalls all the parts of Burke's titles that stress permanence, his long search for essential knowledge, and all of the hundreds of terms and formulas in his work that do the same.

"A Gathering"—a perfect term for all that any critic can hope for, which is to make a gathering, perhaps a number of gatherings, from out of his "scatterhood." Every book is a gathering of time-fixed verbal actions by the critic at a particular point in time. "A Gathering" is both verb and noun, action and substance, the now forever new, beginning and end in one.

"While Everything Flows"—the brute reality, the kingdom of necessity, the history Burke has always acknowledged even as he tried to make a gathering against it. Time, history, flows relentlessly from the past into the present and on into the future producing changes so massive, brought about by causes so complex and widespread, that no single individual has much real power against them. But still you make your gatherings while everything flows. Your gatherings are your books; they stand against time and the flow; they do not stop it. Nothing Burke says about technology is going to prevent technology from fulfilling its entelechy—or, more accurately, nothing is going to prevent human beings from following out their technological genius to the end of the line.

Should this kind of knowledge lead you to cynicism, despair, misanthropy, suicide—no, though all of these are temptations lurking around the edges of our knowledge. Burke could have quit years ago and rested on his gatherings. But he didn't, he hasn't, he won't. He drives on, perhaps more slowly than before, and not just because work is therapeutic and provides one with a daily sense of the renewal of purpose. It is more complicated than that. He drives on because he can't relinquish his belief in the power of knowledge to do good in some way for someone; and he cannot (and many of the rest of us cannot) relinquish his fundamental, irony-tinged American idealism. Why? Because that is *his* entelechy.

Let him speak his own closure from his poem "Introduction to What": "Yours," he says

> for the Light, the Doctrine, the Rebirth, the Promise, the Great
> Praiseworthy, the Over-Flowing through Sheer Abundance, The
> Beginning-and-End-in-One, the Unfolding, the Homecoming, the
> Perfect Turn from Estrangement, the Revelation, the Moment
> Within the Moment (drawn out forever), the Ultimate, the
> Crossing, the Looking Back Into the Future and Forward Into
> Pastness, the Single Irreplaceable Meeting (the one-time miraculous
> combination, the very best of good luck), the Dirt Made Pure, the
> Flash of Blinding Super-Night, the Succession Jammed Together,
> the Forum of Sheer Form:
>
> The Welling-Forth of Absolute Springtime, the Flowering in Winter,
> The Motionless Revolving, The Doctrine Without Dogma. The Law
> Without Lawyers, the Word sans Syllables, the Grant Without
> Strings Attached. . . .
>
> The sunrise at sundown, the New Forever Now. (CP 109)

Notes

This essay was originally written during the winter of 1983–84 for the Legacy of Kenneth Burke Conference in Philadelphia in the spring of 1984, which was the first national conference ever held on the work of Kenneth Burke. It was previously published in a much-revised version (which is only slightly revised here) in *The Legacy of Kenneth Burke*, ed. Herb Simons and Trevor Melia (Madison: University of Wisconsin Press, 1989), 239–61. Some parenthetical citations are given using standard abbreviations for the titles of Burke's works, e.g., RM, CP.

1. See *All Area,* no. 2 (Spring 1983): 4–32. There is a long interview with Burke there, which includes many wonderful pictures of Burke, his family, and friends. The title of the interview is "Counter-Gridlock."

2. See Kenneth Burke, "The Anaesthetic Revelation of Herone Liddell," *The Complete White Oxen* (Berkeley: University of California Press, 1968), 255–310. One section of this story is called "Haunted by Ecology." The story is about the mind-body, self-nature relationships so central to Burke's thought. See Burke's comments on this story in *Attitudes toward History,* 3d ed. (Berkeley: University of California Press, 1984), 391–93.

3. The progression is from anatomy (body) to attitude (mind) to philosophy (mind) to grammar (language) to drama (action) to rhetoric (language).

4. This book is Emersonian because these are also characteristics of such Emerson essays as "Nature," "The American Scholar," "Circles," "Self-Reliance," and "The Poet" and because Emerson also thought of himself as a counteragent.

5. To my knowledge, no philosopher has taken up Burke, and those who have bothered to review his books have not been sympathetic. See the essays by Max Black and Abraham Kaplan in *Critical Responses to Kenneth Burke, 1924–1966,* ed. William H. Rueckert (Minneapolis: University of Minnesota Press, 1969). See also Christian Susini, "Turbulence," *Recherches anglaises et américaines,* no. 12 (1979): 109–25, for an excellent discussion of why Burke can be considered philosophic but not a philosopher.

6. I write as a member of this most conservative profession with many years of experience of trying to discuss Burke with my colleagues. Anyone who has doubts about my remark about trivialization in the profession should examine a program for the annual meeting of the Modern Language Association.

7. Burke's best-known definition is that "man is the symbol-using animal." His most recent definition is that humans are bodies that learn language.

8. Burke began developing a systematic theory of the text as early as *The Philosophy of Literary Form* (1941) in the title essay and in "The Rhetoric of Hitler's *Battle.*" He continued this work in *A Grammar of Motives* in his speculations on substance and constitutions. The famous essay on Keats's "Ode on a Grecian Urn" is clearly written from a carefully worked-out theory of the text, as are the analyses of Ibsen plays. The most fully worked-out examples of Burke's theory of the text are to be found in such essays as "*Othello:* An Essay to Illustrate a Method" and "Fact, Inference, and Proof in the Analysis of Symbolic Action"—both of which were written for inclusion in "A Symbolic of Motives." These essays are most available in *Perspective by Incongruity and Terms for Order,* ed. Stanley Edgar Hyman (Bloomington: Indiana University Press, 1964). Another excellent example is Burke's long

analysis of Saint Augustine's *Confessions* in *The Rhetoric of Religion* (Boston: Beacon Press, 1961), 43–171. All of the single-text analyses in *Language as Symbolic Action* are also excellent examples.

9. Kenneth Burke, *A Grammar of Motives* (New York: Prentice-Hall, 1945), 442.

10. Kenneth Burke, *A Rhetoric of Motives* (New York: Prentice-Hall, 1950), 265.

11. The reference is to Walt Whitman's great poem "A Passage to India."

12. All of Burke's books from *Towards a Better Life* on are arranged in this three-part form in their original editions. Some, like *The Philosophy of Literary Form* and *A Grammar of Motives,* have an appendix. *The Rhetoric of Religion* has an epilogue. Later editions of the books, especially *Permanence and Change* and *Attitudes toward History,* have an afterword or an appendix or both. However, this three-part form is certainly Burke's recurrent and characteristic way of arranging his books, whether they were written all of a piece, as *A Rhetoric of Motives* was, or assembled from pieces written separately, like *Language as Symbolic Action.* Perhaps Burke, always a great lover of symmetry, simply likes the beginning-middle-end arrangement. Few critics have ever tried to analyze the structure of any Burke book as a symbolic action, though this would clearly be a useful and probably revealing critical exercise.

13. *In the American Grain* (1925) is the title of William Carlos Williams's book about what it means to be an American writer. Williams—a longtime friend and neighbor of Burke's—wrote this book in an attempt to explain what it meant to define oneself as a writer in relation to American traditions rather than, as T. S. Eliot did, in relation to European traditions. Emerson and Whitman made similar attempts in their own time, most notably in "Nature," "The American Scholar," the preface to the 1855 edition of *Leaves of Grass,* and "Democratic Vistas." One of the arguments of this essay is that Burke is directly in this American tradition. An elaboration of this argument would require a separate book. However, there are many useful and illuminating ways in which one can see Burke in relation to Emerson, Whitman, Henry Adams, and William Carlos Williams—to name a few of the Americans Burke has written about.

14. Malcolm Cowley (in 1950) was the first to recognize and write about the extent to which Burke was building a dramatistic system in his *Motives* books. Hugh Duncan is perhaps the best example of a disciple who subscribed to this system and tried—in a number of books—to apply it systematically in his own discipline, sociology. Others have tried to use Burke's dramatistic system with various degrees of thoroughness in different disciplines. However, the main response to Burke has tended to be piecemeal: people have taken from Burke what proved to be useful to them in their own disciplines and work. For an account of how Burke has been responded to and used by others through 1966 see my *Critical Responses to Kenneth Burke, 1924–1966.* A bibliographic account of responses to Burke after 1966 can be found in this volume. Other accounts can be found in *Ranam,* no. 12 (1979); in *Representing Kenneth Burke,* ed. Hayden White and Margaret Brose (Baltimore:

Johns Hopkins University Press, 1982); and in Frank Lentricchia, *Criticism and Social Change* (Chicago: University of Chicago Press, 1983).

15. Burke's Helhaven satire and his comments on it can be found in "Towards Helhaven: Three Stages of a Vision," *Sewanee Review* 79 (1971): 11–25, and "Why Satire, with a Plan for Writing One," *Michigan Quarterly Review* 13 (Winter 1974): 307–37. The third edition of *Attitudes toward History* is also a classic example of the self-reflexive Burke with many footnotes from the original edition and its "Afterword to Second Edition," "Appendix: The Seven Offices," and "Afterword: *Attitudes toward History:* In Retrospective Prospect."

16. Kenneth Burke, *Collected Poems, 1915–1967* (Berkeley: University of California Press, 1968), 225.

Chapter 3

. . .

A Field Guide to Kenneth Burke

Kenneth Burke was born on May 5, 1897, in Pittsburgh, Pennsylvania. He knew from an early age that he would be a writer, a man of letters, a Word-Man, and he devoted himself with single-minded determination to achieving that end. Using his own terminology, we could say that he knew his own entelechy early on, and prophesying after the fact, it is quite clear that he achieved it to perfection. Nothing was allowed to stand in his (or its) way, including formal education. By 1918, after brief stays at Ohio State University and Columbia University, Burke had decided that institutional education was too constraining for him, and he set out to educate himself, becoming proficient in whatever other languages he needed (mainly Latin, French, and German) and reading prodigiously in the literature of Western civilization—a process he was to repeat later, in a different way, when he transformed himself from a literary critic and would-be fiction writer into a social critic. The early stages of Burke's career, which are very well documented in the Burke-Cowley letters,[1] may be summarized as follows: like so many would-be writers, Burke was first a poet and then a short story writer and involved himself in any way that he could in the literary life, first at Ohio State and then in New York City. He worked for and contributed to numerous little magazines and finally (in the early twenties) settled into a steady job as an editor with the *Dial,* which lasted until 1929 when the *Dial* ceased publication. Even as he was bringing his desire to be a fiction writer (he wanted to be a Flaubert, he said) to some kind of fruition with the publication of his collection of short stories, *The White Oxen,* in 1924, Burke was beginning to write literary criticism and so was discovering the true nature of his genius (and, I think we should add, coming to realize, just as Faulkner did during the same period, that he was a genius).

The early twenties were decisive for Burke: he married Lily Batterham in 1919, and in 1922 abandoned the city for the country when he bought the first of his houses in rural Andover, New Jersey. He was to live in Andover the rest of his life and he was to live there for many years in a countrified way, with an outhouse and no running water in the house (well into the sixties) and no electricity until 1951.[2] Though he divorced Lily in the early thirties and married her sister, Libbie, in 1933, he never left his original place in Andover, but simply moved down the road into another house. He was eventually to establish a kind of Burke compound there that included his three daughters (by Lily) and two sons (by Libbie) and numerous grandchildren. The significance of Burke's commitment to the country and family should not be underestimated, for both played an important role in his life and the development of his thought.[3]

The early and midtwenties were decisive in other ways. Though Burke was to publish another work of fiction in 1932—his important novel, *Towards a Better Life*—it became increasingly clear to Burke himself that criticism, not fiction, was his true calling, and that theoretical criticism and the development of a resourceful methodology (as in the "Lexicon Rhetorica") were his real strengths. *Counter-Statement,* Burke's first book of literary criticism, was published in 1931 and brings the first major stage of Burke's development to an end. Though it would seem that his novel should be treated as the terminal point in this first stage of development, it is so clearly both a terminal and a transitional work, symbolically enacting a major transformation in Burke himself, that it is best treated separately. The dismal failure of this novel with the public and critics marked the end of Burke's career as a fiction writer, though he was to publish one more "story" (more an autobiographical fragment than a story) in 1957, entitled "The Anaesthetic Revelation of Herone Liddell."

The end of the twenties and the early years of the thirties were crisis years for both Burke and the country. By the early thirties, Burke had committed himself to full-time writing as a career and was to make his living thereafter from his writing and various part-time teaching jobs. As was to be true throughout the rest of Burke's writing life, the troubles that afflicted the country and, later, the world, were to have a profound effect on what Burke wrote and how he conceived of his purpose as a critic. The apparent collapse of capitalism as an economic and political system caused Burke to turn his mind to economic matters and to the relationship between economics, business, and the social good. Like many American writers and thinkers during this period, Burke began a serious study of Marx and other writers on social, political, and economic theory and history. As he turned from literary criticism to social criticism, he read widely in this new field in order to equip himself for his larger role as a social and cultural critic.

Even as he was doing this, his personal life was undergoing profound changes. Burke has written often about the psychological and emotional requirements of the breaking up of one significant relationship with a woman (or vice versa) and the beginning and development of another.[4] All of what he has said on this subject most certainly has a bearing upon the significance and importance of his divorce from Lily and his marriage to her sister, Libbie, in 1933. The importance of Libbie to Burke's life and work is made perfectly clear in the Burke-Cowley letters and was abundantly clear to anyone who knew Burke during the thirty-six years of his marriage to Libbie. All of his major *books* were written and published during this period (1933–69) and most of his major works—that is, the uncollected essays of "A Symbolic of Motives" and many other important essays—were also written and published during this period, as was most of his poetry. Burke has not published a new book since Libbie's death in 1969, so that it is quite legitimate to speak of the post-Libbie period in Burke's development—or, roughly, the period from 1970 to 1984, when the new editions of *Permanence and Change* and *Attitudes toward History* were finally published by the University of California Press.

Burke's shift from literary to social/cultural criticism—which was his way of responding to the stock market crash of 1929 and the depression—was signaled by the writing of *Permanence and Change,* a book he says he had completed by 1933, though it was not published until 1935. As soon as he finished this book, Burke began work on *Attitudes toward History,* which was published in 1937 and is certainly the major work of the thirties. That the tentative, exploratory nature of *Permanence and Change* is replaced by the certainties of *Attitudes toward*

History is most clearly indicated by the development of the comic attitude, which was to stay with Burke from this point on, and the certainties of the "Dictionary of Pivotal Terms." The other work of the thirties, *The Philosophy of Literary Form,* which mostly collects Burke's essays on literature and brings his literary and social criticism into a conjunction in the theory of symbolic action and the critical methodology he was later to call indexing, brings the second major phase of Burke's development to a close. I think we can safely say that Burke discovered his life's work in the thirties, especially in the seminal *Attitudes toward History* and in the major essays of *The Philosophy of Literary Form*—such as the title essay, the essays on Freud, "The Rhetoric of Hitler's *Battle,*" and "Literature as Equipment for Living." Burke never deviated from the main tenets of the theory of symbolic action; and the four-part methodology developed in the title essay was the one he would use in all of his major textual analyses. Marx and Freud, Bentham and Nietzsche, so prominent in all the books of the thirties, would remain central to all of Burke's thought.

The next major phase of Burke's development—the central, mature phase, and the most productive in Burke's now very long and productive career—begins in the early forties when he starts working on *A Grammar of Motives* and begins teaching at Bennington, where many of the ideas developed in *A Grammar of Motives* and *A Rhetoric of Motives* are first tried out on his students. This phase lasts until 1966 and the publication of *Language as Symbolic Action*. The five major works of this period are really all of a piece, with one developing out of the other and the whole making up what we now know as dramatism/logology. With a few exceptions, all of Burke's major ideas are developed and ramified during this period, and the tetralogy of motives he projected early on—the grammar, rhetoric, poetics, and ethics (in imitation of Aristotle)—was really thought through and completed in one way or another. It was a massive undertaking and a truly remarkable achievement. Upon it Burke's real claim to fame rests.

However, it would be a mistake—and it is a very common one—to think that Burke's development and career end here in 1966 just because no new theoretical/critical book has been published since that date. There are three more phases to Burke's development and I want to insist that we should acknowledge them, seriously, if we wish to have a comprehensive understanding of Burke's development and achievements. Burke's last published new book is his *Collected Poems* (1968), which is dedicated to Libbie Burke and was published a year before her death. This book collects the relatively small number of poems Burke wrote up till 1954, which were originally published in his *Book of Moments* (1955), plus the large and varied number of poems he wrote from 1954 to 1968. With the exception of his long "Eye Crossing" poem, written during the last sad year of Libbie's life and originally published in 1969, most of Burke's poems are collected in this volume. As Tim Crusius (1981) has so persuasively argued, we would be foolish to ignore Burke the poet, for it is in his poems that we can see almost more clearly than anywhere else the comic, ironic, and satiric spirit that is at work everywhere in Burke's work as a critic and that is so well known to anyone who has heard Burke speak and perform.[5] I would identify this poetic phase, one that is a product of the most creative and productive years of Burke's life, as the fourth major phase of his development.

The fifth phase begins after the death of Libbie with the work that Burke began publishing in 1970. I will call it the Helhaven phase because his Helhaven satire is one of the major works to come out of it. In that satire and in other essays published during this period, Burke arrives at the conclusion that because humans are symbol-using animals and because technology is made possible by symbol-using, humans' entelechy is technology, and high technology (or post–atom/hydrogen bomb technology) is essentially and potentially both ultimately homicidal and suicidal. In other words, after many years of thinking and writing about technology (a theme that appears as early as *Counter-Statement*), Burke arrives, during this late phase of his development, at a kind of ultimate, ironic, satiric vision of the ultimate, essential nature of the human species. This final tragic vision of humankind is the counterpart of Burke's earlier comic vision, but it is not really separate from it, for Burke has argued all along that criticism is essentially comic, and it is only by critically scrutinizing the human condition that one arrives at this ironic tragic vision wherein our genius may be our undoing.

The final phase of Burke's development—though perhaps it is presumptuous of me to speak of a final phase until Kenneth Burke lets go and leaves us and we have access to the work he has been doing over the past nine years (since 1985 and the "In Haste" essay that appeared in *Pre/Text*)—*lasts* from the late seventies to the publication of the new editions of *Permanence and Change* and *Attitudes toward History* in 1983–84 with their new afterwords—their Retrospective Prospects. The works of this period consist of summarizing essays Burke wrote—

such as "Variations on Providence" (1981)—in which he tried to reduce his major ideas to a few essential theses or propositions. Another example of such a summarizing essay is "(Nonsymbolic) Motion (Symbolic) Action" (1978) which, like the end of "Variations on Providence" is also written as a series of paragraph-long propositions.

Burke has been writing and publishing now for seventy years. That is a tribute not only to his longevity but also to his persistent creative energy. Only a couple of years ago, into his nineties, he was getting ready to embark on yet another project, to have one more go at arriving at the ultimate answers he began seeking in the thirties when he first understood not only that he was a genius but what the nature of his genius was and what the burden of it would be. Burke certainly knew when he was writing *Attitudes toward History* that his genius was to be a critic—not just a literary critic, which, in a sense, he has been all of his life, but a critic in the larger sense, a critic-at-large as Simons and Melia like to put it. He probably knew even then that the burden of the critic is knowledge and that, in the resonating line from De Gourmont he quotes in his "Eye Crossing" poem, "Intelligence is an accident, genius is a catastrophe."[6] Why? Because in Burke the critic's case, genius is intelligence pushed to the limit; it is the compulsion to use this intelligence no matter what burden of fulfillment and knowledge is placed upon you as you go on fulfilling your genius to the end of the line, to the end of your time even if it means that you arrive, near the end, at catastrophic knowledge. Though he must have wanted to and been tempted to at some point after Libbie's death, Burke has never relented in his quest for humankind serving (if not saving) knowledge, has never given up the most fundamental of all the critic's beliefs—which is that knowledge can and, hopefully, will save us. The negative of this, of course, is knowing that knowledge won't and can't save us from ourselves, which is an irony close to the essence of Greek tragedy and to Burke's tragicomic vision of the symbol-using animal that is, thanks to its genius, "rotten with perfection."

Part 2

1924–31

The White Oxen (1924) is Burke's first published book. The fifteen stories that made up the original book were written between 1919 and

1924, as were the three shorter stories he added to *The Complete White Oxen* (1968). The final story in *The Complete White Oxen,* "The Anaesthetic Revelation of Herone Liddell," was written and published in 1957. These stories, plus Burke's novel, *Towards a Better Life* (1932), make up his total output as a fiction writer. Read in the context of Burke's overall development and career, *The White Oxen* tells us some interesting and valuable things about Burke's beginnings. His earliest serious aspiration as a writer was to become an American Flaubert, or a writer whose whole life was dedicated to his craft and whose craft was the carefully written, well-made story or novel. To borrow the title of the first essay in *Counter-Statement,* he wanted to become an "Adept of Pure Literature," or literature that was written solely for its own sake, as a kind of formal and rhetorical exercise. In a sense, that is what he achieves in *The White Oxen.* Without exception, the stories are immaculately written and well-made; and the stories as a group are exercises in different styles and different fictional modes. The progression from "The White Oxen," the first story, to "Prince Llan," the final story, is a progression from the completely realistic and ironic to the completely fantastic and symbolic. In between, there are other stories in the realistic mode and in the symbolic mode, stories in which realism and fantasy are alternated, stories with recognizable characters and consecutive plots and stories with disjunctive plots or three completely separate plots and unrecognizable characters like Treep and Arjk; some of the stories are comic; many are ironic or have an ironic twist to them; some are broadly satiric; many are extremely witty. Overall, inventiveness, experimentation, and variety are clearly operative principles as Burke works his way through a range of short fictional styles and modes. When one finishes this book of stories, one has a sense of having read a book with almost no content by a writer with a very witty, cerebral, and playful mind. The Burke one meets in these stories is the Burke one meets many years later in the poems, the Burke who loved to tinker with the medium, to create humorous, often ironic effects, who could never resist a satiric jab here and there, whose mind both saw and played around corners.[7]

I do not mean to suggest here that the stories, or, later, the poems, are frivolous, because they clearly are not. The stories are serious writing of a particular kind, writing that is more interested in itself—what it is doing—than it is in saying something. It affirms what it is by what it does, which is, as Burke says in *Counter-Statement,* to create certain effects. When Burke began to abandon his aspirations to become an adept of pure literature and turned to literary criticism (to writing about literature rather than writing it) he shifted the whole focus of his aspirations and energy. When he returned to fiction writing in 1928 and began his semi-autobiographical and highly symbolic novel, *Towards a Better Life,* he was far beyond the formal exercises he put himself through in writing the stories that make up *The White Oxen,* even though one can recognize some of this same motive in the early, elegantly written "declamations" that make up the first part of the novel. In between these two fictional works Burke conceived and wrote the essays that make up *Counter-Statement,* the book that signals that he has found his true vocation—criticism.

Counter-Statement is really Burke's defense of the seriousness and serious *social* function of art, the artist, and the critic. Literature (which is usually what Burke means by art) is equipment for living, as he shows in his essay on Mann and Gide (CS, 92–103) and in the theoretical essay "Program" (107–32). As Burke tries to show everywhere in the book, writers are counteragents and their works are "counter-statements"—or should be—in the sense that they tend to respond to the excesses of their own time and place and work against them to either promote change or to restore a healthy norm. It is this countermanding role of the artist and of art that Burke the *critic,* first the literary and later the social/cultural critic, will adopt and perfect. Reading *Counter-Statement* again after reading and rereading all the rest of Burke, it is not so much the theory of form or the critical machinery of "Lexicon Rhetorica" (though both served Burke very well in the years ahead) but Burke's defense of Mann, Gide, and De Gourmont and his defense of the revolutionary humanistic function of art in the "Program" essay that seems significant now. Burke's lifelong battle against overindustrialization, against technology, against scientism, against the oversimplifications of fundamentalism, fanaticism, and bureaucratization begin in this book and form the basis of his defense of the writer and literature, and, roundabout, of the critic. "Certainties," Burke says in "Program," "will always arise, impelling men to new intolerances. (Certainty is always cheap, it is the easiest thing of which a man is capable. Deprive him of a meal, or bind his arms, or jockey him out of job—and convictions spring up like Jacks-in-the-box.) Thus, we can defend the aesthetic as anti-practical, anti-industrial, anti-machine because the practical, the industrial, the mechanical is so firmly entrenched" (113). Burke is not just being perverse here, nor is he playing the devil's advocate. He here states—as he does in the title of his first book of criticism—one of the themes of all of his later work and describes with great accuracy what the function of critics is to be in relation to their own society and time.

It seems unlikely that one could have predicted Burke's future development from *Counter-Statement*. After the fact, we see certain obvious connections; before the fact, it is quite another matter. Though it was not published until 1931, *Counter-Statement* is basically a work of the twenties, a kind of precrash, predepression work that belongs to Burke's life as a man of letters—a would-be fiction writer, a sometime poet, an editor of a literary magazine, a music critic, and a literary critic. Though *Counter-Statement* addresses the question of the relationship between literature and society, it never does so with the seriousness and intensity that was to characterize all of Burke's work in the thirties and after; it remains, after the fact, a work by a literary critic who has not yet developed a real sense of the larger social context we find at work in *Permanence and Change, Attitudes toward History,* and *The Philosophy of Literary Form.*

1935

The change from *Counter-Statement* to *Permanence and Change* is a huge one as is the later change from *The Philosophy of Literary Form* to *A Grammar of Motives*. It is easy to say that Burke changed from being a literary critic to being a social/cultural critic: that is, from the smaller to the larger domain of the critic whereby literature and the function of the critic are absorbed into a much larger, more inclusive context. But this hardly indicates what happened to Burke. For one thing, all of his references change, indicating that he again underwent a massive program of self-education in preparing himself for his new role as a social critic. In a transitional study written in the early thirties called "Auscultation, Creation, and Revision,"[8] Burke uses a metaphor that is much to our purpose here. The metaphor in the first word of the title suggests a comparison between the critic and a doctor who is listening to the patient's internal symptoms with a stethoscope. The patient would be society and the doctor-critic would be Burke, who was in the process of changing from a literary to a social critic. The patient/society is sick, and the critic/doctor is going to determine the nature of the illness and prescribe a cure—a process that is clearly suggested by the second and third words of the title. That is exactly what Burke sets out to do in *Permanence and Change.* He is not now going to tell us what literature is all about, how it functions, what literary form is and how we may analyze and interpret it: he is going to tell us what Western history and modern society are all about, what is wrong with American society at the present time (early thirties) and what the requirements of the good life are—that is, he is going to write about ultimate matters such as human purpose, about what the permanent human needs are throughout history and how they have been and may now be adequately satisfied in the flux and change that is history. But we should never think that Burke is going to abandon his first love—literature, poetry—and he never really does until much later.[9] Instead of analyzing individual works, as he does in *Counter-Statement,* or discussing literary form, he here turns poetry and the poetic motive into metaphor(s) for the good life: they become the corrective "rationalization" needed to counter the dangerous, combative misemphasis of the current capitalistic and "scientific" rationalization and the inadequacies of the old religious one (the church, Burke says, is "like a big deserted building, with broken windows and littered doorways"—PC 65). The "corrective philosophy" Burke proposes in this book will be one in which "the center of authority . . . [is] situated in a philosophy, or psychology of poetry rather than in a body of poetry"; it will be a "rationale of art" whose purpose is to promote an "art of living" (66).

Burke makes these statements at the end of part 1 of *Permanence and Change* and ramifies them throughout the other two parts of the book. Burke not only has an extraordinarily retentive memory but an amazing ability to bring apparently completely unrelated writers and ideas together to make his points. This is why he calls the middle section of the book "Perspective by Incongruity"—a phrase that well describes an analytic technique Burke was to use in all the rest of his books and talks and that tended to make many of his more conservative readers and listeners angry, resentful, and distrustful. By the end of this book, Burke has worked out the cooperative creative moral-ethical "philosophy of Being" (a conception of the "good life," of the "poetry of action") which he will adhere to in all the rest of his books and essays. This position, and its commitments, is well summarized in the conclusion to *Permanence and Change,* where Burke explains what he means by the poetic or dramatic metaphor as "key" and why it is that the poetic cooperative metaphor must be a corrective to the competitive metaphors (the us versus them metaphors) that have "plagued the Western-world with increasing violence" so long. I think we need to remember, when reading and thinking about Burke, that the Western world and, in a sense, much of the rest of the world, has been at war or engaged in devastating revolutions during all of Burke's adult life (from 1914 on).

Interlude—1932

This is perhaps an ideal place for an interlude in which Burke's important, highly symbolic semi-autobiographical novel is discussed. Burke has said many times that the novel names his number; that one cannot understand him without understanding this novel; that it is about the breakup of his first marriage to Lily and his developing relationship with Libbie, his second wife; that he killed off some highly individualistic and destructive part of himself in the novel in the scapegoat character of John Neal and the profound changes that occur in him in the course of the novel. Burke has written repeatedly about this novel in his letters, in various footnotes and afterwords and forewords; in fact he has written a whole essay about it ("On Stress, Its Seeking") and has argued with most interpretations of the novel.[10]

This elegantly written novel tells the story of one John Neal (or, punwise, kneel), who begins the novel as a cynical, mean-minded, manipulative character given to Nietzschean aphorisms of the most cynical, negative kind. Very basically, it is the story of Neal's relationships with four women, Florence, Genevieve, his wife, and the Girl in White. The kindest way to describe Neal's relationships with all of these women is to say that he is despicable. This is especially true of his relationship with Genevieve, who though she is married, loves him and comes to him whenever he needs her, and whom, repeatedly, he treats most cruelly, especially near the end of the novel when he falsely accuses her of betraying him, puts her to obscene tests of fidelity, sends her out to solicit for him, and finally drives her away. It is this final act that precipitates the great change that occurs in Neal in the last part of the novel. The change is classic, in the sense that as a result of his own actions in his relationship with Genevieve, Neal slowly comes to knowledge of what he was like up to that point in the novel. He was, to put it nicely, a despicable human being, a user of everybody, especially his women. As he comes to knowledge, he is driven more and more into himself and begins to break down—an event many critics take as a sign that he goes mad; but there is very little that is mad about John Neal at the end. In fact, he is all wisdom at the end, when he writes a series of unsent letters to Genevieve in which he acknowledges the cruelty of his behavior toward her; or in the recapitulation chapter in which he again admits his faults and guilt; and especially in the final somewhat disjointed chapter, "Testamentum Meum," where it is even clearer what he has learned, what he has purged out of himself (or, symbolically, out of Burke), what he now stands for, and most important, where he asserts that he will rise again, profoundly changed.

Following Burke's own leads in his theory of symbolic action, could we not say that in this novel, by writing this novel (which we know was a very painful experience for Burke, especially at the end), Burke symbolically purged himself of the negative traits that made him unfit for Libbie (the woman Burke says he adored and for whom, he said, he wrote all of his books just to keep proving to her [and himself] that he was worthy of her)? Could we not say that the symbolic function of this novel for Burke was to purge himself and make himself worthy of Libbie and a better life? The novel preceded his marriage to Libbie in 1933, but it did not precede his relationship with her. In depicting a character who finally does learn to kneel at the end of the novel, Burke depicts a character who goes from a kind of Nietzschean, highly self-centered, and individualistic view of the self that makes him incapable of love to a kind of completely opposite view of the self—the view that is depicted in the last three chapters of the novel as Neal comes to knowledge and undergoes his changes. This change, by the way, is also similar to the one that Burke went through when he changed from an artist to a literary critic and then to a social critic; from the artist who wrote, and the critic who addressed himself to individual works and authors, to the critic who addressed himself to society and with its cooperative needs and behavior.

Towards a Better Life consists of unsent letters—that is, of a series of reflexive acts by Neal—to his "friend" and rival Anthony. Two of the last three chapters of the novel break this form because one chapter is unsent letters by Neal to Genevieve and the last chapter is Neal's testament and is called "Testamentum Meum—Jottings." In both of these, as well as the recapitulation chapter, Neal admits that his character was his destiny; he was no victim of fate or bad luck, but the originator of his actions. Hence, it is his character that must change, and does. It is quite clear that Burke, in the fictional person of John Neal, is addressing his symbolic self throughout this novel and that the novel does function as his symbolic action, allowing him in the mysterious ways of symbolic action to purge himself of his burden (his negative traits) and the guilt that goes with them, allowing him to cleanse himself and make himself ready and worthy for both the new relationship with Libbie and his new role as a social/cultural critic. Whatever Burke says about how to interpret the title of the novel, I think we should take it at face symbolic value and realize that by writing the novel, Burke was able to move toward a better life. Unlike *Permanence and Change,* which he says he put together in order to keep from falling apart, in this book he took himself apart in order to put himself together in a new way, to prepare himself for the new roles he was to enter into with Libbie and as a social-cultural critic.[11]

Part 3: 1937–41

As Burke was finishing *Towards a Better Life* he was casting about for the most appropriate way to begin the second phase of his career. After writing and rejecting various projects, he settled into the writing of *Permanence and Change,* which he says he finished in 1933—the year he married Libbie. *Permanence and Change* is a book of beginnings, an exploratory work in which Burke tries to get his bearings as a social critic and to define his own orientation. Having rejected Communism (but not Marx, whom Burke was to draw upon in profound ways right up through *A Rhetoric of Motives*), Burke commits himself to the poetry of action he describes so eloquently at the end of *Permanence and Change.*

However, it is not until *Attitudes toward History,* which was published in 1937, that Burke moves from exploration to self-assurance and certainty and writes what is his major work of the thirties. Even after fifty-three years, *Attitudes toward History* is still an exciting and thought-provoking book to read (and reread)—especially parts 1 and 3, where we do not have to contend with Burke's somewhat tedious, problematical, and very partial account of Western history. I do not mean to dismiss part 2 of the book, with its economic and political analysis of Western history as a five-act drama culminating in "Emergent Collectivism"; after all, it is at the end of part 2 (166–75) that Burke develops the *comic frame,* which is one of the main achievements of this book and one of Burke's major contributions to our intellectual equipment for living. The same can be said for the "Dictionary of Pivotal

Terms" with which Burke ends the book. Like the "Lexicon Rhetorica" of *Counter-Statement*, the "Dictionary" indicates clearly that Burke has now developed a *terminology* (a set of concepts, a calculus) that equips him to analyze and interpret social dynamics in a way that suits him—that is, in a way that is consistent with his view of the role of the social critic and the obligation of the critic to provide society with the "corrective" knowledge and perspectives that it needs to stay sane or regain its sanity. As Burke says at the end of part 2: "The comic frame should enable people to *be observers of themselves, while acting*. Its ultimate goal would not be *passiveness*, but *maximum consciousness*. One would 'transcend' himself by noting his own foibles. [It] would provide a rationale for locating the irrational and the nonrational" (171).

Another achievement of this book is the way in which Burke again—as he had done in *Permanence and Change* with the poetic metaphor as key in the analysis of social behavior—brings poetry and social criticism together in the section entitled "Poetic Categories." Here he uses poetic categories to define and characterize recurrent attitudes toward history ("strategies for living"). He also uses this chapter as the occasion, early in the book, to define comedy and isolate it as the sanest and most civilized of frames of acceptance. The best of Marx, Freud, and Veblen, he says, is comic. Whatever poetry may be, Burke says, criticism had best be comic (107). Burke himself is often wonderfully comic in the way he writes as in the "comic" interpretation of T. S. Eliot's deadly serious *Murder in the Cathedral* (83–86).

The resourcefulness of this book is hard to pin down. The theory of symbolic action is here in germinal form throughout part 3 of the book. Marx, with his emphasis on class structure and the economic basis of social action (property relationships) is everywhere in the book. Burke's deepening awareness of the significance of Freud is present in all of his many references to literary works and symbolism and to the irrational and nonrational motives that operate in social behavior. The "Dictionary" is a storehouse of useful concepts. The book is full of techniques for the analysis of symbolism, wherever it is found, and everywhere suggests ways of bringing literary and social criticism together, a task Burke was to deal with at length in *The Philosophy of Literary Form*. And finally, emerging out of the whole book, in bits and pieces as one goes along, and in the very way that Burke does things, are Burke's well thought-out conceptions of comedy, a comic vocabulary, the comic critic, the comic attitude toward history as the most persuasive frame of acceptance, as the most "peaceful" and peace-promoting attitude and approach to the drama of human relations. Burke was always a yea-sayer, however dark and ironic some of his perceptions are; he has always been in the great American tradition of James, Whitman, and Emerson, just as his contemporary and fellow critic Lewis Mumford was.

It is hard to let go of this book, just as it is of *A Grammar of Motives:* one always wants to dwell in it and on it for a long time, unpacking its many treasures.[12] Much of what he was to do later is anticipated in this book, as one realizes reading it again with the rest of Burke in one's head. Burke's other work of the thirties—aside from a great many reviews—is *The Philosophy of Literary Form,* which collects essays that he wrote during the thirties, and, in the title essay, shows us the profound effect that teaching, which Burke began to do in the later thirties, will have on his work. It is in this book that Burke goes back to his first love—literature and literary criticism—and works out both the basic theory of literature and the critical methodology that will later be the basis of his poetics as he developed it in his "Symbolic of Motives."

It is in the title essay that Burke works out and applies his theory of literature as symbolic action, mostly in an analysis of the works of Coleridge. In this same essay, he elaborates on the four-part methodology he first used in *Attitudes toward History* and anticipated in the theory of form (the "Lexicon Rhetorica") in *Counter-Statement.* Like most of Burke's methodologies, the one developed here is very simple and extraordinarily resourceful when applied to *any* verbal or symbolic structure. Later, in "Fact, Inference, and Proof in the Analysis of Literary Symbolism" (1954), Burke was to call this methodology "indexing." The way to find out what is going on in a verbal structure, Burke says, is to find out what goes with what, or what equals what or what is identified with what. This obviously would include metaphors. Burke and others have called this cluster analysis. One also has to find out what versus what, or what is opposed to what. Burke has called this *agon analysis.* One must also pay attention to what *follows* what, or to the progressions in a given work. Burke called this *progressive* form in *Counter-Statement,* but it is perhaps easiest to think of it in rather conventional terms as structural analysis that studies the progress or development from beginning to middle to the end of a given text. Finally, Burke says, one must study the *transformations* in a given work, or determine what, if anything, changes or is transformed into something or someone else—as in the case of John Neal. This methodology is used by Burke throughout his career, in the many extended analyses he did for the *Symbolic,* the *Rhetoric,* and *Language as Symbolic Action,* and most extensively in "Verbal Action in Augustine's *Confessions,*" in *The Rhetoric of Religion*.

The theory of literature as symbolic action, with symbolic meaning both verbal and the usual something that is both itself and stands for something else, is Burke's functional poetics and his protest against purely aesthetic theories of literature and the new criticism's tendency to deny both a personal and a social function to literary works. In other words, it is Burke's way of insisting that literature is equipment for living, both for the person who wrote the work and for those who read it. Its function is primarily social for writer and reader. According to Burke, literature has a purgative-redemptive function; catharsis is central to the theory of symbolic action, just as it is to the theory of tragedy Burke later worked out in his essays on *The Oresteia* and *Othello,* which are part of his "Symbolic of Motives." We need to remember here, as we do everywhere in Burke from the thirties on, his deep, humanistic commitment to the proposition that, as in the comic frame of *Attitudes toward History* and later in the motto of *A Grammar of Motives,* resolving conflicts by means of words, that is, symbolically, is usually better than resolving them by actual physical means. To put it as simply as Burke sometimes does, it is better to write a poem about killing somebody, or to settle your scores verbally, than it is to go out and actually kill them. Diplomacy is always better than war.[13] Burke has spent most of his mature years as a critic trying to warn us—one of his favorite words is *admonish*—against the causes of war and killing. The *Grammar* and the *Rhetoric* are catalogues of these causes. As every reader of Burke knows, the motto of *A Grammar of Motives* is toward the purification of war; and one of Burke's most frequent reminders to us is that books should be written to promote tolerance and speculation. Burke must have been shocked by the death sentence laid on Salman Rushdie by fundamentalist Muslims for writing a novel, just as he has always been disturbed by the ideological rigidity, the fanaticism, the lack of imagination displayed by the fundamentalists in any religion and by the ethnic and racial hatreds that have led to so many killings in our time. What does all this have to do with literature as symbolic action and catharsis: well, quite a lot because few critics have ever taken literature and the powers of the word quite so seriously as

Burke nor argued quite so persuasively for its therapeutic personal and social functions in the many text-centered analyses and interpretations that he has done in his role as literary critic.

Before leaving the thirties and this text, I want to point out that *The Philosophy of Literary Form* is a lot more than the title essay and Burke's attempt—or second attempt, really—to formulate the first principles—the philosophy—of literary form. Also included in this book is the admonitory essay "The Rhetoric of Hitler's *Battle*," which is really a kind of paradigm of/for all of Burke's later work on the seductive, destructive inducements of ideological and political rhetoric that comes to a head in part 3 of *A Rhetoric of Motives*. There is also the essay "Freud and the Analysis of Poetry" in which Burke not only acknowledges the importance of Freud in his work but indicates, by way of Freud, why he too is so interested in what he calls the Demonic Trinity, or, as he so wittily puts it, in showing that sewers are what churches are for (259). Burke's obsessive concern with the hidden, the disguised motive behind the expressed one, with the secret, often guilt-ridden, and destructive motives behind apparently straightforward, often altruistic, and seemingly innocent actions begins in the thirties, especially in *Attitudes toward History*, and figures prominently in all the work of the next period.[14] Finally, we should not forget such basic Burke texts in *The Philosophy of Literary Form* as "Semantic and Poetic Meaning," where Burke again pits poetic against scientific, and the apparently very simple but extremely important "Literature as Equipment for Living," which states the most basic of all propositions for Burke's thinking about literature.

Part 4: 1941–66

Burke's central period began in the early forties (when he also first began teaching at Bennington College) and lasts through 1966. There is no way in which the five works of this period can be dealt with adequately in a short, omnibus essay such as this one. The five works are *A Grammar of Motives* (1945), *A Rhetoric of Motives* (1950), "A Symbolic of Motives" (done, really, by the late fifties and published as separate essays but never assembled by Burke into a book), *The Rhetoric of Religion* (1961), and *Language as Symbolic Action* (1966). Out of this period, and as the culmination of the work he began in the thirties, come dramatism and logology, the twin towers of the inclusive language-centered system and methodology Burke worked out between 1940 and 1966. Dramatism had as its overall object the working out of a language-centered grammar (a logic; a dialectics), a rhetoric, a poetics, and an ethics. The first three were completed and, though no "Ethics of Motives" exists as such, Burke certainly worked out the moral/ethical basis of dramatism in such essays as "A Dramatistic View of the Origins of Language" (LASA, 419–79), which locates the genius of language, and hence of humans, in the moral negative and in the tour de force that concludes *The Rhetoric of Religion,* "Epilogue: Prologue in Heaven," where Burke lays out the essential features of the drama of human relations according to dramatism/logology. Logology has as its ostensible object a working out of the relationship between the Word (Christian theology) and words, on the assumption that since theology is the perfection of the use of words, it can be used as a paradigm for the study of all uses of words. Logology in its ordinary meaning is simply the study of words (words about words), but as Burke develops and uses it, throughout *The Rhetoric of Religion* and everywhere after 1961, as the main resource of his criticism, logology takes on a whole array of special meanings peculiar to Burke's way of looking at and talking about the world (the natural, the human, the sociopolitical, the supernatural, and, of course, the verbal).

In 1963 (or thereabouts) Burke writes his extended definition of humans as the symbol-using animals (LASA, 4–24) and this action, more than anything else, tells us what the real purpose of dramatism/logology is.[15] It is not so much that Burke spun his system out of this definition as it is that, at the end—or near the end—of working out his system in *A Grammar of Motives, A Rhetoric of Motives,* "A Symbolic of Motives," and *The Rhetoric of Religion* Burke is able to make what he considers to be a definitive statement about the nature of humans, the human condition, and the drama of human relations. This definition is both the culmination of all his previous work and a point of departure for all the work that will follow in the next twenty-five years. In other words, Burke is not just a critic who enters and leaves history periodically with an essay here and a book there, as the occasion demands or will and energy make possible. He is a critic who enters history and plans to make his mark and become a significant permanent part of history by making an original contribution to our knowledge and understanding of ourselves and the drama of human relations. Burke's motives were to follow and use his genius to creative and constructive ends, however eccentric these ends might at first seem. For years, many people regarded Burke as a maverick, someone who was very difficult to place, hard to read, and nearly impossible to understand. He was thought of as a literary critic long after that had ceased to be his primary concern; it was many years before people in many disciplines began to understand the profound corrective social purpose behind his work and its wide range of applications. Burke did not live the way other critics did; he refused to be institutionalized; he was self-taught and often distrusted by the bureaucratized intellects of other formally educated critics; he was, in many ways, so far ahead of his time that other critics had a hard time figuring out what he was doing and why or what they could do with it. It was not really until the seventies that the establishment in many different disciplines finally began to understand what Burke was about and to recognize and honor him and his achievement.

In 1961 Burke ended his twenty years of teaching at Bennington and took his one-man show on the road, crisscrossing the country many times with his wife Libbie. He has been on the road ever since preaching the dramatistic/logological word. Many of the essays in *Language as Symbolic Action* were first given as talks; and almost everything that Burke has published since 1966 was first given as a talk and in one way or another is either an explanation of, or a defense of, dramatism/logology as a system and methodology against all comers—against N. O. Brown in an MLA confrontation, against Marshall McLuhan, Buckminster Fuller, B. F. Skinner and behaviorism, against scientism and reductionism of any kind, against more technology as a solution to the problems caused by technology, against purely formalist literary criticism, against Northrop Frye, against archetypal criticism and myth criticism, against any explanation of the human condition and the drama of human relations that Burke considers an oversimplification. One oversimplification is any scheme that denies the dualism (mind/body, motion/action, verbal/not verbal, nature/language, symbol using/animal, humans/nature) Burke has insisted upon from the very beginning as necessary to an adequate account of the human condition and the drama of human relations. Others are any account that shifts the stress off moral action and drama as the key to the human drama or any account that fails to acknowledge the primacy of words, of language as the essential characteristic of the human animal, or, odd as the converse of this may seem, any account that fails to acknowledge that we are *bodies* that must learn language.

Why stress this adversarial part of Burke's development and career? Because it is such an essential part of all that Burke has done since 1945 and it is a function of Burke's quite dogmatic assertion, part of a somewhat paranoic conviction that he must fight his way out of the corner he is always being backed into. After 1945, he felt more and more strongly that he had in fact, in dramatism/logology, discovered and formulated truths about the human condition, the drama of human relations (especially in the sociopolitical scene), humans' relationships to nature, supernature, and counter-nature that are so essential, so basic, so important that they can and should be pitted against—seen in relation to—other prominent views on the same topics put forth by his contemporaries.

Briefly, synoptically, here are some of the high points of the five works from this period.

A Grammar of Motives (1945)

In the pentad and the ratios and the other terminological resources of Burkean dialectics worked out for us as analytic tools in *A Grammar of Motives;* in the carefully worked out philosophy of action that forms the conceptual center of that book (in chapters 3 and 4 of part 2 of the book); in the theory of substance that Burke says is what he was trying to work out in the *Grammar;* in the theory of language and the assertion that the study of language is the key to knowledge of the human species; in the carefully worked out and often restated conception of the nature and role of the critic (the whole book embodies—or as Burke would prefer—enacts the critical intelligence at work); in the conception of criticism as comic, as hypochondriasis—that is, the study of our own human foibles, of our diseases that we may better understand and live with them; and in the conception of criticism as cure (it works, always, toward the purification of war): in these we find some of the main contributions this book has made to our intellectual equipment for living and to our own conception of ourselves as critics. And, finally, in them we encounter some of the early permanent tenets and methodologies of dramatism (*before* logology).

A Rhetoric of Motives (1950)

In moving from the *Grammar* to the *Rhetoric*, or from logic, dialectics, and substance to rhetoric, to identification and persuasion to action or attitude, Burke moves from "philosophy" to the sociopolitical scene. Burke's interest in rhetoric dates back to the twenties and *Counter-Statement* and persists all through the work of the thirties. The theory of literature as symbolic action is essentially a rhetorical theory in which literature functions as self-persuasion and as a persuader of the reader. The theory of identification as the chief persuasive device in rhetoric goes back to *Attitudes toward History* and the work Burke did there on cluster analysis and symbols of authority; it is also one of the essential parts of the four-part methodology Burke develops in the title essay of *The Philosophy of Literary Form*, there going under the name of equations, or what equals or goes with what. Burke argues in *A Rhetoric of Motives* that it is through the manipulation of identifications (sometimes overt and sometimes covert) that one persuades others to the attitude or action that one desires. And he says that it is in the sociopolitical realm that we should really study this because not only is politics impossible without rhetoric but all kinds of hidden, secret, and often dangerous identifications act as hidden persuaders in most of our sociopolitical life. Much of this is certainly not new with Burke, as he acknowledges in the first third of the book.

It is when Burke comes to the sociopolitical hierarchy, by way of Marx, Bentham, and Carlyle, that he adds a whole new dimension to dramatism and the role of the dramatistic critic. By its very nature as a hierarchy (a graded social order of higher and lower classes) the sociopolitical order or hierarchy is charged with highly symbolic identifications and is intrinsically persuasive, with those in the lower classes always being powerfully attracted to and persuaded by what is identified with the classes above them to mount or move up the hierarchy. Burke says that this causes a pervasive, widespread hierarchic psychosis and results in members of one class wooing members of another class, usually higher up, but not always, for members of higher classes often woo those in a lower class, as with gods and humans (the extreme case of reversal) or aristocrats and peasants or higher classes and rural types. Burke's conception of hierarchy and the hierarchic psychosis, joined up to rhetoric (identification and persuasion, whether active or passive) is so fertile a concept that once Burke has finished exploring or ramifying it in his typical fashion (in parts 2 and 3) by working his way through what he often calls the "range" of meanings intrinsic to the concept, he convinces us that hierarchy and the hierarchic psychosis are everywhere in both benign and malign forms and that we must arm ourselves against the malign identifications and persuaders inherent in any hierarchy, and especially in the hierarchically infused rhetoric we use and assaults us in our daily lives by way of the media. Burke develops a methodology he calls "socioanagogic criticism" for analyzing the social mystery that is present in hidden symbolic form in all hierarchic schemes whether they are ethnic, religious, political, ideological, or sexual. He does this in part 3 of *A Rhetoric of Motives,* the densest, most difficult, often most obscure part of this book—even for a veteran Burkean. Much of the obscurity comes from the fact that Burke—always afraid of, always the enemy of war and victimization in any form—is convinced that in every hierarchy, at every level of it, there are secret identifications that are in reality inducements to violence and victimization, to what he calls the "kill."

The book begins with examples of how poets symbolically kill off parts of themselves in their poems, thus adopting the resources of poetry and symbolic action to nonviolent solutions to their problems, much as Burke did in his novel, *Towards a Better Life*. The book ends with a section entitled "The Rhetorical Radiance of the 'Divine' " and is filled with examples, mostly from literature, of how this powerful persuader from the very top of the hierarchy (doing things in the name of God) is used for good and ill. *A Rhetoric of Motives* ends with this eloquent passage, which probably renders better than almost any other passage in Burke his conception of the role of the dramatistic critic and the passion of his commitment to this task.

> But since, for better or worse, the mystery of the hierarchic is forever with us, let us, as students of rhetoric, scrutinize its range of entrancements, both with dismay and in delight. And finally let us observe, all about us, forever goading us, though it be in fragments, the motive that attains its ultimate identification in the thought, not of the universal holocaust, but of the universal order—as with the rhetorical and dialectic symmetry of the Aristotelian metaphysics, whereby all classes of beings are hierarchically arranged in a chain or ladder or pyramid of mounting worth, each kind striving towards the *perfection* of its kind, and so towards the kind next above it, while the

strivings of the entire series head in God as the beloved cynosure and sinecure, the end of all desire. (*A Rhetoric of Motives,* 333)

"A Symbolic of Motives" (late 1950s)

Burke's "Symbolic of Motives" was really mostly finished by the midfifties, though parts of it were not published until later. For example, "On Catharsis, or Resolution" was published in 1959; "Catharsis—Second View" was published in 1961; and "The Thinking of the Body (Comments on the Imagery of Catharsis in Literature)" was published in 1963. However, these three essays were written long before their publication and are part of the manuscript "Poetics, Dramatistically Considered," a 391-page typed text, which Burke was circulating to his students of the Indiana School of Letters in the early and midfifties.[16] As Burke says in a letter to Cowley, he was distracted from assembling and completing his "Symbolic" in book form (a most uncharacteristic action by Burke) by his discovery of and working out of logology, which resulted from a series of talks he gave at Drew University in 1956 and 1957 on theology and language. It was these talks, which he expanded into the three main essays, that make up *The Rhetoric of Religion,* mostly during his stay at the Center for the Advanced Study in the Behavioral Sciences at Stanford University in 1957–58. The "Epilogue: Prologue in Heaven," in which Burke lays out all the coordinates of human history, according to dramatism, was not finished until 1960.

We will never know what else Burke might have written as part of the "Symbolic" had he done the usual careful introducing, revising, and shaping that was always part of his final preparations of a manuscript. Nor will we ever know, alas, exactly how he would have arranged the existing material into his usual tripartite division. What we do know is that, as with the first two motives books, most of the material for the "Symbolic" was conceived and written during a five-year period from 1950 to 1955, just as the material for *The Rhetoric of Religion* was conceived and written during the next five years and *Language as Symbolic Action* was both written and put together during the next five (1961–66). One is tempted to say that Burke had a series of five-year plans, all but one of which came to fruition in published books. The "Symbolic" did not come to fruition as a book, for reasons only known to Burke, but Burke's dramatistic poetics is certainly "complete" in the sense that all the essential elements of it are present in the existing published essays—

some of which were included in *Language as Symbolic Action,* some in the Hyman-Karmiller double volume, *Perspective by Incongruity and Terms for Order,* and some of which remain where they were originally published.[17] In other words, anyone who wishes to study the "Symbolic"—certainly Burke's major statement on the nature of literature, its function and significance as an act of language, and his most comprehensive presentation and demonstration of the methodology developed for the dramatistic analysis and interpretation of literature—can readily do so. No account of Burke's development and significance as a critic could be complete without making the achievement of his poetics a part of that accounting. Because it does not exist as a book—just as Burke's work since 1966 is not yet available to us as a book—does not mean, as some of Burke's critics seem to assume, that he has no dramatistic poetics or he has done no significant new work since 1966 and the publication of *Language as Symbolic Action.*

The central concept in Burke's poetics is catharsis, just as it was in his theory of literature as symbolic action, and its representative anecdote is tragedy, because tragedy, better than any other kind of text, best illustrates Burke's dramatistic theory (as developed in the third part of *A Rhetoric of Motives*) that the hierarchic psychosis is everywhere with us and everywhere a threat and that in *imitating* various forms of this hierarchic or social *tension,* tragedy activates and releases this tension in us, and purges off, vicariously, as imitations (not realities) do, the more dangerous parts or aspects of it. Literature thus has an essential social function as equipment for living. The classic texts for the study of Burke's dramatistic poetics are "*Othello:* An Essay to Illustrate a Method," "Form and Persecution in the *Oresteia,*" "The Language of Poetry Dramatistically Considered" (which includes the *Faust,* part 1, essay), and "Fact, Inference, and Proof in the Analysis of Literary Symbolism" (which lays out the methodology called indexing).[18] Reading these essays, and the others that make up the "Symbolic," one can readily see why, when he wrote this material, Burke thought of poetry and of his poetics as the culmination of dramatism. In the first place, the scourge of the drama of human relations—the hierarchic psychosis first introduced and developed in *A Rhetoric of Motives*—is confronted and purged off in literature; and in poetry, because of the freedom that goes with the exercising of the imagination, human beings are able to perfect the use of language, to go to the end of the line with any set of possibilities, verbal or otherwise, and in this way follow out the genius of the entelechial principle (which is what makes us rotten with perfection). Finally, the critic, in analyzing and interpreting great literary texts, can practice and preach the corrective comic perspective of criticism (first introduced in *Attitudes toward History,* refined in *The Philosophy of Literary Form,* perfected in *A Grammar of Motives*), which always involves a movement toward knowledge and the fundamental secular assumption of all Burkean criticism, which is if it can't save us (which is what religions promise to do), at least it can help us.

So why did Burke abandon his "Symbolic" and develop logology? In a sense, he didn't really do that at all: he completed his "Symbolic" and moved on, in the next five-year plan, first to logology (1961) and then to the completion of the whole dramatistic enterprise by 1966, when he finishes the final five-year plan of this productive period of his life. He is sixty-nine when this period comes to an end, seventy-two when Libbie Burke dies in 1969, and still as feisty and vigorous as ever.

The Rhetoric of Religion (1961)

Logology, which Burke first develops in *The Rhetoric of Religion* and then uses in almost all that he writes after 1961, sometimes as if it existed by itself and sometimes in conjunction with dramatism and its coordinates, is, ostensibly, the study of words and is based in the most fundamental of all dramatistic assertions: that humans are symbol-using animals and that the best way to study humans is through an intensive study of their distinctive trait—language, with the stress on symbol-using as an action. However, by the time Burke is finished working out logology he has decided that it is in theology, not poetry, that we find the perfection (the entelechy) of symbol-using, and by working out a series of analogies between Christian theology (symbol-using that comes to a head in the Word—the Logos) and symbol-using that comes to a head in god-terms, or in something like Plato's Forms, Burke establishes the main coordinates of logology as a methodology and perspective. The rest of *The Rhetoric of Religion* consists of Burke's applications of logology to two Christian texts—St. Augustine's *Confessions* and the first three chapters of Genesis—and his comic "Epilogue: Prologue in Heaven" (imitating the beginning of Goethe's *Faust,* part 1), which consists of a dialogue between TL (The Lord) and S (Satan) before the Creation and Fall, and translates or transmogrifies the whole history of humankind from the beginning to the end of time, from Genesis to

Revelation, into dramatistic and logological terms. In some way, *The Rhetoric of Religion* is one of Burke's most definitive texts, as well as one of his densest and most complex.

It is definitive because so much of it seems so final: logology is Burke's final methodology for the study of words; using Christian theology as a paradigm for the study of words allows Burke to discuss first and last things over and over again in his own terms as he works his way, chapter by chapter, through the *Confessions* and, in almost tortuous detail, through the Christian or biblical narrative account of the Creation, Fall, covenants, redemption by way of the sacrificial Christ, and Apocalypse, and the timeless cycle of terms implicit in the idea of order which he says is intrinsic in this narrative or rectilinear account;[19] and the "Epilogue: Prologue in Heaven," where The Lord explains to his cooperative interlocutor, Satan, the whole mighty moral drama of human relations as it develops inexorably from the dramatistic fact that humans are the symbol-using animals. No purer Burke in his maturity can be found anywhere else, and Burke in his maturity is almost always dense and complex, often pursuing a hidden agenda you have to figure out, analyzing texts with exhausting thoroughness and intellectual ingenuity, and writing, when it suits him, as it does in the "Epilogue: Prologue in Heaven" with great wit, humor, irony, cleverness, and inventiveness on the most serious of topics, reminding us, as he does himself, that we better take things seriously, but not too seriously lest we puff up and burst in our self-satisfied pride.

Language as Symbolic Action (1966)

A great text; a great moment in Burke's development. What follows is something of an anticlimax, but only in relative terms, for *Language as Symbolic Action* is really the most complete single-volume presentation of mature Burke that we have or are ever liable to have until someone does a reader. It is probably Burke's most carefully arranged, most thoroughly annotated, and most diverse and representative book. After the fact, it seems like the most perfectly planned and timed book that Burke could have done at this date. It is a book that sums him up or, more accurately, sums up the achievements of the four previous books and moves forward from them, in some of its essays, by applying logology and, especially, by applying the dramatistic poetics to a variety of new texts. It is good to remember, when thinking about *Language as*

Symbolic Action and what is and is not included in it, that in 1964 Hyman and Karmiller edited and published *Perspective by Incongruity and Terms for Order,* which consists of essential Burkean selections from *The White Oxen* through *The Rhetoric of Religion* (1961) *and* includes some of the most basic essays from the "Symbolic," but omits any selections from either *A Grammar of Motives* or *A Rhetoric of Motives.*

What Burke does in selecting the material for *Language as Symbolic Action* is include all the major essays he wrote and published between 1961 and 1966, most of which are developed from either dramatism or logology or a combination of both and many of which were written as attempts to finish off the "Symbolic"—which Burke kept announcing as forthcoming during the early sixties. In addition to this material, Burke includes essays from the early fifties that were written for the "Symbolic," such as "Form and Persecution in the *Oresteia*" (1952), "Goethe's *Faust,* Part 1" (1954–1955), "Vegetal Radicalism of Theodore Roethke" (1950), and "The Thinking of the Body" (1963), which was written in the early fifties but published later. And finally, because it is so essential to dramatism and the whole moral/ethical drama that is central to it, he includes the four-part "A Dramatistic View of the Origins of Language" (1952–53).[20]

Part 5: Collected Poems (1968)

With *Language as Symbolic Action* we come to the end of this long productive and creative period in Burke's development. After 1966, Burke was never to return to literary criticism or literature in any significant way, though he was to continue to write poetry into the seventies and in the early seventies conceived and partially wrote his satiric piece "Towards Helhaven: Three Stages of a Vision." Many people seem to think that Burke's career and development end after 1966—in part because they do not take his poetry seriously and in part because there are no further books to deal with and *Language as Symbolic Action* seems, falsely, I think, so inclusive. Burke's *Collected Poems* was published in 1968. If we added his "Eye Crossing" poem, which was originally published in 1969, the year Libbie Burke died, and later, in 1973, in a longer version, with an elaborate commentary on the poem by Burke, and the few poems he published after her death, we would have, if not all the poems Burke wrote, at least all that he has been willing to publish.

Anyone who really wants to understand Burke should read his poems. There is the critical self and the poetic self, both of which (or whom) have comedy and the comedic in common. Wit, humor, irony, satire, self-irony, mind play, verbal play, puns, a love of formal tinkering and of aphorisms, a sense of the absurd, including the absurd in his morbid, sickly "selph," therapeutic laughter, comedy, including the comedy of the human barnyard—all of these are part of Burke's poetry, as they are of Burke's performing self and, in different ways, of his "comic" self—as in "Epilogue: Prologue in Heaven" in *The Rhetoric of Religion*. Though it is not as obvious as it might be from the letters that Paul Jay selected for inclusion in the Burke-Cowley letters, these are also traits of Burke's letter-writing self, including, no doubt, the many letters he wrote when angry or somewhat tanked or "alkylined" and put in his unsent letter file.

The *Collected Poems* is a joyful, high-spirited book, appropriately enough dedicated "To Libbie," who brought so much joy into Burke's life.[21] It was Libbie Burke who arranged the puzzlelike Flowerishes that appear in this book on pages 88–92 and 297–300, and which, taken as a whole, represent the essential ironic nature of Burke's mind, critical perspective, and final vision, as well as his belief that there is no unearned wisdom. Irony gone sour becomes cynicism and debunking, neither of which Burke ever allowed himself to lapse into—though he must have been tempted at times, especially after the death of Libbie. But Burke had his final say against the destructive debunking in *The Philosophy of Literary Form* and he was always saved from cynicism by the laughter that was a part of his irony. Burke's lasting fame will certainly not depend upon his poetry nor, for that matter, upon his novel, both minor works in relation to his criticism, but works nonetheless, which name his number for us because they are also his symbolic acts and some part of the complex personality of this American genius; some of the burdens that go with being a genius get expressed and purged when the fictional and poetic voices speak and Burke uses himself as a text. This is probably nowhere more obvious and illuminating than in Burke's last "story," "The Anaesthetic Revelation of Herone Liddell," an obviously autobiographical "fiction" he wrote after a traumatic, but minor, hernia operation when he was sixty and which he describes as a kind of symbolic "recovery" sequel to his novel, *Towards a Better Life,* another fiction about other traumatic events written twenty-five years earlier.[22] And returning to the poetry, it is certainly obvious in another symbolic work where Burke also uses himself as text, the "Eye Crossing" poem Burke wrote while he and Libbie were living in Brooklyn during the last painful year of her life, and Burke, in a reversal of roles he must certainly have understood and appreciated, literally became Libbie's keeper. As Burke has said so often about the writers he has studied, we would be foolish to ignore and not make use of the evidence provided us about Burke, and his motives, by these fictional and poetic works. As he said long ago in *The Philosophy of Literary Form:* the critic should use all that is there to use in trying to understand what the great creative minds are doing in their works and how any or all of it impinges upon our own lives. Burke's most productive period began in 1933 with his marriage to Libbie and the writing of *Permanence and Change,* his first symbolic act as a social critic. This transformation is certainly symbolically enacted in *Towards a Better Life.* It is, therefore, most appropriate and significant that his last published book, after thirty-six wonderfully productive years, should be a book of poems dedicated to Libbie and that his last major poem, "Eye Crossing," should come out of a "context of situation" in which Burke has become the keeper of the woman who changed his life, at a time when she is clearly dying from an irreversible, untreatable, fatal disease—and one which must have driven both of these wonderful, always active and creative people to the edge of madness. Fortunately, Libbie died before she became completely helpless—that is before she had lost the use of all her muscles, including her tongue (but remained mentally alert yet helpless) and finally would have choked to death on her useless tongue. Burke, of course, went on and, as I write (January 1990), he is still going on.

Part 6: 1970–

By way of closure, I want to consider what Burke has done (and not done) since 1970. What he has not done is as important as what he has done because it is responsible for the fact that we will not be able to adequately assess the final stages of his development and career until he is dead and we have access to all the work of this period. To use his own phrase, Burke has chosen to exist in his scatterhood ever since the death of Libbie because he has refused to assemble and publish any new books. Instead, he has traveled around a lot, even going to Europe for the first time, shortly after the death of Libbie; he has spoken, performed, and been in residence at a great many different places; he has been the subject of numerous conferences devoted to him and his work and has become the subject (or object) of numerous new books, dissertations, and essays on him and his work by people in many different disciplines, including European scholars, who finally discovered him; special issues of journals have been devoted to him, as have special sessions at regional and national conferences. And finally, during this same period, as Burke has almost literally scattered the seeds of dramatism and logology all over America, he has been rewarded by receiving many honorary degrees—this critic who never even bothered to get a B.A. degree—and many awards in acknowledgment of his achievements. In sum, and somewhat ironically, it is during this period after the death of Libbie that he finally became what he set out to be in the twenties: a famous person, an acknowledged authentic American genius, like Faulkner, with every bit of his fame *earned* by the labors of his mind and the power of his written words.

But let me return briefly to Burke in his scatterhood: Burke has simply declined to put his "Symbolic" together as a book the University of California Press (or many others) would gladly publish,[23] and has refused to, and refused anyone else permission to, put together a collection of the important major essays he has written since 1970, a collection that, like *Language as Symbolic Action* or *The Philosophy of Literary Form,* would have summed up the work of the last twenty years and would have put an end to the common delusion that his development came to an end in 1966, with his last published book. Basically what Burke has done since 1970 is turn himself into his own best advertisement for himself and his ideas. This is all well and good, but in a sense Burke has scattered himself instead of gathering himself, as he had done in the past, into a book, or books, which could be read and reread, studied and absorbed in relation to his other books. I have discussed the lost "Symbolic"; let me here discuss the essays Burke has published since 1970, up to and including the "In Haste" piece in *Pre/Text* (1985).

The work since 1970 can be divided into two groups and discussed rather briefly because all of it is based upon the achievements—that is, the coordinates—of dramatism/logology and most of it consists of attempts on Burke's part to sum himself up as concisely as possible or attempts to take dramatism/logology as a way of thinking about the world to the end of the line. The first group consists of what I will call the Helhaven (or language/technology) material after the title of the satire Burke published first in 1971. When Burke conceived this antitechnology satire is not clear, but it figures prominently in the two lectures that make up *Dramatism and Development* (1971, published in 1972) and in the 1974 essay "Why Satire, with a Plan for Writing One," which is his most complete version of the satire and one of his major statements on the relation between language, rationality, and technology, and what we need to do about the threat posed by high technology.[24] In this material, Burke moves his thought forward in the following manner and arrives at what is surely an essential part of his final ironic vision of humankind and the drama of human relations. If language and hierarchy were the major themes and concern of Burke's work in the forties and fifties and if language and theology were the major concern of his work in the late fifties and sixties, then we can say that language and technology were the major concern of his work in the seventies. Burke's interest in and concern with technology—especially the high technology that develops during and after WWII—goes way back to the thirties. It is a central concern in *A Grammar of Motives* and becomes a specter haunting Burke's mind from the atomic/hydrogen bomb on. However, it is not really until the late sixties and early seventies that Burke begins to explain technology, and especially the high technology of Western culture and America in particular, in dramatistic and logological terms. That is, he links it to symbol-using and gradually works toward his ironic formula that human beings' entelechy is technology. Human beings' specific genius is for symbol-using; the final genius of symbol-using is no longer the god-head, but high technology is; in and by means of high technology, humans have arrived at the ultimate secrets of life and matter and so have the capability of creating and manipulating new life and of destroying life itself, or at least all human life, and perhaps the planet earth as well. Humans, in other words, thanks to symbol-using and technology, have become the god-head because they have, as a result of their genius—their desire to know and understand and control everything—arrived at the knowledge that gives them the powers once attributed to God.

This final vision of Burke's is most clearly worked out and presented in the second Helhaven essay, "Why Satire, with a Plan for Writing One" (1974), and in his bicentennial lecture, "Towards Looking Back" (1976). In both of these essays, Burke makes extensive ironic use of Whitman and the romance of technology so prominent in his poems and essays and in nineteenth-century America's view of itself—generally.

Whitman's dream has become our nightmare, Burke says, and the only real question anymore is whether we will be able to use all the knowledge and power we now have for good or ill. More technology will not solve the problems already created by technology; only a neohumanistic (poetic, comic, and antitechnological) corrective vision or perspective can bring an end to our slow pollution and destruction of the earth and its atmosphere, and us along with it. And Burke, ironist that he is and good ecologist that he has always been, must doubt whether such a corrective vision would have any persuasive power in the seats of real power: science, economics, and politics.

Burke has moved some distance in his thought beyond the hierarchic psychosis that so dominated his thinking in the fifties and early sixties. As has been typical of his development from the very beginning, when he moved from smaller (literary criticism) to larger (social criticism and later, from social to global), Burke has consistently tried to take on larger and larger questions and move his thought toward the all-inclusive, ultimate questions. In his Helhaven works, or those essays that are concerned with language and technology, Burke has certainly arrived, by his own dramatistic/logological route, at the final, ultimate question about humans, the symbol-using animals: will the creative genius of humans, a function of their innate inherited genetic endowment, their ability to originally create symbol-systems (primarily language) and their ability to learn and use symbol systems (we are bodies that learn language, Burke says)—will this creative genius take us to the holocaust, the apocalypse; or can we use our knowledge and power to save ourselves from ourselves, somehow controlling both the suicidal and homicidal motives that seem intrinsic to the drama of human relations.

These are among the last questions Burke asks; and though they may seem like questions of the seventies, they seem less and less historically limited as we enter the nineties, plagued and harassed, even as we are served and helped, by technology and its products, especially by the products of electronic technology. I don't wish to present Burke here, toward the end of his career, as a doomsday thinker. He's not, nor has he ever been. Even as he contemplates our possible self-caused doomsday, he satirizes it and proposes, as usual, his comic corrective neohumanistic perspective. In doing both, he is fulfilling the admonitory role of the critic, a role he adopted in *Permanence and Change* and to which he has been faithful ever since. Burke's Helhaven satire is basically very simple and well worth contemplating if we wish to understand some of the end thoughts of this remarkable man. In the satire, Burke has the lords of high technology—the small elite group that has benefited the most from high technology and its products—build a space bubble on the moon—Burke calls it counter-nature—that exactly reproduces what they are used to on earth. But of course it is all artificial. At the point where the lords of high technology have polluted or destroyed most of planet earth and made it uninhabitable, they get in their spaceships—themselves products of high technology—and set forth for Helhaven—the ironic punning name of the space bubble on the moon, also a product of high technology. There they will live happily ever after in their counter-natural setting.

Whither after this, one might ask? Well, in a sense, Burke returned to himself and his own development after Helhaven, summing himself up, exploring the implications of his refinement of his dramatistic definition of humans (from humans the symbol-using animals to we are bodies that learn language), defending dramatism/logology as a system or position against his traditional adversaries (scientism, the simplifiers, the behaviorists, the warmongers and polarizers, and the politicians, the technocrats, and any others who did not appreciate the merits of the dramatistic/logological perspective). His defense of himself can best be seen in an essay such as "(Nonsymbolic) Motion (Symbolic) Action" (1978) and his summing up of himself can best be seen in an essay such as "Variations on Providence" (1981), which ends with a section entitled "Counter-Nature: Fulfillment *via* Technology" and consists of thirteen summarizing logological propositions. And, finally, as he has been doing here and there ever since "*Curriculum Criticum*" (1953) was added to the second edition of *Counter-Statement,* Burke recapitulates his own development, most notably in the extensive interview which appears in *All Area,* no. 2 (1983), in the two long afterwords he adds to the new editions of *Permanence and Change* and *Attitudes toward History* in 1984, and the long "In Haste" piece written for the special issue of *Pre/Text* (1985) devoted to him.

Epilogue

And, of course, many others have been commenting on him and summing him up since the great revival of interest in his work began in the mid- and late seventies, a revival that has thus far resulted in four important new books on Burke (with more forthcoming),[25] the formation of the Kenneth Burke Society, numerous conferences devoted to him and his work, especially by those in communications, and a flood of essays.

One would have to say, now, in 1990, that Burke has finally gotten his just rewards (recognition and appreciation, understanding) for a long creative and productive life. However, the returns are not all in yet, nor will they be for some time to come—certainly not until the archives at Penn State and elsewhere are more complete. There must still be a treasure trove of material in Burke's house at Andover, as well in the thousands of still uncollected, unpublished letters. The Burke-Cowley letters, valuable as Paul Jay's selection of them is, represent but a partial selection from that long and important correspondence. The last forty-five years of Burke's life—1943–88—are inadequately represented in Jay's collection (which stops at 1981) and many crucial events in Burke's life and in the history of his time never figure at all in the published letters. No one really knows (except the poet himself) how many unpublished poems Burke still has in his files, nor how much other material there is that he wrote but never published. And there are his so-called papers—the voluminous notes he is always referring to and the drafts of his essays and books. No one has yet written a biography, and Burke, for reasons of his own, has always refused to write anything but bits and pieces of his autobiography. No one has ever really written about Burke as a reviewer—he wrote more than 150 reviews in his life—and only a few of these many reviews have been collected and published (in *The Philosophy of Literary Form*). I do not mean to suggest that Burke should be picked apart and worked over the way Faulkner has been, only that large quantities of essential material (including tapes, videotapes, interviews, remembrances, notes on and accounts of his many lectures, performances, and prolonged stays at various institutions—to name a few) remain to be collected, assembled, sorted out, and, where feasible, published in book form if we are ever to arrive at a comprehensive view and assessment of this remarkable man's achievements.

Burke the published critic is one thing; but Burke the man or, rather, Burke the person and personality is another, and as such has had a powerful effect on many of us. He would not want to be, nor should we really want to (though some have tried), turn him into a cult figure and lose him in the inevitable vagaries, vulgarities, and sentimentalities of personality adulation—a tendency we can see quite clearly in the

1985 *Pre/Text* special issue devoted to him. He is a great man as well as a great thinker; he is a person of extraordinary generosity toward all those who were genuinely interested in his work; he is a person of great integrity, who has lived what he believed in, affirming in his life-style at Andover with Libbie and his family what he argued for and against in his writing; he is a person of great honesty, often telling us the truths about ourselves, our country, and our times that we did not really want to hear, but which we knew to be true; and he was a great teacher for those willing to pay attention to what he said and did in and out of his writing, with the doing (the actions of the mind, the way he went about things) as important as the saying (the truths, the ironies, the aphorisms, the pronouncements scattered through his works and conversations).

Finally, no one (since my own efforts in *Critical Responses* twenty years ago) has undertaken the extensive and difficult task of reviewing and evaluating the now rather considerable amount of scholarship that has been done on Burke, going back to the pioneering works and coming forward to the huge amount of work done in the seventies, eighties, and nineties by scholars in many different fields, here and abroad.

Notes

All my references to and quotations from Burke's books are to the University of California Press editions of his works. The original dates of publication are given in the body of the essay.

I want to note here that I have made no *serious* attempt to acknowledge or in any way to argue with the considerable amount of work now in print about Burke, either in the body of the essay or in the notes that follow. This "field guide" is based on my reading and rereading of primary works by Burke, including his letters to me, and on many years of thinking and writing about Burke. It is now possible, I think, to meditate on Burke as a whole, and that is what I have tried to do here, taking no specific doctrinal or "discipline" approach and trying to acknowledge and account for all of his significant works.

This essay, here slightly revised, is reprinted by permission of the University of Alabama Press from *Extensions of the Burkeian System*, James W. Chesebro, ed. © 1993 the University of Alabama Press. This volume consists mostly of essays that were originally prepared as position papers for the first national conference of the Kenneth Burke Society, which was held in May 1990, at New Harmony, Indiana, to coincide with Burke's ninety-third birthday on May 5.

1. *The Selected Correspondence of Kenneth Burke and Malcolm Cowley,* ed. Paul Jay (New York: Viking, 1988). I have drawn upon this invaluable collection of letters throughout this essay. My only regret about this selection is that so much of it is devoted to the early years and not enough to the amazingly productive (for Burke) years from 1943 to 1981. Hopefully, someone will do a second volume of selections from this rich exchange of letters between these important but quite different American men of letters.

2. I first visited Burke in Andover in the early sixties after *The Rhetoric of Religion* was published and last visited him there in 1968, during the last year of Libbie Burke's life. By then, Libbie was in a wheelchair and Burke had modernized because of that. He put in a regular bathroom, ran water into the house, had a well dug and a septic system put in. During all of my other visits during the sixties, he was still using his outhouse and carried all of his water into the house in galvanized pails from his well next to the house. Libbie Burke was a truly remarkable and wonderful person who understood Burke and his genius perfectly and knew exactly how to deal with and get along with this volatile and difficult man. They were an amazing couple. We used to visit them with our pack of kids and dog, whose name was Burke. Dealing with my dog at Burke's house was, to say the least, highly comical.

3. Burke gradually bought up all the land between the original two houses, as well as land across the road, where his pond and tennis court are located. He also bought and restored a pig barn across the road where his daughters and guests stayed. His grandchildren built a house down the road. Libbie had a studio (she was an excellent painter) in the woods up behind the house. The original house was down the road from where Burke and Libbie lived. My memory of my visits there is one filled with people, especially family. Burke's daughters lived in New York City and would come out on weekends, as would some of the grandchildren. Burke's sons were still around when we first visited. I remember long evenings of eating, drinking, and talking. Then, as now, Burke was a fabulous talker and arguer, as well as a truly remarkable drinker. He also loved to walk, especially at night, after hours of drinking and talking, and would take you out for long walks on the dark country roads, talking all the time, as vigorous as ever even as you were about to drop from exhaustion and alcohol.

4. He did this especially in *Attitudes toward History,* the title essay of *The Philosophy of Literary Form,* and "Freud and the Analysis of Poetry" in *The Philosophy of Literary Form.*

5. See Tim Crusius, "Kenneth Burke on His 'Morbid Selph': *The Collected Poems* as Comedy," *CEA Critic* 43 (May 1981): 18–32. I have only read a manuscript version of this essay, but I assume that the published version is essentially the same. Crusius has also written brilliantly on *The White Oxen* and *Towards a Better Life,* but has apparently not published either of these essays. Again, I read them both in manuscript and am somewhat puzzled that they are not in print.

6. See my essay "Kenneth Burke's Encounters with Walt Whitman," *Walt Whit-*

man Quarterly Review 6 (Fall 1988): 61–90, in which I discuss this poem and the Helhaven satire at length.

7. Armin Paul Frank, in his *Kenneth Burke* (New York: Twayne, 1969), 28–43, has written an illuminating account of these stories. For some reason, we tend to overlook Frank's excellent book on Burke, with its many fine insights into Burke and his work. He writes about Burke with considerable wit and wisdom and brings a welcome European perspective to bear upon this unique American critic.

8. See "*Curriculum Criticum*," *Counter-Statement*, 213. The work is transitional because it comes after *Counter-Statement* and before *Permanence and Change*. The manuscript was published for the first time in *Extensions of the Burkeian System* along with Greig Henderson's commentary on it. Timothy Crusius has written a fine analysis of the manuscript and its implications for the study of Burke. See his essay "Kenneth Burke's *Auscultation:* A 'De-struction' of Marxist Dialectic and Rhetoric," *Rhetorica* 6 (Autumn 1988): 355–79.

9. Burke's last significant essays in literary criticism are all in *Language as Symbolic Action*, even though he did, occasionally, return to the subject of literary criticism in some of his essays and reviews after that date.

10. This essay has been published. See Kenneth Burke, "On Stress, Its Seeking," in *Why Men Take Chances*, ed. Samuel Z. Klausner (New York: Anchor Books, 1970). Burke sent me a manuscript copy of it (thirty-eight typescript pages) shortly after he wrote it in 1966 on the occasion of the republication of his novel by the University of California Press. See also his prefaces to the first and second editions of the novel, his preface to *The Complete White Oxen*, his afterword to *Attitudes toward History, Language as Symbolic Action*, 338, and the many references to the novel in the Burke-Cowley letters, as well as Paul Jay's comments on it in his introduction to part 2.

11. An adequate account of this novel as symbolic action would require a long, carefully documented analysis of the text, using Burke's own methodology, especially of all those scenes and passages involving John Neal and his women, particularly Genevieve, and of part 3, where the transformation of John Neal occurs, along with the strange episodes involving Alter Ego, which are vaguely homosexual, and the episode with the Mad Girl in White, in which John Neal seduces an essentially helpless female. See chap. 6 for such an account.

12. Burke, of course, has made it even harder to let go of this book with all of the additions he has made to it since the first edition. Not only do the many long footnotes take one off in many different directions, but the "Dictionary of Pivotal Terms" is deliberately designed as a nonsequential stimulator and recapitulator at the end of the original edition of the book. To the first edition, Burke added an introduction, an afterword, and the "Appendix: The Seven Offices" when the second edition was published by Hermes in 1959; and to all of this he added the long (fifty-five-page) "Afterword: *Attitudes toward History:* In Retrospective Prospect" to the third edition published by the University of California Press in 1984. Much

could be made of the original and final structure of this book. See my keynote address "Criticism as a Way of Life or Criticism as Equipment for Living," *Kenneth Burke Society Newsletter* 6, no. 2 (Oct. 1990): 7–15.

13. Burke never denies that some wars and revolutions have to be fought; he only argues that many large and small-scale wars are senseless and need never be fought. Many of these senseless wars and killings take place because of ideological differences that have hardened into implacable fanatical commitments, often supported by literal-minded interpretations of "holy" texts, whether political or religious. Lebanon would epitomize what Burke means by senseless wars: There, Muslims fight Muslims, Muslims fight Christians, Christians fight Christians, both fight Jews; but all of this is also happening in other parts of the world: Muslims fought Muslims in the Iran/Iraq war and killed each other in the millions. Muslims fight Hindus in India; Catholics fight Protestants in Ireland. Ethnic, racial, religious, and political strife (killing) occur all over the world these days, and much of it is due to the way in which words are used and interpreted and the apparently incurable human desire to group together with one's own kind *and* exclude or destroy those who are different—whether of a different color, a different race, a different religion, a different ideology. When Burke dedicates a book to the purification of war and writes at length about dialectics, and the basic principles of discussion and debate so central to democracy as a political system and criticism as a way of life, he is writing out of and pleading for one of the most profound aspirations of all thoughtful people in the twentieth century, a century in which hundreds of millions of humans (and who knows how many animals and other living creatures) have been killed in wars in the name of the state, in the name of God, in the name of democracy, in the name of communism, in the name of right, in the name of racial purity; he is writing out of desire for peace, out of a deep desire that a way can be found to minimize the polarizations and, in many cases, the goals of empire that have caused all these wars and killings. The February 1990 developments in South Africa are a splendid example of Burke's assertion that we can purify war by means of talk—discussion, debate, negotiations.

14. Burke's interest in these matters is certainly compulsive and obsessive and comes to a head in his relentless pursuit of evidence of the presence of the Demonic Trinity (the fecal, sexual, and urinal) where one might least expect it. Burke's search for evidence of the Demonic Trinity is often a hidden agenda in many of his analyses of texts and is based on his assumption that there is always some form of sin and guilt hidden in every text (and life) that must be purged. This explains his frequent search for puns and his development of the technique he calls "joycing"—which he uses to phonetically coerce words until they become images of the Demonic Trinity. His most notorious example of this, and one that outraged many critics, is his assertion that the famous lines from the end of Keats's "Ode on a Grecian Urn"—"Beauty is truth, truth beauty" really mean "body is turd, turd body." His most extended discussion of this matter can be found in "The Thinking of the Body" and

"Somni Ad Urinandum" in *Language as Symbolic Action.* He also says *towards* in the title of his novel contains punwise "tords," or "turds."

15. Parts of this definition—that is, phrases of it—were written much earlier, and Burke was to tamper with and modify his definition somewhat in later years by saying that we are bodies that learn language, rather than symbol-using animals, and that we are unique because, of all other species, only humans have a foreknowledge of death. Still, my point is essentially correct and is corroborated by Burke who says that you do not ever really start with a definition like this one, but arrive at it, bit by bit, phrase by phrase, until it suddenly comes to you whole and you realize that it is your title of titles and sums up all the essential parts of your thinking. Only after you have arrived at such a definition can you then start from it in the work that follows—which, of course, is exactly what Burke has done since 1963.

16. Interesting as this manuscript is, it is clearly only a *draft* of Burke's poetics. See my discussion of Burke's "Symbolic" in *Kenneth Burke and the Drama of Human Relations,* 2d ed. (University of California Press, 1982), 230–37, 288–92. Burke was a great reviser, and it seems perfectly clear that any final version of his *Poetics* would have been much different from this draft.

17. It seems likely that Burke would have included "Symbolic Action in a Poem by Keats" in the "Symbolic." This essay was also included in *A Grammar of Motives.* In the Hyman-Karmiller volume, the following selections in *Perspective by Incongruity and Terms for Order* are part of the "Symbolic": "From Three Definitions" and "*Othello:* An Essay to Illustrate a Method"; and from *Terms for Order,* the following selection is part of the "Symbolic": "Fact, Inference, and Proof in the Analysis of Literary Symbolism."

18. This is somewhat misleading. I say these are the classic texts because two of the essays develop the theory of tragedy and the theories of imitation and catharsis that are so central to Burke's poetics; one essay lays out the basic methodology (indexing) in great detail through an analysis of Joyce's *Portrait;* and the fourth essay lays out Burke's whole theory of poetic language and the freedom he associates with it; develops his theory of the text; and, finally, applies both in a brilliant, detailed analysis of Goethe's *Faust,* part 1. However, there is considerably more to Burke's "Symbolic" than what one finds in these four classic essays.

19. No one-sentence account of this essay on the first three chapters of Genesis can possibly render the complexity and ingenuity of Burke's dialectical spinning out of the tautological cycle of terms he says is implicit in the idea of order. The beautifully symmetrical chart in *The Rhetoric of Religion* (184) gives some idea of the complexity of this endeavor and the ways in which Burke tries to relate the dramatistic account of the creation and the drama of human relations to the biblical account. This whole essay pursues at much greater length a distinction Burke first made in *A Grammar of Motives* between logical and temporal, or between the ways in which a narrative or rectilinear account of things simply lays out in terms of scene-agents and actions what was logically prior to the temporal account. To show how this is

true, Burke generates the whole biblical account of Christian history from Creation to Apocalypse from an analysis of the cycle of terms implicit in the idea of order.

20. This essay is certainly the culmination of Burke's dramatistic thinking about the nature of language—a way of thinking that he began in *A Grammar of Motives*. Had he written his projected "Ethics of Motives," this essay would have been central to it. In asserting that there are no negatives in nature and that it is language that adds the negative, especially the moral negative but also the kind of negative we get in irony and abstractions, Burke makes crucial distinctions between nature and language: the preverbal (nature before humans), the verbal (nature with language and humans added), the postverbal (language and language-created concepts infused back into nature by humans), and the metaverbal (the realm beyond language, arrived at by means of language).

21. Burke also dedicated *A Grammar of Motives* "To Elizabeth Without Whom Not" which, symbolically, at least, is the perfect pairing for the motto of that book. Burke's other dedications are sort of interesting: three books—*The Philosophy of Literary Form, A Rhetoric of Motives,* and *Language as Symbolic Action*—are dedicated to his patron and friend, James Sibley Watson, who, with Schofield Thayer, provided the chief financial support for the *Dial.* When I say Watson was his patron, I mean that he provided Burke with a fixed amount of money for many years, beginning, I believe, in the thirties, and probably helped make it possible for Burke to devote himself full-time to writing. Burke dedicated *The White Oxen* to his first wife, Lily, and *Permanence and Change* to his mother and father. His first short book of poems, *Book of Moments,* he dedicated to his "sparring partners." All the rest of his books are without dedications, which has always seemed a little strange to me. And only *A Grammar of Motives* has a motto; but then, it might well be the motto for all of Burke's critical works. The dedication of *A Grammar of Motives,* "To Elizabeth Without Whom Not," proved to be somewhat prophetic in the sense that no further *new* books by Burke have been published since her death in 1969.

22. Except for some of his long poems, such as "Eye Crossing," "On Flood Times of Sinkership," and "Introduction to What," the Herone Liddell story is probably the most obvious and the best example of Burke using himself as text—something he also does in some of his essays. In this story, Burke starts out with his hysterical and certainly paranoic reaction to the minor hernia operation, with all of its bodily indignities, that he is about to, and does, undergo. All the first part of the story is body obsessed and somatically concerned. The second part of the story deals with the revelation and Burke's (Herone's) dreams, and is psyche-centered. Who but Burke would analyze his own dreams for us or tell us how important it is to listen to one's unconscious? In the third section of the story, entitled "Haunted by Ecology," Burke (Herone) explains that being so obsessed with his body and its mortality naturally got him to thinking about symbol-using and humans' specific genius. In this section, we have a brief summary of dramatism, which Burke then uses to explain himself to himself, especially the relationship between psyche and soma and human beings'

duality. From this, in good Burke fashion, he finally gets to ecology and the ways in which humans, because of their symbol-using genius and especially because of the technology that symbol-using makes possible, are destroying nature. So from his initial concern with his own body, Herone (Burke) finally moves to the much larger concern with human beings' relationship to nature. This movement from the concrete, highly particular, and personal to the global is most characteristic of Burke, especially from *A Grammar of Motives* on, as is the analogy he works from between the mind and body, the psyche and soma, and humans (the mind) and the world's body. The last part of the story has Herone (Burke and Libbie) in Florida recuperating by the sea. Most of this section of the story is about Herone reading and meditating on the dying Keats's letters. If we remember that Keats, like Burke, is a Word-Man, a symbol-user, this reading of Keats's last letters will make more sense to us. Many of these letters are concerned with poetry, with symbol-using at a high and refined level. Herone recovers at the end of the story, in part by having young Keats die for him from his bodily affliction, which was consumption. A lot can be learned about Burke from studying this story, just as it can from the study of any of his other fictions and poems where he deliberately confesses to us by using his private self as his text—whether in disguised form, as in the story, or in frankly open, undisguised form, as in the long poems. Burke's commentary on his "Eye Crossing" poem, which he wrote in response to student analyses of the poem solicited by his friend Henry Sams at Penn State, is revealing, especially since it is written so soon after Libbie's death.

23. In fact, Burke has probably lost, or lost sight of, the original conception of the "Symbolic" he was working with in the fifties. See the list of what Burke thought might be included in the "Symbolic" in 1978 in my *Kenneth Burke and the Drama of Human Relations*, 2d ed., 291–92. The logic of this list is hard to figure out, except that most of the items have something to do with literature and anything published in *Language as Symbolic Action* is omitted. Basically, it would be another omnibus collection of Burke's uncollected essays and would resemble *The Philosophy of Literary Form* in the sense that it focuses on literature and literary criticism.

24. I have written at length on much of this material in "Kenneth Burke's Encounters with Walt Whitman" and in chapter 6 of *Kenneth Burke and the Drama of Human Relations*, 2d ed.

25. These four books are *Representing Kenneth Burke*, ed. Hayden White and Margaret Brose (Baltimore: Johns Hopkins University Press, 1982); Frank Lentricchia's *Criticism and Social Change* (Chicago: University of Chicago Press, 1983); *The Legacy of Kenneth Burke*, ed. Herbert W. Simons and Trevor Melia (Madison: University of Wisconsin Press, 1989); and Greig E. Henderson's *Kenneth Burke: Literature and Language as Symbolic Action* (Athens: University of Georgia Press, 1988). The second edition of my 1963 book on Burke, *Kenneth Burke and the Drama of Human Relations*, with a long new chapter covering Burke's work from 1963–81, was also published during this period (1982). These books have certainly altered the way we think about Burke. Lentricchia's book, an aggressive defense

of the social function of criticism that uses Burke as a basic text, is especially suggestive; and Henderson's book finally makes an attempt to see Burke in relation to other language theorists of his time. The other two books are collections of essays that provide ways of reading Burke by people in a variety of disciplines. In addition to these books, a number of highly sophisticated critical minds have made extensive and interesting uses of Burke; among these are Hayden White, Clifford Geertz, Sherman Paul, Harold Bloom, Bernard Duffey, Wayne Booth—to name but a few. Richard Thames's "Selected Bibliography of Critical Responses to Kenneth Burke, 1968–1986," in *The Legacy of Kenneth Burke*, 305–15, gives some indication of the range of work done on Burke as well as the range of his influence. However, his bibliography is far from complete and much good work has been done since he completed it and much interesting work is in progress by a new generation of Burke scholars.

Part 2

Individual Texts

Chapter 4

• • •

Criticism as a Way of Life: Kenneth Burke's *A Grammar of Motives* Forty Years Later

I first read this book thirty-three years ago in 1952 when I was twenty-six years old. I was a hot-shot graduate student then, old enough and smart enough to understand much of what this book said and knowledgeable enough to use it with the irresponsible bravado of a young punk intellectual who needs to seem smarter than he is. But I was certainly not old enough, wise enough, or experienced enough to understand and appreciate what this book did and represented. That came only much later.

Back then nobody had written much about Burke and many critics seemed either awestruck or annoyed by the gymnastic qualities of Burke's mind, his formidable eclectic learning, his spinning out of terms, his dazzling reading of texts, and his cranky style. Today, we are all used to these things in Burke. I mean, anybody who can read Derrida, Lacan, de Man, or deconstructive criticism can read Burke and wonder why we ever made a fuss about his style and difficulty. Forty years after it was first published, *A Grammar of Motives* has become a classic, Burke has become an institution, and we are now—finally—in a good position to read this great text with a very high degree of accuracy and assess it with an equally high degree of fairness. I will attempt a little bit of both here today. It took me a long time to unsettle my earlier, rather limited readings of this book enough to reread it in a way that now seems more accurate; and it took even longer for me to understand

and appreciate just how this book is a critical action upon a historical scene—a kind of quintessential action of the critical mind.

Burke is unquestionably one of our great modern critics. At first we thought of him as a literary critic (a role that is continuous throughout his career); then we thought of him as a social/cultural critic (another role that is continuous); then we thought of him as a language critic (not a linguist, but a critic who approached the study of human relations through the study of language); then we thought of him as a dramatistic critic (not a dramatist, but a critic who had constructed his own dramatistic system as a conceptual frame for the study of human relations); then we thought of him as a logologer, a critic who studies words; and more recently, I think—for he has been with us for a long, long time—we have begun to think of him as a critic at large, a kind of roving intelligence whose subject is the human condition as he perceives it in his own time. I want to argue here that Burke has been this all-purpose critic from the very beginning, and the epitome of what it means to practice criticism as a way of life is to be found in *A Grammar of Motives*.

The sustaining action of Burke's career has been his commitment to criticism as a way of life, just as writing novels was the sustaining action of Faulkner's career and the writing of poetry has been the sustaining action of W. S. Merwin's career. Burke has been many other things in his life—editor, fiction writer, poet, teacher, lecturer, reviewer, performer, sage—but these are incidental (not accidental) to the role that he has played in our intellectual and cultural life since the twenties. In the most general sense, criticism is the application of mind, intelligence to any subject, the object of which is to produce something more than purely factual knowledge. Passing judgment or producing dogma and doctrine are much less important to criticism than the action of the critical mind itself and the production of knowledge. Judgments and dogmas are always subject to the vagaries of history and taste, but knowledge endures; and the action of the mind that produces this knowledge is one of the single most useful and important resources any human being can develop.

Burke exemplifies what it means to be a critic in the large general sense of this term; he is not a private critic, which all of us are to some degree, but a public one whose compulsion—whose profession—is to produce as well as publish and share his knowledge with the rest of us in the belief that community is an essential part of a sane and civilized life. Sharing your knowledge is not just an egocentric or economic matter (we all love to have our books published and acknowledged and every dollar we make from them is a great source of satisfaction)—it is more complicated than that: you have to believe in a kind of epistemological idealism; you really do have to believe that the knowledge you produce and the means by which you spread it—the written word—will help to purify war, promote tolerance by speculation, and foster the principles of wonder, resignation, tolerance, and sympathy that are necessary for sound human relations (GM 305). You have to believe, as Burke does, that a mind like Freud's "deserves the eternal respect of mankind because of the profound imaginativeness and methodical skill by which he widened our powers of meditation" (GM 305). *Purify* war, *promote* tolerance by speculation, *foster* the principles of wonder, resignation, and sympathy, *widen* our powers of meditation—all these process terms referring solely to the actions of the mind as the end result of the critical action of the mind locate us in a limbo between knowledge and action in the sociopolitical world and raise many of the crucial ethical questions about the value and function of criticism that Lentricchia has tried to deal with in his book *Criticism and Social Change*. Burke addresses this question everywhere in the *Grammar* by precept and example. Overwhelmed by the methodological virtuosity of this book and by its terminological resourcefulness as a supplier of tools for thought, we have often tended to ignore or undervalue Burke's many discussions of why he is doing what he does and why it is necessary and important. It is clear from a study of these discussions that Burke is not a philosopher but a critic and that he had a very clear and carefully worked-out conception of the function of the critic in a democratic society—a conception he had been developing since *Permanence and Change*. Burke tried and rejected political action earlier in his career: he was much too smart for politics; he was too truthful. Had he been less idealistic, less socially and politically conscious, he might have stuck to literary criticism or gone on with his fiction and poetry. But he didn't; he chose to be a critic.

Genuine criticism, of the kind that Burke believes in and practices, requires freedom in order to flourish and is consistently opposed to dogma, dogmatism, doctrinal evaluations, fanaticism, fundamentalism, dissipation (isolationism, a retreat from engagement), ostrichism, insistence upon conformity and orthodoxy, the cult of empire, extreme ambition in any form, "naively perverted religiosity"—and many other human tendencies Burke discusses in the *Grammar* because he thinks they prevent thoughtful humans from achieving the humanistic goals that are important and necessary for a sane and healthy life.

This is just another way of saying that criticism without a humankind-serving motive to sustain it is hard to conceive. With all due respect to our own efforts here, there is no way that Burke could have achieved his goals within the limited confines of literary criticism. Critics cannot really be merely self-serving or even text-serving, though many are both. They have to acknowledge and work from the larger idealistic motive. What criticism actually does for humankind is quite another matter. Has Burke altered history, has he purified war, has he brought about significant social change? Of course not. Critics serve humankind in a different way. Burke has altered many individual minds, purifying some of them, and certainly equipping many of them more adequately for the endless war of words that makes up a major part of our lives. Criticism is written for those who can read and think and believe in the powers of the critical word. That is a very small percentage of any population. Criticism is part of the thinking person's way of keeping in trim. Critics are word and mind people and appeal to other word and mind people. Criticism deals in knowledge, just as the stock exchange deals in money. Knowledge alters attitudes. Attitudes are the prelude to action, whether symbolic (that is, purely verbal) or physical. Criticism believes absolutely, if somewhat ironically, in knowledge and the power of the written word, just as politics and religion believe in the power of the spoken word—the sermon and parliamentary debate. Criticism always responds to the world out there and to the written word with written words. It is seldom spontaneous or extemporaneous. It originates from the contemplative, meditative, speculative centers of the mind. Criticism is exclusively concerned with the human world. One does not write criticism about nature, but about what humans have done or are doing to nature. The humankind-serving motive of criticism is the appeal to mind, "reason," the appeal to humankind to use mind and knowledge as a guide to its actions in this world. Criticism for Burke is always tied to some conception of the possibility of a better life.

Reading *A Grammar of Motives* now, Burke-fashion, looking for the key terms that reveal a critic's deepest concerns, one cannot help but notice the following repetitions: *admonish* in all of its forms, *ambiguity, paradox, irony, puns, complexity, foibles, reduction, scope;* one notes a whole range of thought terms, such as *contemplation, meditation, speculation,* and *dialectic* in all of its forms; one notices the many system and placement terms, such as *calculus, grammar, network, logic,* and, of course, the *pentad* and *ratios;* one notices, especially, the many seek-out-what-is-hidden terms, such as *covert, lurking, surreptitiously, concealed,* and *reduced to;* and, finally, the many important attitudinal terms, such as *resignation, acceptance, tolerance, comic, ironic, skeptical, neo-stoic, neo-liberal,* and *appreciation.*

As a way of understanding the relationship between these terms and of coming to some understanding of what Burke is doing in this book, let us take a relatively simple and very representative sentence from the *Grammar* and subject it to a kind of Burkean analysis. The sentence is almost dead center—page 235—and was picked from hundreds of variations of it in the book. "We are," Burke writes, "*admonished* to be on the *lookout* for the *covert workings* of the *action-motion ambiguity.*" Let us look at the key terms and phrases in this sentence. *Admonish,* in all of its variations, is one of Burke's favorite terms. It occurs everywhere in his work from the *Grammar* on and is present as a critical motive from *Permanence and Change* on. It identifies one of the primary functions of critics: they are admonishers, they warn us, counsel us against something, caution us, notify us, incite us to duty. Critics have discovered something they think the rest of us thinking people ought to pay attention to. They warn us to be on the *lookout for* it—as if we were in danger—and of course we *are,* if we do not pay attention to critics and use our minds and knowledge as part of our equipment for living. Awareness has a very high value for Burke. His mind is clearly better than ours and it seldom sleeps. In fact, if critics did not have superior minds capable of relevant perceptions and knowledge, we would never pay attention to them.

Critics warn us to be on the lookout for *covert workings.* Covert workings are concealed, secret, disguised—all key terms for Burke everywhere in his career. If they are covert they are working in ways that we are not aware of and they presumably impair us or threaten us in some way. The theory of covert workings is a basic assumption of psychoanalysis and much literary criticism. The critical action, then, is one in which the hidden is found, the secret made known, and the disguise stripped off. It is a seeking and revealing action. The assumption is that knowledge is a good thing and that if we know what it is we can deal with it. Burke's whole theory of symbolic action is that all great texts—for example, St. Augustine's *Confessions*—function covertly for the author and that it is a useful and beneficial critical action to try to find out what these covert workings are. For example, did Keats really mean that body is turd, turd body when he wrote "Beauty is truth, truth beauty"? Burke believes that we can't deny the body, and there is more to this famous and somewhat outrageous essay on Keats than meets the eye. All of Burke's work on victims and victimization in *A Rhetoric of Motives* tries to reveal the covert workings of various destructive principles and warns us about them. His attempt to purify war is another attempt to expose and neutralize other covertly working principles, on the assumption that this knowledge will somehow have an effect upon our actions.

We are warned here to be on the lookout for the covert workings of the *action-motion ambiguity.* An ambiguity is a doubleness or uncertainty of meaning, an unavoidable source of confusion. It is another one of Burke's all-time favorite terms, just as *admonish* and *covert* are. What is the action-motion ambiguity and what is so dangerous about it that we have to be warned of its covert working? Well, it has something to do with a confusion between motion and action—as staunch a pair of Burkean terms as you will ever find. Bodies move, things move: minds act, humans act. Burke has spent half a lifetime studying the action/motion, mind/body pair, opting always for accounts of the *human* condition that favored action, as dramatism does. To favor action is to favor freedom, some principle of authority, will, choice, the moral-ethical, language, and knowledge. All accounts of the human condition that feature motion and conditioned responses demean us as human beings and do not provide an adequate account of who and what we are. Probably the worst villain for Burke is behaviorism; but there are others: determinism, uncritical scientism. Burke does not want to do away with ambiguity; it is a necessary part of human reality: he wants to warn us about it so we will recognize it and be able to discount it. He wants us less naive, linguistically and otherwise: he wants us to have an adequate account of what we are and to be able to resist and compensate for the relentless human tendency to reduce and simplify everything, to reduce the plenitude of possible answers to the one true answer. Burke has given a lot of thought to this age-old dilemma, and though he would have liked to come up with the one true answer—and perhaps tried to in dramatism—the very possibility would have been offensive to his critic's mind. Burke likes answers that are true without being reductive and methodologies, like the pentad and ratios, that are resourceful without being overly prescriptive or restrictive. The whole of the *Grammar* can be seen as an attempt to develop both, though it would be a great mistake not to realize that everything Burke does in this book can be sorted out in relation to what he "believes." What he believes is more a position than a doctrine, more a set of mutually reenforcing attitudes than a systematically worked out doctrine. The position guides and motivates the work of the critic. I'll turn to it next.

"We demand," Burke says, "a fully worked out version of the ways of homo dialecticus in contrast to the scraps of dialectical lore now scattered about the literary landscape, with each typical modern verbalizer digging in some one thin vein as though it were a bonanza." "Fully worked out version" and "ways of homo dialecticus" give us, first of all, the essential characteristic of Burke's endeavors as a critic, which always places a strong emphasis on adequacy, scope, as full a range of possibilities as can be worked out; and, second, the object of these endeavors, which is basic, essential knowledge about and for thinking humans. Again, we must remind ourselves that Burke is not writing for, nor is he writing about, the person on the street or the majority of people I encounter when I go to the supermarket or Ames department store. All of Burke's criticism is addressed to the speculative portion of the mind, and much of the *Grammar* is addressed to those of us who want to and are able to think, on a global scale, about what is happening to us in the twentieth century. Burke says that he wrote the *Grammar* in the firm belief that a kind of

> "Neo-Stoic resignation" to the needs of industrial expansion is in order. . . . For better or worse men are set to complete the development of technology that will require such a vast bureaucracy (in both political and commercial development) as the world has never before encountered. Encountering a global situation, to what extent can we avoid the piecemeal response of dissipation (that is, content simply to take whatever opportunities are nearest at hand) and the response of fanaticism (that would impose one terminology of motives upon the whole world, regardless of the great dialectic interchange still to be completed)? To what extent can we confront a global situation with an attitude neither local nor imperialistic? Surely, all works of good will written in the next decades must aim, somehow, to avoid these two extremes, seeking a neo-liberal, speculative attitude. To some extent, it will take an attitude of hypochondriasis: the attitude of the patient who makes peace with his symptoms by becoming interested

> in them. . . [and in this way develops] an attitude of appreciation. (GM 442–43)

This passage can hardly be examined closely enough if one is to understand both what Burke is doing as a critic and the noble, idealistic, and highly moralistic reasons why he is doing it. It is also a passage that makes one appreciate his prophetic abilities and the admonitory nature of his criticism: the development of technology Burke predicted has gone far beyond what even Burke could have imagined, the political and commercial bureaucracies that he prophesied in 1945 are monsters, and human beings are even more completely enslaved by and to the machines they invented to serve them than even Burke's great capacity for ironic perception could have suggested.

Everything Burke predicted has come true—with a vengeance. The very responses he admonished us to avoid or curtail—dissipation and fanaticism—are with us on a global scale in worse and more threatening ways than ever before; in this country, and elsewhere, we have tended to try to confront the global situation Burke describes with attitudes that are militantly both more local and imperialistic. We can hardly claim to have purified war very much; and demonic ambition, especially in the commercial world, seems more strident than ever. The distortions and misconceptions of purpose that Burke so feared seem as prevalent as ever.

What, then, has Burke's great critical action upon the historical scene accomplished after forty years? What actions have come of this critical action except more critical actions such as what I am doing right now? How has humankind been served by this critical action? Has *A Grammar of Motives* brought about ameliorative social change? No one could possibly answer this question in any accurate way because the empirical evidence is not now, nor will it ever be, available. Burke is not a politician and his ideas are not translated into action in the same way that political, social, scientific, or even religious ideas are. Burke's ideas will not eliminate starvation in Ethiopia, poverty in India, or terrorism in the Middle East. Fanatics and fundamentalists would hardly be receptive to Burke's neo-liberal approach, nor would they like to be told that they are acting upon a faulty or limited terminology of motives. A fanatic would probably just as soon shoot you as change ideologies.

The critic serves humankind by addressing individuals. The inside of the head is Burke's domain—and not too many heads at that—even here at this MLA meeting. Those of us who have been receptive to Burke can testify to what he has done to the inside of our heads, or to what reading him has enabled us to think, do, and be that we could not have thought, been, and done before he came into our heads and lives. That would take us into a domain most people in this profession do not like to talk or even write about. We prefer to stick to a stricter, more limited conception of criticism, one that serves the text, the author, the period, or the genre. Though the *Grammar* has served all four of these with equal brilliance, it is the larger question we must ask if we are to understand what it means to make criticism a way of life—as Burke has done.

Critics are always in a dialectical relationship with history. Everything they write and publish is both a critical action—or interaction—and the end result of that action, or the production of knowledge. Both the nature and quality of this critical action as well as the knowledge that it produces can have a profound effect on the reader. The way in which Burke goes about analyzing the dialectic of constitutions is as important as what he says about them. Even if the knowledge in a given critical text becomes outdated, the critical action may still be usable to produce new knowledge; and even if the goals of a given critical text have not been met—if war has not been purified, if demonic ambition has not been cured, if we have not yet arrived at a proper attitude toward bureaucracy and technology—those goals may still need to be pursued, especially in one's own life, and the attitudes promoted by the critical action may still be worth acquiring. Any critical book is always more than it says: the specific dialectical relationship between the critic and history may be a role model we wish to adopt and practice as part of our way of being in the world. A great text, such as the *Grammar,* may become a model for other critical minds to follow, not purely as doctrine, but as action. And even if, following such a model as *A Grammar of Motives,* we discover that we can't often act upon our knowledge and acknowledge this most fundamental paradox of criticism, we may still decide, as Burke surely did, that we still want to maintain a critical attitude toward ourselves and the world and keep our mind in shape by doing so. After all, what other alternatives are there for a thinking person?

Forty years after *A Grammar of Motives* was published, Burke—amazingly—is still at it. In his long life as a critic, Burke has never been a cynic, he has never been a debunker, he has never lost his epistemological idealism. He maintains his belief in irony, comedy, admonition, satire. From the very beginning—and especially in this great text—he has been a true critic and upheld, even as he practiced it, one of the highest and most persistent ideals of the human mind: this ideal is that the human mind is capable of arriving at knowledge, true wisdom; that this knowledge has power; that somehow, someway, if this knowledge is shared, it will benefit others and be transformed into constructive actions by individuals. I testify to the truth of Burke's lifelong commitment.[1]

Notes

This essay was originally written for a special session on Burke at the 1985 meeting of the Modern Language Association in Chicago. Some parenthetical citations are given using standard abbreviations for the titles of Burke's works, e.g., RM, CP.

1. The following question about the nature of Burke's criticism was asked, repeatedly, by Herb Simons, the moderator of "The Legacy of Kenneth Burke" conference in Philadelphia in the spring of 1984. "Does Burke show enough 'warrantable outrage' given the injustice his critical inquiry reveals?" What follows is my attempt in 1986 to briefly address this question for the *Kenneth Burke Society Newsletter.* This attempt appeared there as "Forum—Response to H. Simons on Burke and Warrantable Outrage" in 2, no.1 (July 1986): 2. I thank the *Newsletter* for permission to reprint it here.

First of all, "outrage" is not a very useful critical response and rage, in general, is debilitating. Critical inquiry may begin in outrage—and it often does—but it should not end there. Anybody who knows Burke personally knows how outraged he is by injustice, pollution, behaviorism, scientism, technology, real politics, and war and how prone he is to express this outrage in conversations. Many of the injustices that Burke's critical inquiry reveals are such that irony and comedy—not outrage—are the best written responses. Burke is a critic, not a politician, and inquiry rather than action is his proper business. Criticism has been Burke's way of life since the twenties. Burke is also a poet and in his poetry he has often shown his tempered outrage at injustice and human folly. However, outrage is not a very useful poetic device either. Instead of outrage, Burke has more often responded in print with irony, laughter, and stoical resignation. Injustice is intrinsic to the drama of human relations. You can reveal it but you cannot make it go away. Irony, comedy, and dialectic are probably more useful than outrage as linguistic devices and intellectual resources. The fact of the matter is that Burke has always shown plenty of "warrantable outrage," but it has always been tempered with language, style, and dazzling dialectic. Outrage is inarticulate. No critic can afford to be inarticulate. Nor can any poet. Criticism and poetry are often the transformation of outrage into style. Unmediated outrage leads to murderous actions. Burke has spent a lifetime trying to purify war. He would never promote outrage. He peddles knowledge, not outrage. Politicians often peddle outrage. Burke is not a politician. To wish that he were a politician is to misunderstand the nature of his critical endeavor and to want something from him that he never tried to or wanted to give us. We have enough outrage in our heads without getting any more from Burke. Even Burke's most overtly political writings—"Waste, the Future of Prosperity" and the Helhaven satire—are just that: writings, stylized critical responses to intolerable outrageous situations. What could be more outrageous than our systematic pollution of our planet and only home. But Burke's satires do not promote outrage—even "warrantable" outrage; they purify it. How can one purify outrage? The same way one purifies war: by transforming it into symbolic action so that the causes of it can be contemplated. Does this prevent or abort action? No. It slows it down, encourages action based on knowledge rather than outrage, and, where action is not possible, teaches one how to "accept" the outrageous and intolerable. Surely these are among the primary functions of critical inquiry. It is outrageous that more politicians do not read Burke.

Chapter 5

• • •

Comic Criticism: *Attitudes toward History,* 1937–84

Criticism generically is not a derivative or secondary activity. It is a primal and natural expression of language and thought.

"Poetics, Dramatistically Considered"

Whatever poetry may be, criticism had best be comic.

Attitudes toward History

Any terminology is suspect that does not allow for the progressive criticism of itself.

The Rhetoric of Religion

Criticism is important because people are entities capable of symbolic action and to varying degrees they can be addressed, reasoned with, petitioned, persuaded. Things can but move or be moved. One does not negotiate with nature.

The Rhetoric of Religion

Smiling Hypochondriasis: the attitude of the patient/critic who makes peace with his symptoms by becoming interested in them—and in this way learns to appreciate them.

A Grammar of Motives

Criticism is written to purify war, to promote tolerance by speculation, to foster the principles of wonder, resignation and sympathy, and to widen our powers of meditation.

A Grammar of Motives

By Way of Introduction

My original plan for this essay was to take up *Attitudes toward History, A Grammar of Motives,* and *The Rhetoric of Religion* so that I could discuss comic criticism, dramatistic criticism, logological criticism, and their relationship to each other. After writing more than a hundred pages in an attempt to get all of this worked out, I realized the futility of my plan in relation to the time available and, when the end of March approached and I was still writing, I succumbed to hysteria, quit writing, and took inventory of my options. I had a whole talk on the third edition of *Attitudes toward History,* half a talk on *A Grammar of Motives,* which could easily be expanded, and three quite different talks on *The Rhetoric of Religion,* plus many meandering pages of tentative conclusions about the continuities of comic criticism over a fifty-year period.

With so many options open to me after my midwinter logomania, it was hard to make an intelligent choice—even after reading everything over many times. So I decided to follow the pleasure principle and pick the piece of work that had given me the greatest amount of satisfaction. That clearly was the new thinking I did on *Attitudes toward History,* beginning with the 1937 edition and then working my way through the additions Burke made to it between 1955 and 1984. This allowed me to sort of achieve my original goal, which was to move from comedy to dramatism to logology—and beyond—and to clearly establish the continuities of comic criticism from its origins in *Attitudes toward History* to its continuation and culmination as the main perspective of both dramatism and logology.

What follows is an account of my most recent encounter with *Attitudes toward History,* a text that has been with us now for fifty-three years and seems as fresh, exhilarating, and applicable as ever after all this time. Most of my talk is devoted to it and to the nature of comic criticism. The last part deals with the additions Burke made to the original text: three for the second Hermes edition in 1959 and the long afterword he added to the 1984 University of California Press third edition. The first group of additions connect comic criticism to dramatism and its vision of the drama of human relations; and the second, final addition connects comic criticism to Burke's later logological vision of the human condition and the drama of human relations.

1

Without casting any aspersions on the four books that preceded *Attitudes toward History*—two of fiction, one of literary and one of social criticism—I think we can accurately say that *Attitudes toward History* is the first true flowering of Burke's genius as a critic. In the structure of *Attitudes toward History* we have a map of Burke's mind. The book is in three parts and has many apparently digressive footnotes that allow Burke to radiate out from, or range out from, any particular point into a wide variety of examples and ramifications. This radiating out from is one of the most characteristic actions of Burke's mind, which is a mind that seldom moves in a straight line in the manner of a philosophical argument or a regular, orderly expository mode. It is a mind that likes detours and has a very unusual, original, and sometimes baffling way of putting things together. The three parts of this book have a repetitive structure in the sense that each section ends with a discussion of the comic frame of acceptance that is, Burke argues, the corrective frame social critics should adopt and apply at that particular point in history if both the critics and our sick society are to be restored to sanity and health.

In trying to think about the function of criticism for Burke, we should not forget that every one of Burke's books and major essays also functioned for him as symbolic action in rather complex ways. In a letter to Cowley after his wife Libbie died, Burke says that he wrote all of his books after they met in order to keep proving to her that he was worthy of her. He has not published a new book since she died. Of *Permanence and Change,* Burke says that it was a book he put together to keep himself from falling apart. He also says of *Permanence and Change* that, not knowing who he was or where he was in his head, he wrote the book to discover some answers to these questions. Of his novel, *Towards a Better Life,* he says, among other things, that it names his number and that by writing it he was able to purge himself of many of his negative and destructive character traits and prepare himself for a better life. He also says that if we but knew how to read this novel as symbolic action, we would discover that it is really all about his relationship with Libbie. It seems obvious now that *Attitudes toward History* was as much addressed to Burke himself as it was to his readers and that he was clearly trying to make himself over in the positive, affirmative image of the book he was writing. He was never to abandon the comic perspective he first developed in this book.

The book begins with a consideration of universal frames of acceptance and rejection as they are embodied in the written word. (And we should always remember that Burke is primarily a critic of the written word.) These frames—that is, these attitudes toward history—may be embodied in poems (Whitman), in essays (Emerson), philosophical texts (James), and other kinds of written texts—including works in all of the different poetic categories, such as comedy, tragedy, and satire. Comedy is singled out in the first section of the book as the best of all possible frames of acceptance, as exemplified in the works of those great nineteenth-century American affirmers Emerson, Whitman, and James. We are also told that the best of Marx, Bentham, and Veblen is "high comedy." Prophesying after the fact, we can certainly say the same of the best of Burke. Criticism and comedy are later joined up in Burke's assertion that "whatever poetry may be, criticism had best be comic." The whole book is an extended definition and demonstration of what comic criticism is and a highly persuasive argument as to why the comic perspective should be adopted by the social critic.

Part 2 shifts from the universal to the historical, which is another characteristic movement of Burke's mind, whether he does it by going from the logical to the temporal, from the timeless cycle of terms implicit in the idea of order to the rectilinear narrative of Genesis 1–3, or from the particulars of a specific text to the philosophy of literary form (or the reverse—say from the essence of tragedy to *Othello*). More specifically, in part 2 Burke traces the curve of Western history from its beginnings to the 1930s in America—that is, to his own particular time, place, and society—using the rather startling metaphor of the five-act play to organize and enliven his presentation. Burke's conclusion is that the comic frame of acceptance and comic criticism—what he calls comic correctives—are what is needed to cure the ills from which America and Western society are now suffering. Thus, the movement of part 1 is repeated in part 2, but quite different material is used and the comic perspective is explained at much greater length almost at the very center of the book. Again, it is very characteristic of Burke to always address specific historical problems (what is happening at his point in history) and to also address the larger, timeless, universal problems. In this way, he can consider the extent to which the *Now* is a deviation from some ideal norm of the good life he has in his head and speculate on what could or should be done to correct this deviation.

Part 3 is the most radical section of the book and the one that tells us the most about Burke's genius and his methods as a critic. The corrective comic frame has been laid out in some detail at the end of part 2. We expect it to be applied in part 3. But there is an abrupt shift in part 3, chapter 1, to the analysis of symbolic structures and the "general nature of ritual." Most of what is in this chapter consists of the analysis of symbolism in literary works, especially covert private symbolism of the kind that was to figure so prominently in Burke's theory of literature as symbolic action, with its obsessive interest in the ways in which symbolic verbal structures function as purgative-redemptive rituals of rebirth for those who enacted them. In a sense we are back where the book began with its brief analyses of the ways in which the symbolic structures of Emerson, Whitman, James, and others functioned as rituals of acceptance and rejection by locating and taking a position in relation to symbols of authority. We are back to the way in which texts function as part of our equipment for living and, more specifically, to the ways in which critics, by making use of a comic critique of social relations as they find them presented in various texts, can develop poetic symbols and critical formulations that help us size up the important factors of reality and to adopt workable attitudes toward them. It is in this sense that criticism also functions as part of our equipment for living—something that it most certainly did for Burke during his long and varied critical life. Critics are mediators between the symbolic structures and us readers; they share their knowledge with us, not because they think we are stupid, but because they see things in these texts that we don't and they are convinced that their knowledge will be useful to us. It is in this way that the mediating function of criticism becomes creative and justifies its existence.

In part 3, chapter 2, there is another abrupt shift when Burke turns to the "Dictionary of Pivotal Terms," which forms the real conclusion to the book—insofar as any book by Burke has a conclusion. These are called pivotal terms because taken together they constitute the terminological cluster comic critics need for their analysis of society and the symbolic structures, or texts, that shape and guide our lives in society. Since the advent of writing, we have lived by the ideas expressed in the *written word,* and this has always been Burke's special domain. He is not an anthropologist and does not really do fieldwork. He seldom works without a specific written text, sometimes even creating his own texts or stories, as in the "Epilogue: Prologue in Heaven" and the Helhaven satire, and sometimes analyzing his own texts, as in "Stress, Its Seeking," where he uses his own novel, *Towards a Better Life,* or in the commentary on his "Eye Crossing" poem; and sometimes, he even uses himself as text.

It was certainly an act of genius on Burke's part to arrange the conclusion to this book in accordance with a scheme that does not follow logic or any kind of orderly principle of exposition but follows a purely arbitrary alphabetical scheme that has the effect of making all the terms equal and equally implicated in each other. It also allows Burke to do what he does best, which is to make unexpected and new connections between the terms as he goes along. To arrange the terms in this way is to arrange them in a timeless order rather than a narrative or logical order, so that each term implies the other and all terms imply each other. Most of the terms in the dictionary have been used over and over, often in quotes, in the preceding parts of the book. The one major omission in the dictionary is the term *comic* or any variations thereof. The whole book defines comic, and all the terms in the dictionary belong to the terminological cluster comic critics need for their social criticism. The brief conclusion following the dictionary does return to comedy, thus completing, by reaffirming, the repetitive structural symmetry of the book as a whole.

Much of this book—most of Burke, really—is about the need to have an adequate, pliant range of terms for discussing a given text or situation. As Burke later pointed out in one of his most notable phrases, every term is simultaneously a reflection, selection, and deflection of and from reality. What is needed is a full, pliant terminological cluster such as Burke tries to generate here, and most certainly does generate in the great terminological diversity of *A Grammar of Motives* and dramatism in general. This master at analyzing and dismantling other's terminological clusters and screens in deconstructive critical actions that preceded deconstruction itself (without the powerful negative bias or starting point of deconstruction) *begins* here what was to be a lifelong attempt to develop or generate a variety of pliant, "liquid" terminological clusters for his comic criticism, an endeavor that came to its first real fruition in dramatism, to a second, later fruition in logology, and to a final fruition in the conflation of dramatism and logology. We should note here that once he named and characterized it, in *Attitudes toward*

History, Burke insisted ever after in calling his criticism comic, even, as he says, when the subject of it is tragedy or his own later tragic logo-technological vision for the word-using species. The informing spirit of his criticism is always comic, right up to 1985, and it is good to always remember this.

The whole of the "Dictionary of Pivotal Terms" is Burke at his best, at his wittiest, most inventive, and freewheeling (to borrow an automotive term from the thirties), most comic, most aphoristic and formulaic. It is like the Burke we find in the "Epilogue: Prologue in Heaven," which forms the ironic, witty, comic conclusion to *The Rhetoric of Religion* and has the same kind of certainty and assurance that the "Dictionary of Pivotal Terms" does. In fact, we could compile a later and equally definitive dictionary of pivotal Burkean terms from the "Epilogue" and *The Rhetoric of Religion* as a whole. And a dictionary of pivotal terms for Burke as a whole would be a wonderful way to do Burke in his own fashion.

To illustrate his own point about terminological clusters, Burke starts the dictionary with *Alienation* and ends it with *Transcendence.* Start with *Transcendence* and you are going to get to *Alienation* at some point, not by logic in the usual sense, but because, as Burke is so fond of demonstrating in *The Rhetoric of Religion,* if transcendence, then something that needs to be transcended, and hence alienation. If alienation, then something that is causing it, and so forth. Turn to *Lexicological,* where the dictionary is used to define itself: "An argument (as in a lawyer's brief)," Burke writes, "is nothing but a set of interrelated terms and one's real job as a critic is to disclose and discuss these interrelationships, thereupon testing their relevance by applying them to the interpretation of events" (ATH 293). Any set of interrelated terms can be taken and arranged arbitrarily on a sheet of paper so that you can start anywhere and will have moved through the *set* of terms by the time you finish, but never in any prescribed order. As such, these terms do not constitute an argument, but a range of terms necessary to discuss a subject.

Let us, for example, generate the terminological cluster from *Attitudes toward History* that defines comedy, the comic, the comic critic, the comic corrective, the comic perspective and frame of acceptance. We'll do this from the text as a whole rather than from just the "Dictionary of Pivotal Terms." Burke begins constructing the comic cluster on page 39 when he first discusses comedy as a frame of acceptance and the most civilized form of art. Burke is not really interested in comedy as a dramatic form but as an attitude toward history, a habit of mind, a perspective, a critical/analytic way of looking at and examining the drama of human relations as it unfolds in history.

The motto of this book might be Everyone a comic critic, for like all of Burke's other books, this one is addressed directly to individual readers and urges them all, tries to persuade them to make themselves—their minds—over in the image of the comic critic. Burke knows very well that society does not read books, individuals do, and it is the inside of the head of these individuals that you want to try to change with your criticism—rather than, say, the institutions, which is what politicians try to change. Though he was always a highly idealistic thinker and critic, Burke was always a political realist and certainly knew who he was writing for and what sort of effect his books would have. The uneducated do not read Burke and only a small, elite segment of the highly educated read him and take him seriously. It is hard—impossible, really—to imagine Burke on the political circuit or out trying to organize the workers. Though he never really abandoned some of the important things he learned from Marx, Burke did flirt briefly with communism (which is always dedicated to institutional changes), but soon abandoned it and its party line to pursue his own highly individual and original program of social thought. Burke was never going to take orders from anyone. As he said in one of his wonderful offhand remarks to one of his adversaries: "Well, you don't *have* to think the way the Pope does." Criticism has to be free to be itself, and no established orthodoxy would ever appeal very much to, or be able to restrain, Burke's ever ironic and always questioning mind. This is the critic, we should remember, whose comic inspiration it was to put his own words into the mouth of The Lord.

Comedy, Burke says, in this oft-quoted passage, is the most civilized form of art because it depicts people not as vicious or criminal but as mistaken and foolish. Anyone can be mistaken and foolish at times. If mistaken or ignorant, you can be corrected by being brought to knowledge; if foolish, you can be taught the manners necessary to be less foolish. Shaw's *Pygmalion* is one of our archetypal comedies. Comedy shows us, Burke says, that every insight contains its own blindness, and so works against arrogance and pride, against believing that one is always right and has the right to be right and impose it on others. Comedy teaches humility (we are all sometimes mistaken, foolish, wrong, wrongheaded) because in realizing our errors (and correcting them) and in being able to laugh at ourselves we realize that we are not better than everyone else, but just like everyone else in some ways. Comedy promotes integrative, socializing knowledge. Why is comedy so civilized? Well, for one thing, people do not kill and victimize each other or commit suicide in comedies, as they do in tragedies; people are not punished in comedy but corrected by dialogue and dialectic.

One comedy in which people are punished (forever) because they are beyond being corrected is Dante's *Divine Comedy;* but Burke makes the point over and over in *Attitudes toward History* (in all his work, really) that the comic frame (like logology) is secular and deals with people in society, not with humans in their relationship to God and divine justice. In fact, *The Divine Comedy* would be just about the furthest away from Burke's comic perspective that one could imagine. The idea of the unforgivable, eternally punished sin is certainly foreign to the comic perspective; it is a frame of acceptance dedicated to the amelioration of individual lives in society, largely by means of knowledge of human error and a whole series of salvation and transcendence devices that stress a both/and rather than an absolutist either/or, US versus THEM attitude. It is a mind-set committed to negotiation, education, and peace; one that is always opposed to the closed confrontational mind-set that so often leads to violence, killing, and war. In fact, Burke even says that war and the comic perspective are incompatible, which may be why he dedicated *A Grammar of Motives* to the purification of war.

Against the comic frame, Burke consistently and repeatedly sets the *euphemistic,* the *debunking,* and the *polemical. Euphemistic* is Burke's euphemism for the church or any frame that is based upon a supernatural scheme that hides or covers up or misnames the real ills of life in society and promises a better life in the next world. As Burke points out here and elsewhere, this promise may make people feel better, but it does nothing to change the causes of their poverty, misery, enslavement, their alienation and their rejection, their inability to be a significant part of society. By *debunking,* Burke means any frame or attitude that is consistently negative and simply attacks things in order to discredit or destroy them without putting anything better or positive in their place. To understand Burke's dislike of debunking, one should remember his two long essays on this tactic in *The Philosophy of Literary Form.* By *polemical,* Burke means any absolutist frame that allows for only one point of view that is always defended as the only correct or true frame or doctrine. As *The Rhetoric of Religion* makes clear, Burke has not really changed his mind about the euphemistic frame, in spite of his great admiration for its formal beauty and symmetry; but it is the debunking/negative and the polemical/absolutist frames that are Burke's real enemies because the first simply destroys without offering constructive or creative alternatives; and the second tends to eliminate freedom of thought and action. Without freedom of thought there can be no criticism and hence no mavericks like Burke to stir up our minds with his many perspectives by incongruity and ironic examples of the bureaucratization of the imagination. And Burke has always insisted that without freedom there can be no authentic action. Working within a closed value system, as the debunker always does, eliminates alternatives, just as the absolutist/polemicist does, whether the doctrine is religious, political, ethnic, or philosophical. Burke found both of these approaches to words and reality intolerable and unacceptable and strenuously opposed both all of his critical life.

The comic frame tells the mind that it must equip itself to accurately name and confront its situation. It cannot oversimplify (give only one name) or misname the situation, nor can it assume that it will always be able to change the situation or eliminate what caused it. It is just as likely that the mind will have to change its attitudes in order to confront and learn to live with the situation. We must sometimes learn to change or perish, Burke reminds us, and we cannot act in 1937 in America as if it were the fourteenth century in Europe; nor can we try to keep on using a frame that has died out of history even though it is being kept alive by a well-established bureaucracy even after history has clearly contradicted it.

Many of the modifiers for *comic* are terms that stress the need for a *wider* frame, a need to *broaden* one's terminology, a need for a *well-rounded* frame, one that is an *amplifying* device rather than a diminishing or reductive one; there is a need for a perspective that includes an awareness of *ambivalence* and *irony*, that promotes the ability to see double, to use and recognize metaphor, to see around corners, to take multiple approaches. In other words, the comic perspective must acknowledge that life—reality—is not static but is always in process and that we must adopt a frame that accounts for the true complexity of the human situation and resists the mind's compulsion to reduce this complexity to an oversimplified, orderly set of terms. Over and over again in *Attitudes toward History* (and right on up to the present), Burke reminds us that all the returns are not in yet, and probably never will be. As Burke The Lord says at the end of the "Epilogue: Prologue in Heaven," it is always more complicated than that. The work of the critic is never done, can never be finished: there are no final solutions. The main solace for the critic is to know that one is not condemned to have to live forever. The irreversible flow of time always contains a promise of freedom. Others will come after to continue the work of criticism.

In trying to characterize the comic perspective, Burke says that it should be a frame that is charitable but not gullible, and thus promotes humility; it is a frame that stresses maximum awareness of the forensic (the public dialogue, debate, discussion, criticism itself); it should promote a realistic sense of one's limitations. The comic frame should acknowledge the basic truth of ecology, which is that everything is related to everything else; applying this to social relations, Burke says that one should strive for a balance or symbiosis of the material and transcendental in human affairs, a point that later will be basic to the whole conception and argument of *The Rhetoric of Religion*. The comic frame takes nothing at face value—it is not a literal-minded view of things and is not subject to naive verbal realism, but assumes that there is always some symbolic content, that some covert motive may be lurking in even the most overt and explicit of statements and actions.

A comic perspective must be admonitory and should treat the so-called lore of errors as an aspect of truth, as corrective errors. A comic critic must know how to discount, must realize that things are not as they seem. One has to learn how to see double, recognize and use irony and ambivalence, read symbols, and recognize the deceptions of literal-mindedness. The comic perspective disregards categories and aims at a perspective of totality, using perspective by incongruity to transcend categorical, logical barriers. As Burke argued in *Permanence and Change,* the comic critic must turn metaphor into a perspective. The comic critic considers human life as a *project in composition,* hence it is always subject to revision and correction, depending upon the findings of the critic. The comic perspective stresses the maximum opportunity for the resources of criticism as equipment for living and is committed to using all that is there to use. It does not believe in absolutes, in categorical NOs, in logic as an absolute criterion for truth, in any kind of rigidified doctrine or in the kind of fanaticism that supports terrorism around the world, whether it is ecoterrorism, antiabortion terrorism,

Marxist terrorism, Islamic terrorism, fundamentalist Christian terrorism, democratic terrorism, fascist terrorism, or racial terrorism.

Comic criticism is a social instrument; it allows one to both act and observe one's actions. It heightens self-awareness and social responsibility at the same time. Comic critics must be analytical (rather than, say, purely evaluative) so that they can speculatively reassemble in a new way what they have taken apart as they work with the documents (texts) left by other people's perspectives. The comic critic must develop a diagnostic technique Burke calls a tempered form of hypochondriasis.

Hypochondriasis is another medical metaphor Burke used to characterize one of the essential attitudes and activities of comic critics. It is similar to the auscultation metaphor he used in his abandoned manuscript of the early thirties when he was making his shift from literary to social criticism. Hypochondriasis is also a good example of Burke's tendency to coin terms that carry his own special meaning. This mouth full of harsh sounds means that one should study the symptoms and causes of one's own illness in order to better understand it so that one can learn how to treat it and live with it. Much of Burke's writing consists of the application of this diagnostic form of criticism to himself and to his own times. It is an essential feature of all dramatistic criticism, especially in *A Grammar of Motives* and in the third part of *A Rhetoric of Motives* where Burke diagnoses and discusses the hierarchic psychosis. His story "The Anaesthetic Revelation of Herone Liddell" is a classic example of his application of hypochondriasis to himself, as are many of his poems and many analyses of his own dreams.

Comic critics must develop critical formulations that enable them to size up the important factors of reality by means of a comic critique of social relations and to adopt workable attitudes toward them. Our times—Burke says in 1937—require maximum analytic and critical efforts because terminology itself has produced an analytic world—hence no other instrument but analysis can confront it with the necessary precision. This is the main reason why Burke became a comic social critic rather than, say, a poet or a fiction writer or even a purely literary critic. Comic criticism should be integrative and stress synthesizing attitudes. It tries to make one at home in the complexities of modern relativism and pluralism. One needs "liquid" attitudes, by which Burke means ones that go with the flow. "While Everything Flows" was a title Burke contemplated using for *The Philosophy of Literary Form* and the title he would use, he says, for a collection of his essays since 1970.

The thirty-three pivotal devices or terms of comic criticism all stress that getting along with people—rather than hating or vilifying or excluding or victimizing or killing them—is a primary object or goal of the good life. Later, Burke will add getting along with nature as part of the good life, especially in his later work. Picking up one of the main themes of *Permanence and Change,* Burke says that comic criticism stresses that more of the artistic or poetic (creative) should be expressed in vital social relations so that we can cultivate an art of living well. The obverse of this, and of just about everything Burke proposes in *Attitudes toward History* and in his later books, is killing, victimizing, and destroying those you can't get along with, whether human or animal. We have seen a lot of this in our time, not just because there is a lot of it, but because the media makes it all so readily available to us. Even as Burke was writing this book, the purges were going on in Russia and the prelude to World War II (the Spanish Civil War) was in progress. Though radical in his thought and in the way he thought, Burke was never a revolutionary writer and never a proponent of actual revolutionary action. Peaceful social change—the way of democracy—was always Burke's goal. You do not have to completely destroy an old order—which is the goal of most revolutions— to construct a new one. Even in the thirties, Burke was trying to devise ways of purifying war. Burke saw with great clarity what the real threats of Nazi fascism and Hitler were, and refers to both often in this book, and warns us at length about these dangers in "The Rhetoric of Hitler's *Battle.*"

This classic Burke text will perhaps help get us to the crux of the dilemma that is central to comic criticism and really to all of Burke's criticism and his conception of the role of the critic and the function of criticism in a democratic society.

Burke is a specialist in admonitory, preventive knowledge. In his analysis of Hitler's text, Burke shows that one of Hitler's major rhetorical political strategies was to unify a defeated and depressed Germany around hatred and fear of a common enemy. The Jews became this enemy of the state and were victimized by being turned into human scapegoats who were literally sacrificed in the name of national purity and unity. Burke shows how Hitler and the Nazi party skillfully manipulated a variety of deep, recurrent needs, fears, and tendencies to their own totalitarian political ends. Among these are guilt, with the corresponding need to purge it; alienation and the corresponding need to find some way to unify the self; fear of contamination and the need to find a way to destroy or control the contaminant; and the always powerful desire for racial, ethnic, and national coherence and power. Guilt and the need to purge it; alienation and the desire for unity; the desire to act in the name of and believe in some higher purpose are among the deepest and most urgent of human needs. Religion and art normally minister to and satisfy these needs, usually in benign ways, making use of symbolic rather than real living scapegoats. Burke's argument is that the Nazis perverted these normal psychological and religious needs and desires by directing them against real humans as opposed to symbolic victims and using them to totalitarian political ends—a strategy that eventually resulted in the death of six million Jews as well as millions of other enemies of the state. Burke wrote this essay before the Holocaust. We read it after that terrifying event, and many other genocidal actions that were also taken in the "name of the state" and might also be "explained" as rhetorical strategies that serve political ends. Here is Burke's conclusion to his essay: "Our job, then, our anti-Hitler battle, is to find all available ways of making the Hitlerite *distortions* apparent, in order that politicians of his kind in America be unable to perform a similar *swindle*" (PLF 219). Burke's analysis and diagnosis of the rhetoric of Hitler's *Battle* is as persuasive an admonition now as it was in the thirties. However, the word *swindle* brings us up with a start in any post–World War II reading of this passage. What Hitler and the Nazis did, and what numerous politicians here and elsewhere have done, is more than a swindle—more than just the actions of con artists. No amount of hypochondriasis can ever explain away or justify this event. It is not an illness. The problem of evil may often be met and dealt with by transcendence, as Burke says in *Attitudes toward History,* but this is an event that cannot be transcended: we acknowledge it, even though we don't really want to, because we have so thoroughly documented the horrifying reality of it. And similar events continue to happen all around the human world. Comic criticism can call this a *distortion* and a *swindle,* but in so doing it only identifies a problem that Burke, like St. Augustine, has always had trouble with—which is the problem of evil itself. Burke's problem was not with the origin of evil, as it was with St. Augustine, who had God to deal with, but what to do about it beyond warning us about it and how it works—especially in the organized killing and victimization of other human beings. Like Freud, Burke is an implacable dualist and has always known that evil originates within humans. The devil did not make Hitler and those who ran the death camps do what they did, nor did any abstract Manichean principle of evil do it. Burke has perhaps always believed too much in the power of words in the sense of believing that the constructive/reconstructive and destructive powers of words are equal. This does not always seem to be the case. It was a problem that also troubled Freud, who was never really certain that Eros could or would triumph over Thanatos.

I do not mean to cast a pall over comic criticism here, or even to discredit it; I only want to identify a problem that seems intrinsic to it and persists right on through dramatism and logology and what Burke has to say about the hierarchic psychosis and technology. Knowledge may be able to correct errors and dispel ignorance; it may prevent swindles and correct distortions, but it cannot make evil go away. Hitler and the Nazis knew exactly what they were doing. Nothing could have been more rational, more carefully thought out than their plans for the extermination of the European Jews. The same can be said of Stalin, of Mao, of the Khmer Rouge, of the drug barons, or of the Muslim terrorists.

But enough of this. Comedies always have happy endings so let us return to the comic perspective of *Attitudes toward History*, which tells us, with characteristic Burkean irony, that our stupidities are ever born anew and that even the most accurate, astute, and comprehensive of sciences would not be foolproof. Hence, there must be in comic criticism a constant stress on the knowledge of limitations—as for example, the fact that any structure develops self-defeating emphases (inner contradictions) and unintended by-products. Burke often refers to this as a neo-Malthusian admonition and gives as an example the question of how much longer the concept of progress, or limitless growth, can continue to engross humankind. Another example he gives is the comic perception that all bureaucratizations and bureaucracies such as the Kenneth Burke Society—say—eventually reach their Malthusian limits. Other examples are the comic critic's admonition that we must learn how to "socialize our losses" by saying to ourselves not "I'm guilty" but "*All* people are guilty." Comic critics should devise ways of putting things together by establishing modes of convertibility (perspectives by incongruity) between economic, religious, and esthetic vocabularies of motives—or between material, transcendental, and imaginative or creative terminologies—so that one can show that they are not so different as they might seem. The major emphasis in comic criticism is always reconciliatory and constructive.

The comic perspective, Burke says, is halfway between the extremes of iconoclasm and hagiography, which is a nice way of characterizing what he is doing in *Attitudes toward History.* An iconoclast is basically a *debunker* like H. L. Mencken, bent on destroying cherished beliefs by showing that they are based on error or superstition or absurdities; and a hagiographer is an unquestioning venerator of saints and the miracles and orthodoxies that are usually a part of the church and transcendental sainthood. Following Emerson, the comic critic should try to make these extremes meet in some middle ground where neither would have to be completely denied. As Burke's satiric poems and essays show, he might have been a great debunker and iconoclast; but as his many critical books show, he was also a great idealist of the intellect and the powers of knowledge and a moralist whose most basic, often transcendental, values were ones he shared with many great Western religious and ethical thinkers. Terms like love, charity, humility, the good life, the way, peace, goodness, and truth appear all through Burke. Faith and hope are operative terms everywhere in Burke, but they are always to be understood in secular terms, as faith in the power of truth and knowledge (of dialogue, dialectics, and criticism); and hope, always, that we can move toward the better life and achieve the good life—not through the descent of the godhead into our world, but through the good offices of the critic, that dispenser of truth and knowledge, who keeps the dialogue going.

In this respect, Burke resembles other great humanistic thinkers. This is especially obvious when one comes on some of Burke's many "comic" aphorisms in *Attitudes toward History*—such as the following one near the end of the book: the ideal of the comic frame is to continue to search for a vocabulary that could provide humility without humiliation, which is actually a quote from Gide, but might have come from any humanistic thinker. Humility is one of the many antipride, antiselfaggrandizing, anticapitalistic, knowledge-of-one's-limitations terms one finds in Burke. It is what John Neal acquires at the end of Burke's novel, *Towards a Better Life.* It is a term born of irony and self-knowledge in Burke, whose formidable intellect and verbal powers must always have tempted him away from humility toward humiliation. Humility defines the condition all tragic protagonists must achieve after they have suffered their losses and come to knowledge of their death dealing pride, arrogance, and errors of judgment. Oedipus, Creon, and Lear are perhaps the classic examples.

Humiliation is one of the many victimization terms one finds in

Burke. Humiliating another person is a function of power, as is all victimization, whether of a minor variety, as in putting someone down, or of a major variety, as in the Holocaust. The Nazis were always careful to humiliate—to degrade—the Jews they exterminated before the actual extermination, in any way that they could. It was part of the reduction-to-zero—from humans to nothing—process the Nazis put them through. It is one reason people are tortured before they are killed.

In polarizing humility and humiliation, Burke, ever the dualist, even sometimes, as he says, a schizoid dualist, has given us creative and destructive terms and in so doing has clearly identified the major emphasis of comic criticism, which is always creative and cooperative, always upbeat, no matter how negative the knowledge it conveys may be. If ever there was a heads I win, tails you lose kind of attitude and approach, comic criticism has to be it. Just look how long it has kept Burke going.

2

So much for *Attitudes toward History* and 1937. Now, I want to look at the additions Burke made between 1955 and 1984 to the second and third editions of this text. They show very clearly that Burke has remained true to the basic terms and values of comic criticism right up to the present.

In 1955 Burke added a brief introduction to *Attitudes toward History* as part of the second Hermes edition. In it he says that if comedy is his attitude of attitudes then the process of processes that it mediates upon is the bureaucratization of the imagination which is, he says, what happens universally when humans try to translate a pure, transcendental vision or aim into material terms. The pure vision is necessarily corrupted in its material embodiment. A classic example of this is what happened to Christ's vision when it was progressively bureaucratized by Paul and the church. Burke does not use the term *corrupted:* he says, more mildly and comically, as is his practice, that "*vexing* things happen when humans try to translate vision into action." Comic criticism, he says, *meditates* on this process. Later in the introduction, Burke addresses the historical changes that have occurred since he wrote *Attitudes toward History,* most notably the invention or discovery and use of the atom bomb and the awesome destructive potentialities in the event of a nuclear war between the superpowers—or any nuclear powers. Burke says that this has brought about a "truly new situation, which makes it all the more imperative that we learn to *cherish* the *mildly charitable* ways of *comic discount*. For by nothing less than such *humanistic allowances* can we hope to *forestall* (if it can be forestalled) the most idiotic tragedy imaginable: the willful ultimate poisoning of this lovely planet, in conformity with the *mistaken heroics of war*." At the end of this remarkable passage, every key term of which could be examined at great length, if we but had the time, Burke says that he equates tragedy with war and comedy with peace. We can certainly conclude from this passage that one of the main functions of comic criticism is the purification of war and the promotion of peace.

Burke's second addition to *Attitudes toward History* is a brief afterword, which was presumably written at the same time as the introduction. The most significant point, for our purposes, is the following: In his later books, Burke writes, the problem that is here discussed in terms of bureaucratic order is treated in terms of the sociopolitical pyramid, with its corresponding "hierarchal psychosis." This motive bears an important relation to tragedy. Thus, it might even be said to call for a "tragic" frame of interpretation rather than for a "comic" perspective. But as the issue looks from a comic point of view, however tragic tragedy may be in itself, the critical analysis of tragic motives is in essence comic. First of all, the sociopolitical pyramid, the hierarchal psychosis, and socioanagogic criticism are introduced into dramatism in *A Rhetoric of Motives*, part 3, and dominate much of Burke's work from that point on through many of the essays in *Language as Symbolic Action*. The major theoretical essay in *The Rhetoric of Religion*—"The First Three Chapters of *Genesis*"—is centrally concerned with the sociopolitical order and the timeless cycle of terms intrinsic to it. Furthermore, the hierarchic psychosis—Burke calls it the tragic tension—is central to Burke's theory of tragedy and catharsis as he developed it in the early fifties in the various essays that were to be part of his "Symbolic of Motives." Even as Burke's perception of things became more and more "tragic" after *A Rhetoric of Motives*, his criticism always remained, as he says, in essence comic. To understand this remark, one should read Burke's great critical essay on *Othello*, in which he uses the tragic tension of possession, as it is imitated and purged in that play, to do what comic criticism always does, whatever kind of text is being used: to bring us to knowledge and to warn us, not just about the tragic potentialities inherent in overpossessive love, but about the possession of every kind of property in any kind of sociopolitical order. Admonition is one of the most fundamental duties of comic criticism, as the next two additions will make clear.

Burke's third addition to *Attitudes toward History* is his essay on the "seven offices," which was originally published in 1958. Comic criticism and the comic perspective are never mentioned in this essay, but the comic attitude that was born and named in *Attitudes toward History* is simply renamed and prevails here, as it does everywhere in Burke. Burke's term for this attitude in the essay is *neo-stoic,* a term he used frequently in *A Grammar of Motives*. Burke sometimes also calls this the neoliberal ideal or attitude (354). The same kind of historically urgent question that is posed for the critic in *Attitudes toward History* is posed here for the educator as follows: "The ideal question for education *today* (as distinct from education always) would be: How *adapt* man to the needs of worldwide empire progressively made necessary by the conditions of technology." This question is answered in the essay entirely in dramatistic terms, which go far beyond the pivotal terms of *Attitudes toward History,* with the whole discussion now being based in the dramatistic definition of humans as symbol-using or word-using animals, with all that goes with it in Burke, including especially victimization by the sociopolitical order and technology. By 1958, when dramatism was pretty well completely formulated and written out and he was working on logology, Burke had begun to think in global rather than purely national or Western terms, which is one of the notable differences between his work of the thirties and his later work.

The seven offices of the title need not concern us much here except to point out that the comic critic and comic criticism are mainly concerned with teaching, curing, and consoling. If I could add an eighth office, it would be admonishing. However, the end of this essay does require our careful attention since it restates the aims of comic, dramatistic criticism in terms of education. Burke's three-part conclusion is as follows: The overall aim of secular education would be to discover just what it means to be a symbol-using animal. Such would be the grand aim of education, Burke says—and, we might add, of dramatism, logology, and comic criticism in general. The basic educational problem at *this stage of history* would be: How best *adapt* the symbol-using animal to the conditions of world empire that are being *forced* upon us by the *irresistible* "progress" of technology. (Such would be the global aim of education.) And, finally, beginning with either of these propositions: To locate the typical source of *individual anxiety,* in not more than three moves, we should get to neo-stoic *contemplation* of the Hierarchic Psychosis (or Rat Race), that is the reflex of the need for a pyramidal or ladderlike order in human "offices."

First of all, we should note the ironic determinism and fatalism that are present here, as elsewhere in Burke: the *conditions* of world empire are being *forced* upon us by the *irresistible* "progress" of technology; the hierarchic psychosis and individual angst are the *reflex of* the *need for order* in human life. We must learn to *adapt* to the first and can only contemplate the second with neo-stoic resignation. We should also note the focus of criticism here: in the first part, where the overall aim of secular education is stated, the emphasis is clearly on discovery and the acquisition of knowledge, for its own sake, pure and simple. We should know who and what we are, in empirical terms. In the second part the emphasis is still upon knowledge, but this time on the kind of knowledge that will enable us to best *adapt* to worldwide conditions that are of our own making but probably not to everybody's liking. If there is one thing you can count on in Burke, it is an insistence that we are the cause of our own problems. In the passage about adapting to what is inevitable and cannot be changed, the job of criticism is to teach people what can't be changed or cured and to console them in whatever way one can. We should also note here that the ingredients of tragedy are implicit in the conditions of world empire being forced on us by the irresistible progress of technology. This point became Burke's primary concern after 1970. And finally, in the third part we should again note the stress on knowledge: individual anxiety is inevitable and we can only deal with it by means of neo-stoic contemplation. *Contemplation* is such a key Burkean term, so central to what comic criticism is all about, we should dwell on it a bit. Contemplation does not necessarily lead to action, so that once again we come on the great modern disjunction between knowledge, action, and power. Neo-stoic contemplation takes us back to adapting (in part 2) and to the sheer knowledge gathering (in part 1). There is no Marxian dialectic and idealism here, no movement from thesis to antithesis to final synthesis: there is learning about, adapting to, and contemplating what is, what has been, and what will be. We might say that there is, finally, only the comic contemplation of the tragic global human situation. Remember that this was in 1958, after Burke had worked out dramatism and while he was working out logology. And note that the occasion for this essay is a conference on education and that the whole thrust of the essay is what we should be teaching our young people to equip them for living and prepare them for the *future.*

The final addition to *Attitudes toward History* is Burke's "In Retrospective Prospect," which he wrote in the early eighties for the third edition of *Attitudes toward History,* forty-seven years after the first edition in 1937. We might say of this new and final afterword that it is post-everything and that it is typical of Burke and comic criticism to still be looking *forward* even as one looks back after all those years of critical endeavor. Like all the rest of Burke's late or post-1970 work, this long afterword is centrally concerned with symbol-using, high technology and counter-nature, or what we might call the logology-technology cluster. Always admonitory, comic criticism here warns us, not about the hierarchic psychosis and the suicidal and homicidal threats posed by life in any sociopolitical order as *The Rhetoric of Religion* does, but about the dangers inherent in another of our human creations: high technology, the Technologic Edifice, counter-nature, all of which are made possible by humans' symbol-using genius, just as all sociopolitical orders, with their laws, are made possible by this same symbol-using genius. The question Burke raises—he is always asking these hard questions—is whether any *worldwide political system* can be contrived that will be adequate to control the uses and misuses of high technology and the Technologic Edifice, which Burke likens to a vast grotesque cathedral (like the church in *Attitudes toward History*) composed of nothing but gargoyles that spurt, not rain water, but a constant downpour of electronic and chemical pollutants that will go on as our bequest to the future, insofar as the human race lets itself have one.

Burke does not answer his own question, but true to the spirit of comic criticism, which has been admonishing us since 1937, just as Freud did, earlier, about our innate divided nature and our apparently equally powerful and paradoxical potential for creation and destruction, peace and war, Eros and Thanatos, Burke, ever the comic critic, says at the very end of this darksome look into our future that "Technology has a kind of built-in hopefulness, not just with regard to the resources and resourcefulness of Technology itself, but even to hoping that a worldwide political system adequate to control its uses and misuses *can somehow be contrived*" (339–40). The point of comic criticism (and Burke has never been anything but a comic critic, no matter how dark and tragic his vision)—is that if we can create the problem, we can also solve it or find ways to control it, as with *contriving* a worldwide political system adequate to control the uses and misuses of our monstrous Technology—always capitalized by Burke, as if it were a god. Uncontrolled or unwisely used, it will surely destroy its creators, whether by accident or design. Never a doomsday critic or a debunker—for that would be antithetical to the spirit of comic criticism—Burke has pointed out that by using our rationality (our symbol-using genius) to create our high technology, we have arrived at the outer limits of rationality and at an ironic and potentially tragic point where rationality is in conflict with itself. The instruments invented and created by humans threaten, now, to destroy the persons who created them. That is what Burke means when he says we are now polarized by the conflict between personality and instrumentality, whether we think of it in terms of computers, recombinant DNA, thermonuclear warheads, the fantastic resources of medical technology (which can keep even the technically dead alive for years), or the wonders of modern chemistry. Burke, of course, votes for personality, comic criticism, neo-stoicism, smiling hypochondriasis, neo-humanism, dramatism, logology, and all those other views that subscribe to the basic view of *life as an education*. We learn by suffering, Burke says, and surely the kind of knowledge he arrives at and shares with us is a form of *creative suffering*, functioning as it does, in an admonitory way, as all pain does. Pain, Burke says, is the sharpest of admonitions any organism learns to choose and thus live by. Freud said much the same thing in explaining the conflict between Eros and Thanatos in *Civilization and Its Discontents*. If we bring Freud and Burke together here at the end, we have left him in good company, for we can say of Burke, as he said of Freud, that a mind like Burke's deserves "the eternal respect of mankind because of the profound imaginativeness and methodical skill by which he widened our powers of meditation."

Note

This essay was originally written as the keynote address for the first national conference of the Kenneth Burke Society in New Harmony, Indiana, in May 1990. It was later published as "Criticism as a Way of Life or Criticism as Equipment for Living" in the *Kenneth Burke Society Newsletter* 6, no. 2 (Oct. 1990): 7–15, and appears here slightly revised.

Chapter 6

. . .

Symbolic Action in Kenneth Burke's Novel, *Towards a Better Life*

Off and on over the years, Burke has told us in letters, prefaces, footnotes, afterwords, comments in essays, and in a whole essay on the subject that his only novel, *Towards a Better Life,* names his number; is a symbolic action that enacts a ritual of rebirth, transcendence, and resurgence for its central character (John Neal) and, presumably, according to Burke's own theory of symbolic action, for Burke himself; is essential to any understanding of what he and his works are all about; is, if we know how to read it, all about his relationship with his second wife, Libbie, who was the sister of Burke's first wife, Lily (or Lie Lie, as he punningly called her in a letter to Cowley); and is an enigmatic inception or early indicator of Burke's devout belief that the "best possible of worlds would have the Comic Muse as its tutelary deity" (viii). These comments by Burke begin in letters to Cowley while he was writing the novel and in the preface to the first edition of the novel and continue off and on as late as 1984 in the afterword to the third edition of *Attitudes toward History.* Burke has told us that the first ten chapters of the novel were written just before the great crash of 1929 and that the last eight chapters were written soon after this traumatic event. He finished the novel in 1931 and it was first published in 1932. We also know that this period was traumatic for Burke: he quit a well-paying job to commit himself full time to writing. He finished *Counter-Statement* and *Towards a Better Life* and began reeducating himself for the writing of social and cultural criticism. His first marriage was breaking up and his relationship with Libbie had begun. His career as a fiction writer, begun in the early twenties with the publication of *The White Oxen* (1924) came to an end with this novel, and his shift from literary criticism to social criticism was in progress. He tells us that he experienced a serious breakdown during this period (1929–32). We know for a fact that after he finished this novel, he divorced Lily and married Libbie (in 1933) and subsequently wrote *Permanence and Change, Attitudes toward History, The Philosophy of Literary Form, A Grammar of Motives, A Rhetoric of Motives, The Rhetoric of Religion, Language as Symbolic Action,* and *Collected Poems,* plus a great many reviews and still uncollected essays that make up his "Symbolic of Motives." Libbie Burke died in 1969 and Burke has not published a new book since that date. He tells us in his letters to Cowley that after she died he had no more desire or driving compulsion to publish any more books because he had written all of his other books to prove and to keep on proving to her that he was worthy of her love. We know what a devastation Libbie's terrible illness and death were for Burke. He tells us over and over again in his letters to Cowley how "crazy" he was about her. Those of us who knew Burke while Libbie was still alive know what a wonderful couple they were and with what genius and devotion Libbie managed their life together.[1]

I mention all of this at the very beginning because I am going to use Burke's own theory of symbolic action, as he lays it out in *The Philosophy of Literary Form,* to help analyze *Towards a Better Life* as Burke's own symbolic action, as a purgative-redemptive fictional work in which he symbolically, fictionally names and purges out the negative destructive characteristics in his self in the character of John Neal so that he can be redeemed and born anew as a self worthy of the love of a woman such as Libbie, who is represented in the novel, I take it, by Genevieve. This means that I am going to take the title of the novel seriously and analyze what happens to John Neal in the course of the novel as a purgative-redemptive action in which he comes to a considerable amount of self-knowledge about his character, his actions, his own responsibility for his actions—especially in his relationship with Genevieve—and show how this knowledge enables him to change, not so that he can achieve the better life right then, but so that he can begin to move toward a better life. The end of the novel is all preparation for a hypothetical future in the sense that John Neal has been purged of his negative traits—his cynical intelligence, his corrosive irony, his mind games, his reliance upon pure intelligence, his inability to understand the true nature of love and to be able to love or be worthy of the love of a good woman—and redeemed in the sense that a new self can now be born in him. At the end of the novel, he is not, as Barry Maxwell has put it, a "silent casualty" (that is, mad and totally defeated) but a "battered survivor." His silence at the end enables him to listen to the cells of his body speaking to him so that he can come to an even fuller understanding of the "burden" within himself—and listen to the "torrent (inside and out) in all its fullness." Burke himself tells us what a nasty unpleasant person Neal was, especially in part 1, but really right up to the moment when he drives Genevieve away in part 3. The novel is, basically, about how John Neal is humanized by having his corrosive mind tempered. It may sound trite to put it this way, but it is love that tempers his mind, and not love in the abstract, but as it is embodied in the person of Genevieve.

Salient Formal Characteristics of the Novel

All this by way of introduction, to indicate where we are going. Let us begin the analysis, as Burke always does, by noting the salient formal characteristics of the novel. It is good to remember, as we begin, that the *towards* of the title is a directional term, suggesting movement away from and toward, rather than arrival at or achievement of the "better life." It is a from/to term, just as the "better life" part of the title is a qualified value term. Most obviously, it belongs to the good-better-best sequence as well as the opposites of all these terms: good/bad, best/worst, and better/worse. At the opposite extremes of the sequence would be the equivalents of hell and heaven, or the worst that there could possibly be and the best that there could possibly be. Good and evil, with their many variants, are also implied by the title. We need to remember when reading this title and when meditating upon the novel as a whole that it would have been possible for John Neal to move toward a worse life. Better than what, we ask; better than what Neal had when he began or was able to achieve in the course of the novel, even though the life he lives in part 2 seems like it ought to be a pleasant, easy, and satisfying life with a wife, two children, and a substantial piece of property. But obviously it is not, or Neal does not think it is, fixated as he still is on Florence at that point. In so far as we are able to say anything about what this "better life" might be from internal evidence, it would have to be based on what Genevieve represents or stands for. But more on that later.

First and most obviously, the novel is narrated from the first person point of view by one John Neal and consists mostly of unsent letters addressed to his friend and rival, Anthony. Part 3, chapter 4, consists of unsent letters to Neal's mistress, whom we assume to be Genevieve, even though she is never named as such. And part 3, chapter 6, is called "Testamentum Meum—Jottings." It is never clear whether this is also addressed to Anthony or not, but it seems to be purely reflexive, without the pretense of the unsent letters. Why the unsent letters are addressed to Anthony is never really clear, though it is discussed a couple of times. The whole novel is really a reflexive action on the part of Neal because letters that are written but never sent never complete their intended purpose, which is to communicate something from one person to another. Hence they become merely a device used by Neal to help him explain himself to himself. Perhaps it helped Neal to imagine that he was addressing Anthony, the only other male character in the novel of any significance and perhaps a variation of the later Alter Ego. Anthony disappears as a character from the novel after part 1 and we would tend to forget about him completely were he not referred to by Neal as the hypothetical recipient of the unsent letters.

The other—or, another—obvious thing about this novel, as Denis Donoghue is so fond of pointing out, is that it is elegantly written from beginning to end. In fact, especially in part 1, one could argue that style overwhelms plot and almost all else so that one is always exclusively focused on Neal, who reveals himself to us by way of the style and his many cynical, Nietzschean aphorisms about life. The style, then, always points beyond itself to the main character and is the chief device Burke uses in the first part of the novel to reveal Neal's unlikable, often cruel, and manipulative character.

Insofar as this novel has a plot, it is generated out of Neal's relationship with Anthony, his friend, fellow writer, and sometime rival, and with the two women in the novel, Florence and Genevieve. Minor episodes are generated out of Neal's relationships with his wife and children, the Mad Girl in White, Alter Ego, and a number of unnamed other characters—such as the man who commits suicide. Neal and his development in the course of the novel is always central. In a sense, there are no other focal points (except for the style) or developed characters in the novel. Though the novel alternates between the city (parts 1 and 3) and the country (part 2), neither setting is developed to a point where we become really interested in the scenic details or the scene-agent ratio. This is not a novel about the individual and society (the principal subject of so many other novels), but about a single individual and his relationship, primarily, with Florence and Genevieve. Neither woman and no other character is developed enough to have much reality apart from Neal. No one but Neal has a last name and we know almost nothing (including what they look like) about any character apart from his or her relationship to him. His wife and children are never named. Most all of the individual other characters who appear remain unnamed (exceptions are Margaret and Hubert) and are simply identified as I knew a man once, or I knew a woman once, or I knew a poet, and so forth. No cities or towns are ever named in the original edition of the novel and the passage of time is always made extremely vague, though we are conscious that time passes and that Neal moves around and changes, usually as a result of purely internal motives (his character) and his own actions, especially in relation to Florence and Genevieve.

Let me say here, early on, that I do not think, as some others do, and even as Burke seemed to suggest in his earlier remarks on the novel, that John Neal goes mad at the end of the novel. In fact, his sanest statements and perceptions all come in the last three chapters of the novel, and his "jottings" in the final chapter are more an indication of a character in transition (from disintegration to reintegration or from an old self to a new self) than of a self gone mad. It is important to make this point early because my whole analysis is based on the conclusion that Neal, at the end of the novel, points ahead, is a portender, as the title suggests, and is thus a hopeful character under the aegis of Burke's favorite tutelary deity, the Comic Muse. He might have been a tragic character, but Burke turns the arrows of his development in the other direction after he cruelly drives Genevieve away and begins to come to knowledge of what he has done and what he has lost. Neal is not a symbolic scapegoat upon whom Burke loads all of his burdens and sends out into the desert to die; rather, he is a character whom Burke loads up with his vices but then purges and redeems by means of painfully acquired self-knowledge and love. This is not the way of tragedy, but of comedy, as Burke so carefully points out in *Attitudes toward History.* John Neal is a hopeful character because he represents the possibility of individual change and amelioration by means of self-knowledge, which is exactly what Burke argues for at length in *Permanence and Change* and *Atti-*

tudes toward History. What John Neal portends, then, is the possibility of the kind of "better life" that Burke works out in his first two books of social and cultural criticism.

The plot of *Towards a Better Life* can be summarized as follows, remembering, always, that we do not have a narrative of a whole life, here, but bits and pieces of a life. The "story" begins in the city at an undisclosed point in time with the triangulated relationship between John Neal (who remains unnamed until page 122), Florence (with no last name and of indeterminate age), and Anthony (of no last name, of indeterminate age and profession). Neal is in love with Florence and is in some sort of relationship with her. Before Florence, we are told in a kind of aside, he had a relationship with Genevieve, but we have no idea how long ago that was, nor how long it lasted. Much of part 1 of the novel is devoted to Neal's strange and certainly masochistic manipulations of the relationship between Florence and Anthony. That is, he seems determined, for reasons that are not really clear, to defeat his own purpose, which is to win Florence by bringing Florence and Anthony together. He does this by arranging for them to act together in a play and by arranging for them to spend the night in his own apartment. By the end of part 1, Anthony has Florence; Neal, in his self-generated despair at the loss, has spent what little money he had and fled the city.

At the beginning of part 2, Neal is in the country, in a village he had never been to before, and is soon to marry a woman of considerable means, with whom he will have two children. Before this occurs, he sends for Genevieve, who then reenters the novel and his life and helps him recover from the despair he experienced over the loss of Florence. When she learns that he has proposed to a woman of the village, she insists on leaving. A few years pass. Neal makes a life for himself in the village. He has a wife, two children, and, thanks to his wife, a considerable estate. He becomes involved in the life of the community, writing a play for the school and arranging for a traveling group of players to come do a performance of *The Merchant of Venice*. Florence reappears as part of this traveling group, playing the role of Portia in the play. She has left Anthony and leads Neal to believe that she has married a wealthy man and travels with the players now and then to amuse herself. Neal, of course, is delighted to have Florence back and renews his courtship of her. At the end of part 2, he finally "wins" her only to discover the truth of what has happened to her and the fact that she was not really what he thought she was nor the woman that he really wanted. She is not married to a wealthy man. Anthony has thrown her out and so has another lover. She is poor, broken, and in need. She asks Neal for help after they finally do make love in the grubby hotel room where she is staying, only to be refused and sent on her way. This leads to his second collapse and second departure.

He leaves the village, his wife and children, and begins a period of wandering. But first, he goes and persuades Genevieve to leave her husband and come with him; as she had done earlier, she once again restores and fortifies him. During this transitional period, Neal takes to hacking unfinished statues out of granite—which are clearly symbols of his as yet undefined self. With the departure of Florence and his departure from the village and the kind of ordinary life he had achieved there, Neal becomes convinced that his life has lost whatever purpose it had and that he must seek a new one. Neal and Genevieve wander aimlessly for an unspecified period of time and finally settle in New York. Much of the early chapters of part 3 are devoted to the relationship between them and the group of friends they make in the city. Neal has consistently driven those with whom he has any kind of relationship away from him and he continues this pattern in part 3, first driving all of their friends away from Genevieve and himself and then cruelly driving Genevieve away by telling her to go out and solicit to raise money for them. This decisive action is the major turning point of the novel, though it takes Neal a while to discover just how traumatic and decisive his actions toward Genevieve will be. Just before he drives Genevieve away, he takes advantage of the Mad Girl in White, luring her off to a hotel room and there "seducing" her. Right after he has driven Genevieve away, he has a brief, strange, and vaguely homosexual relationship with Alter Ego, who abandons him before Neal can drive him away. From this point on to the end of the novel, Neal is alone. The last three chapters of the novel are all concerned with his coming to knowledge of what he has done in driving Genevieve away, of who and what he was that he could do such a terrible thing, of how he alone is to blame for what he did, of what he has lost in losing Genevieve, and of how he must change if he is to be able to move toward a better life. Much of the last part of the novel is about Genevieve and love; or, rather, the nature of love and how completely incapable of love Neal was up to this point in the novel (157), where he lays a curse upon himself as punishment for what he was and what he did to Genevieve and others.

In terms of plot, what we have at the end of this novel is John Neal beginning to learn how to obey the punning imperative in his name (John kneel!). The elegant, cynical, Nietzschean aphorisms of part 1 have been replaced by the rather meek, guilt-laden confessions and apologies of the imaginary letters to his mistress and by the very un-Nietzschean jottings of part 3, chapter 6. Neal is alone, unable to act, driven completely into himself and silence (this man of the destructive word), so that from the inner part of himself, he can learn what he needs to know to begin building a new, more humane self. In a sense, the novel has been a confession, though I'm not sure it started out to be that. Like any confession, the central action is the transformation of the main character from what he was to what he became, or, at least, to a change in his "being" and a new becoming, even if the details of that new becoming are not fully worked out.

No other character in the novel undergoes any kind of change or development or transformation and all are best examined in relation to what happens to Neal. All the other males in the novel are subordinate to the two main women since none of them offers Neal any kind of positive alternate self. Alter Ego is clearly negative. Of the two women, Florence is clearly negative and Genevieve is clearly the positive force.

The Repeating Tripartite Structure

Before looking at John Neal and Genevieve in detail, since their relationship is certainly the key to the novel, either as a novel or as a symbolic action by and for Burke, I want to examine the repeating, tripartite structure of the novel—a kind of structure that we find over and over again in Burke's books. Each of the three parts of the novel ends with Neal in crisis. In part 1, the crisis is brought on by the loss of Florence, a loss that is engineered by Neal himself. In response to the crisis, Neal leaves (flees) where he is and goes elsewhere to regroup and start another life. He is aided in this by Genevieve at the beginning of part 2 when she comes to him in the village where he has settled and "restores" him. She leaves, at her insistence, to give him a chance to start a new life with a woman in the village, which he does. The second crisis comes at the end of part 2 after a long false rise occasioned by the return of Florence and Neal's belief that he has found what he so long sought and desired and that Florence will make him happy. The more or less normal life that he achieved with his wife and two children has obviously not provided him with what he really wanted, especially once Florence comes back into his life. The second crisis is precipitated by Neal's discovery that Florence is not what she says she is and in fact not what he apparently thought she was all these years. She is a beaten, broken-down, rather shabby female—a hunted thing, Neal calls her—in need of a degree of kindness he cannot give her. She has been used and rejected by Anthony and the boxer and is used and rejected again by Neal, who, after his sexual conquest of her, sends her away. With the rejection of Florence, Neal feels that he has lost the motivating force in his life. He feels that he now has "no reason for doing any single thing." Much of this is because he had tied so much of what he did to Florence.

He decides that he must again leave where he is and go seek a new purpose. He leaves his wife and children, persuades Genevieve to leave her husband and come to his aid again, and sets forth with Genevieve on what, in his later notes, Burke calls an "ecstatic pilgrimage."

It should be noted here that once again it is Genevieve who comes to him and saves him and helps him to begin a new life. The pattern that was first established at the end of part 1 and the beginning of part 2 is here repeated with variations. Neal and Genevieve settle in the city (finally named by Burke in his later notes as New York) and begin a life together. But just as the crisis in part 1 was caused or brought on by Neal, so the crisis in part 3 is also a function of his sick, cynical, antinomian mind. Even though he knows that it is Genevieve who has restored and saved him, he begins to turn against her, obscenely tempting her in her sleep to admit that she, the most faithful of women, has betrayed him. He "betrays" her with the Mad Girl in White in another obscene episode and finally drives her away. The crisis with which the book ends is a direct result of this cruel and completely unjustifiable action. As soon as he has driven Genevieve out, he realizes what he has done and runs after her, but it is too late. At this point, Neal says of this action and of himself: "if I were not myself, but something that looked down upon this that was myself, I should brand it, I should in quietude put an effective curse upon it, I should corrode it with the slow acids of the mind" (157).

The next two chapters deal, we are told by Burke, with the "progress of this curse." The first deals with his rather troubling and certainly ambiguous relationship with Alter Ego and the other consists of his unsent letters to his mistress—presumably Genevieve—and deal with his relationship with her. It is clear that Neal is again in crisis, but this time he does not flee (though he does go away briefly with Alter Ego) but turns inward. There is no longer Genevieve to come to his rescue, though he constantly yearns for her return. The crisis finally comes about because he has driven away the one person in the novel who did bring him love, sanity, comfort, fortitude, happiness, strength—and gave of herself, in his times of need, with great generosity, over and over again. There is no part 4 to this novel, so that in a sense the crisis is not fully resolved and we do not have John Neal starting up again, as we did in parts 2 and 3. We have him taken by Burke to the extremity of the crisis and left there with only the promise, or perhaps the suggestion, that the pattern will repeat itself in the hypothetical future of this novel and Neal will be able to keep the promise he makes to the readers (and himself): "*resurgam! resurgam!* I shall rise again! Hail, all hail! Here is a promise: *resurgam!*" (217).

John Neal's Antinomian Character

Burke has said that he concentrated his worst negative traits and vices (including some he invented) in John Neal and used him as a scapegoat in order to purge himself of these traits and vices. He refers many times to Neal as a nasty, unlikable fellow; as a deliberately conceived character so unpleasant the reader could not possibly have anything in common with him; as a character who lacks a "saving touch of humour"; as a character who has an inquiring mind he converts into a liability by using it to arrive "at zero." But a reader of this novel does not have to have Burke to tell him what a destructive character Neal is. Neal does this himself in narrating his own story. So, using Burke's own critical percepts as they are laid out for us in the title essay of *The Philosophy of Literary Form,* let us, by examining the internal evidence, find out what Neal "equals"; that is, let us find out what Neal is "identified" with, realizing that he is the supplier of the evidence we are going to use against him. And let us begin at the beginning, since we are also going to track him through the novel by studying "what follows what" in the unfolding of the novel—that is, John Neal's story, as he tells it.

Neal's obvious characteristic in part 1 is the negative, cynical, destructive, and self-destructive bent of his mind and the disjunction between the operations of his intellect and the rest of him. Put somewhat differently, the emphasis on style places an overwhelming emphasis on the priority of words in relation to experience. This is what Burke means when he says that Neal converts his primary asset—his inquiring intellect—into a liability by a continuous process of conversion downward to or toward zero (and often into negative numbers). Much of part 1 is about how Neal conspires against himself by manipulating others—especially Anthony and Florence. He is so successful in this conspiracy against himself that he arranges for the woman he is in love with to become the mistress of his philandering friend Anthony and so causes the loss that precipitates the first crisis of the novel. This self-destructive and self-abusive behavior on Neal's part only gives us examples of how the negative bent of his mind is translated into actions. But most of part 1 is not actions at all but John Neal's thoughts, especially as he tries to reduce human behavior to the aphorisms that, collectively, make up what Burke calls his "antinomian philosophy." *Antinomian* here derives its meaning from *antinomy* and is meant to suggest a philosophy based upon antagonisms and oppositions, or a kind of agonistic view of human behavior. This would be the very opposite of a philosophy based on love and community. And in fact, through much of the novel, John Neal drives people away from him.

Neal unfailingly locates or focuses upon the negative element—the zero factor, we might call it—in every human event and in human relations generally. It is really his major talent, certainly in part 1 of the novel. When he tells us that because he could not tell the difference between friends and acquaintances, his "converse became a monologue" (5), he gives us one of the salient features of his character, which is to remain isolated, engaged always in a monologue (that is, not listening to or responding to others). This is perhaps why the novel consists of unsent letters or repeated examples of a circuit never opened and completed. Or, referring to the other part of the title, declamations delivered to no audience except the declaiming self. Hundreds of quotations could be assembled to illustrate this pattern. Barry Maxwell has suggested that John Neal is the embodiment of cynical reason and that one model Burke had in mind for him was Jeremy Bentham. Certainly another model was Nietzsche. But no model is necessary, really, since Burke tells us that Neal concentrates all of his own negative traits and intellectual and other vices, including, we have to assume, the way in which he regarded and treated other people, especially women. So, symbolically, Neal must represent a part of Burke, a habit of Burke's mind that he came to dislike and distrust; to study and understand it better so that he might purge it or alter it more completely, he embodied it in a fictional character. This novel is Burke's own act of hypochondriasis: it is the study by the creating self of the symptoms of its own disease so that they may be better understood and coped with.

Throughout much of the novel, John Neal represents the exact opposite of the comic perspective developed in *Attitudes toward History*, and the ironic-comic attitude so prevalent in Burke's later poetry. An antinomian philosophy might be the basis for a tragic perspective, but Neal is really more grotesque than tragic. He is not the victim of a tragic fate and could never be taken seriously as a tragic protagonist. If he is anything, he is a kind of *isolato*, whose principal cause of isolation is his own arrogant mind: the kind of mind that can arrange the loss of Florence to Anthony by giving first Florence and then Anthony (unbeknownst to Florence) the keys to his apartment so that—and note the motive—he could force the "role of intruder" upon Anthony, and then, once the relationship between the two has developed and flourished, can think, "There was gratification in the thought that I might derive even my defeat from within" (55). If such a view of the self is not relieved and partially discounted by irony and comedy then it is sure to become corrosive and more so as it extends its range, as Neal does, to human behavior outside the individual self.

John Neal is so thoroughly dislikable that we sometimes slide right over our reasons for disliking him, especially in part 1 where we are overwhelmed with one cynical observation or aphorism after another. But it is important to be as precise as possible in characterizing his view because it is what must be purged and replaced by another more constructive and generative view. There is no basic change in Neal until after he drives Genevieve away in part 3. The more cheerful and sometimes apparently almost euphoric Neal of part 2 is not a person who has undergone any fundamental change. He has tried a new mode of existence in the village by marrying and becoming a part of the community. For a change, he does not have to worry about money since he has married it. When Florence reappears quite by accident with the traveling troupe of actors, Neal, still obsessed with his desire (or "love") for her, feels certain that he has now achieved what he has so long desired—that is, Florence. And he does finally "have" or conquer the woman he thought he had lost and whose loss was the cause for his flight to the village. But his conquest of her is surely the major anticlimax of the novel. Neal realizes he has pursued a kind of illusion all these years. He is still as ungenerous as ever and sends Florence on her way. Burke is writing after the great crash of 1929 and I think we have to understand what now happens in the novel as symbolic of more than just what happens at the level of plot. John Neal discards all that had given his life purpose up to this point. Florence, who had obsessed him for so long, is gone for good. His wife and children and his role in the life of the village are all abandoned.

But has Neal changed? Not really, or not yet, though he has abandoned one, perhaps two sets of goals or purposes and, as he says, "the fundamental concerns of several years had been rounded off and finished" (131). Florence's rather complicated significance for him is finished, and the mixed motives of love, fear, and vengeance she produced in him are suddenly removed and, as he says, he falls forward into a kind of purposeless void (132). He must decide whether to stay and make a life in the village with his wife and children or leave and seek a new purpose. As he says on page 133: he stays and waits for the call from within that will tell him what to do. He waits and while waiting makes wonderfully symbolic unfinished statues out of stone. The call does come and he leaves, going to Genevieve and persuading her to leave her husband and come with him. We could say, at this precise point, that John Neal is in a position to change and that he is beginning or making the long transition that will result in his changing by the end of the novel. His returning to or turning again to Genevieve is as symbolic as the termination of his obsession with Florence and the termination of his brief relationship with his anonymous wife and children (matrimony, domesticity, fatherhood—none of which will be satisfactory without some fundamental change that has not yet occurred but for which the ground has been prepared.) In terms of the plot, both Florence and the wife and children must be rejected, but so also must the mind-set that so overwhelmed part 1 of the novel but that recedes in the false rise and euphoria of part 2, chapters 1–5. Neal's loss of interest in and dismissal of Florence are in fact somewhat "cruel," but Florence is not the woman who will redeem him, though an act of kindness toward her in her time of need might have helped him to change, especially when she both names him for the first time and implores him to obey the imperative in his name: "Neal, Neal, John Neal" (122). It is Genevieve he needs and who will show him the way, but only after an action toward her more cruel than anything he could have done to Florence. The two women in the novel are not really so much in an oppositional relationship to each other. That is, they are not the classic blond and dark ladies of fiction. Basically, though clearly negative in many ways, Florence is a blank Neal fills with his own illusions, whereas Genevieve is a powerful generative force who finally destroys many of Neal's illusions about himself and others.

Genevieve

Nothing negative is ever said about Genevieve in the novel. From the very first mention of her in part 1 (30) she is always described in positive terms. We learn that Neal had a relationship with her that occurred before he knew Florence. We are told that Genevieve had gone to secret places with him and that she had provided him with "moments of brilliance and tenderness" (30). She is described as "lovely" and we are told that he takes pride in this. She is always "loyal" to him (30). She is "contented and cheerful" by nature, yet, he tells us, he "mistreats" her (31). He brings anguish into her life because he molds and shapes her to his sinister purpose when she is young and unformed (31). She is "delicate and imaginative" (31) and "lavishes her charity" on him (31). She "walks in sweetness" and somehow survives his "rancours" (32). Neal tells us that "she believes unquestionably in 'moral obloquy' "—or that she willingly blames herself for what goes wrong because she believes she has failed rather than that Neal has been cruel or mean. Neal says she is like a tree he has carved his initials into and that she will bear his mark forever (32). This tells us more about him than it does about Genevieve, because it tells us how he treats even such a sweet, loyal, blameless person like Genevieve—who is, from the very first mention of her, his opposite.

We next meet Genevieve in part 2, chapter 1, when Neal turns to her in his time of need after the loss of Florence to Anthony. He describes this as his "compensatory" use of her. He says that it is "perhaps to Genevieve that I owe my life" (66). She has made the "evil" of his life "bearable." She aids him because it is in her character to do so—again a trait opposite to those that dominate Neal's character in part 1. If there are polar opposites in this novel—Burke's what versus what—they are certainly John Neal and Genevieve. Of Genevieve, Neal says: She was "deeply emotional, yet lacking a medium of art in which to embody her emotions, she was compelled to seek her poetry in the disposing of her own person" (66). We may note, again, the opposition here between the cold, calculating intellectualism of Neal and the deep, generous emotionalism of Genevieve. She had a "pronounced gentleness," Neal tells us, which opens her to others (66). She is well-equipped for her "eventual abandonment to his wishes." He "delights in her loveliness" and wishes to "cherish these moments" (66). Finally, after some months of the healing relationship with Genevieve, she insists that she leave so that he can marry the woman in the village to whom he has proposed, and he reluctantly accepts, with the cynical "appearance of speechless regret" (68).

The contrast between Neal and Genevieve is very pronounced here and provides one of the best ways to be precise about what Neal is like. We do not encounter Genevieve again until after Neal's second crisis when he goes and gets Genevieve once again. For the first time in the novel, he regrets some of the things he did to Genevieve in the past. He acknowledges that she is ever "faithful" and "full of virtue" and he realizes the extent to which he draws some of his strength from her (139). She even helps to support them in the city. But Neal has not changed yet. He becomes jealous of her, without cause, and begins to pick away at her in a recurrence of the negative mind-set that was so prevalent in part 1. His meditation on this faultless woman, based on his observation that she "does not have morbidness enough for continued loyalty" (149) is a classic example of how Neal's mind works. His specialty is converting positives into negatives in the alembic of his cynical mind. At the end of this mediation (149–52), Neal attempts to get Genevieve to admit to the infidelities he has invented for her. He does this while she is asleep, caressing her, whispering in her ear, even arousing her sexually while she sleeps, hoping she will whisper someone else's name. Finally, in shame, he abandons these attempts, but he does not cease his cruelty toward her. His next action is to betray her with the Mad Girl in White whom he picks up and takes to a dingy hotel by the river. There, he symbolically seduces her and then sends her away in a scene reminiscent of his seduction and dismissal of Florence.

Just as he has previously driven everyone else away from him or abandoned them so he now drives Genevieve away in what is certainly his most perverse and cruel action. In need of money, Neal sends Genevieve from the room, "telling her that she could get us money from any man" (156–57). She leaves and he never sees her again. This, as it turns out, will be the decisive act for him. It coincides with his meeting Alter Ego, a sinister symbolic character of ambiguous sexual orientation with whom Neal has a short relationship. At this point, Neal brands and curses himself for what he has done to Genevieve and for what he has been up to this point. Most of the rest of the novel will explore the consequences of what he has done to Genevieve. But first he must have his relationship with Alter Ego and be abandoned by him so that he is completely alone, finally, with no actual Genevieve to turn to for help. He does, however, turn to the memory of Genevieve often and it is from her that he learns what he must do to get himself ready to begin to move toward a better life.

John Neal's Letters about Genevieve

In the many search-for-the-self or rituals-of-rebirth novels that exist in our literature, there is always a stripping-away action, a reduction of the self, not to nothing, but to some essential element or elements of the self from which a new self may be formed. No change in the self can occur without this reductive process and no change can occur without the coming to knowledge (of what one was, of what one can become) that is always part of this reductive process and the generative process that follows it. John Neal has one last thing he must do before he bottoms out and can begin the coming to knowledge that will enable him to clear the ground for a new self. He must be rid of Alter Ego, his other self, a possible alternative to what he now is. We should note here that Alter Ego, like Neal's wife in part 2, is "monied" and can thus take care of him. Though it may seem strange to put it this way, Alter Ego is a corruption of Neal, a decadent Neal, a direction in which, at this bitter point in his life, he could go. Like Neal, he is a user of people and he tends to use them for his amusement; when he tires of them, he abandons them, as he did Neal, and moves on to others, in this way always making sure that he is essentially alone. At the end of his relationship with Alter Ego, who is certainly one of the more sinister characters in this novel and perhaps represents what Neal might become if he does not change, John Neal is finally ready to change, and at the end of part 3, chapter 3, he begins the process when he says, "Henceforth, Genevieve, I will deserve you" (168). Then, in the paragraph beginning "Purifyings by ritual, relief by the utterance of a formula, contrivances whereby, after so many sentences, the supplicant becomes a new man, denying such untoward yesterdays as are still recorded in the upbuildings of his tissues—I will not allow that things can be so erased" (168–69), he makes it clear that he is going to open himself to the truth about himself, that he will use no tricks, allow no subterfuges, allow none of the irresponsibilities of faith, forget none of the sins of the past, and never allow himself to believe that simply by acknowledging God or Allah he can be forgiven and saved.

In part 3, chapter 4, in the unsent make-believe letters Neal addresses to his "mistress," who is quite clearly Genevieve or some sort of surrogate for her, his confession and purgation begin. This long chapter must be examined in detail if we are to understand the transformation that occurs in him at the end of the novel, a transformation in which he moves closer and closer to the values that are represented by Genevieve in the novel. The title of this chapter is "A Story by John Neal," but the chapter does not tell much of a story. It dwells mainly on the relationship between Neal and Genevieve and Neal and the wooden policeman, who, like most of the secondary male characters in the novel, is a symbolic adjunct to Neal. He is now completely alone and unwilling or unable to enter into any human relationships. The best he can do—somewhat comically—is relate to his "kinsman" the wooden policeman who is, he says in one of the few jokes in this novel, a "real dummy." His unsent letters to Genevieve, along with the imaginary replies, which he then answers, are primarily confessional and expiatory: they also express a wish that he knows can never come true, which is that, as before, Genevieve will return and save him. She does not return, nor will she, but she does help to save him, because in confessing his cruel and perverse rejection and loss of her he comes to understand what she meant to him and thus comes little by little to understand something about the true nature of love.

There is much in these letters about Neal's loneliness, a condition he has brought upon himself and which he must endure while he learns that it can only be brought to an end by becoming worthy of being loved. In the first of the letters (which are written over a seven-month period), Neal says that he "can promise you nothing, nothing but the abject tributes of one who loves you, 'like the little bird that picks up crumbs around the door'" (172). In the same letter, he writes of "the loneliness that will undo him," with the *him* referring to the hero of the fiction that he is writing, so that we have a fiction within a fiction functioning to tell us something about Burke's fictional hero. In the second letter, Neal says that his "genius resides in loving you abjectly" (174), and right after that, again using the device of the fiction within the fiction, he says, "I swear I would never touch this desolate work again were it not that I must earn you, that I must make some visible thing which entitles me to you" (174). This is obviously a very different John from the one we have seen in the first chapters of part 3 and in all of the earlier parts of the novel. Later, in this same letter, again thinking about his relationship with Genevieve, he writes: "For each lack in me, you brought the corresponding fulness; . . . wherever I was in need, you had the fitting kind of charity" (176). And a few lines down, "I did not now regret my particular ills, since they turned me with such avidity to you as the cure for them" (176). In the third letter, Neal returns again to his need to make himself more worthy of Genevieve, which, again, we should think of in contrast with the manipulative way he treated her earlier, especially when he refers to her as a tree upon which he has carved his initials. Toward the end of this same letter, we find this: "Oh, I am tired—tired of trying to deserve you, tired of writing you so constantly and so unmanfully. May you come soon, to repair all this—may you come, that I may nestle against you" (180).

Three months have passed since Neal began these unsent letters. It is now January. He goes on with his expiatory confession, speaking of himself, as he often does, in the third person.

> I know of a man who, in a moment of blind self-interest that undid its own purposes, had sent away a lovely woman. Needing money, he had suggested sullenly that she procure some as best she was able, yet there had been much delicacy in his possession of her. She left the room without reproaching him, but he never saw her again thereafter—and with each succeeding month he understood more bitterly the destitution he had brought upon himself. He found that she alone had upheld him, for there was no pliancy in him that had not come from sources within this woman. He remembered how they had crept together, with the city roaring about them like a monster; how he had felt the warmth of her while she slept, as though they alone were spared from a cataclysm, as though all mankind, torn by madness, were fleeing from danger, while they lay safely in sweet segregation, enclosed in the Ark of their four walls, and the torrents of the metropolis pounded outside their windows. (183–84)

Then, after describing the changes that took place in this man after his loss, Neal, in a rare instance of self-irony, hopes that what happened to this man does not happen to him. He hopes that he will not "gradually lapse into this man's strangeness," but he admits that he fears "lest all that smiled readily in me has been taken from me" (184). It is a masterful sequence that tells us much about the kind of self-knowledge he is coming to as he becomes more completely reduced to his solitary self.

The next letter is dated March 8 and is addressed to his "dead Mistress." The salutation is completely accurate in the sense that she, Genevieve, is dead for John Neal because she will not come to him again, ever, no matter what he tells himself in this "make-believe correspondence" he carries on between them, "writing letters you never receive, and answering letters you never sent" (185). He knows this "make-believe correspondence must come to an end because it is a subterfuge," but it goes on a bit longer because Burke needs to tell us a few more things about what is happening to Neal. In this same letter, he tells us he has been "cursed by Selfhood" and "deprived of Emanation"—in a paragraph filled with fragments from Blake. In the letter of March 28, also addressed to his "dead Mistress," he describes how his relationship with the wooden policeman becomes more obsessive as his loneliness becomes more acute. "A sweet woman once took delight in the touch of me, and I sat in many ordinary places conversing with strangers readily enough, and people did not think it odd—but now, I can approach no human thing without remarkableness" (187–88). The problem clearly lies with him, and he begins now to try to characterize it. "I am in a vicious circle," he says to two complete strangers in the park; "there are accounts of such vicious circles in folk-lore— . . . a once handsome prince locked up in a repellent form . . . the Prince will not be freed until the love of a beautiful woman has freed him—and how, short of magic, can a beautiful woman love him until his true form is revealed?" (188–89). We cannot help but understand this fairy tale symbolically with Neal as the prince who is locked up in the repellent form—or, more accurately, the repellent self of the previous parts of the novel—but who will be freed by the love of a beautiful woman who loved him in spite of his repellent self. There is a way out of the vicious circle short of magic, and Neal will discover it before the novel is over: he can purge what is repellent out of himself and be born anew with the help of love.

In the next letter of April 3, also addressed to the dead mistress who will save him, Neal tells us that he has a clenched fist in his brain. "It is as though my mind had muscles, and these muscles would not relax" (189)—a wonderful image of the kind of distress that he has been in since he drove Genevieve away. In the next to last letter of April 7, addressed "To my dear, dead Mistress," Neal, deep in his painful introspective journey of self-discovery, writes that his "life is a funnel—and with each day I am squeezed farther into its narrow end" (191). In the last part of this letter, he writes "Memorandum: Rules to Self," which consists of classic paranoic responses to the world outside the self and is a further indication of the extent to which he is completely isolated from the kind of relationships that will reconnect him to humanity. The narrow end of the funnel is an image for this being squeezed into the self, or the reduction to a kind of seed of the self from which a new self can be born. John Neal lists his alternatives: being reduced to madness, suicide, drugs (perhaps), faith (which he has rejected), travel (which he has tried), or regeneration, "*resurgam.*" The images all through here are images of pain that anyone who has experienced great distress will immediately recognize.

In the final letter of April 8, now addressed to his "Dear Mistress," is another image familiar to anyone who has suffered great psychological distress: "Oh, I am very tired. I should like to fall into a deep sleep, and on awaking, find every single thing around me altogether different" (194). This Rip van Winkle wish can never come true, as he acknowledges in the last paragraph of the letters, where he says good-bye to Genevieve and acknowledges that though she may have shown him the way, he must travel it himself. "I must not think of writing you," he says, because "probably it was the weakness of these make-believe letters that first started me on my course into the funnel. I must put myself under severer rules. I must deny myself all these little subterfuges that pamper me. This is the last word that passes between us" (194). And it is, though this is not the last of Genevieve in the novel. What is "the weakness" of the make-believe letters? It is the false hope that Genevieve will come again in person to pamper him and to prop him up before he has made himself worthy of her. He must do things the other way around: He must change and make himself worthy of the love of someone like Genevieve and then he can go to her; he must earn what he gets; he must do what is necessary to change the prince from his repellent form back into (or perhaps, coming out of the fairy tale, just into) a handsome self worthy of the love of a beautiful woman.

The Man Whose Antinomian Purpose Never Failed

We come now to the penultimate chapter of the novel, "In Partial Recapitulation," which Burke tells us is "a selective, and amplified review" of John Neal's life.

Since Neal is telling his own story, we have to decide when to believe him, when not to believe him, and when to discount what he says. He has a tendency to "lie" to himself since all the unsent letters are really addressed to him. For example, in part 2, he leads us and presumably Anthony, to whom the letters are ostensibly addressed, to believe one thing about his relation to Florence and who and how Florence is, only to correct the false impressions he has created in the last chapter, where we learn the truth about the relationship and Florence. There is some of this same tendency in this chapter of part 3, which is also addressed to Anthony and where again Neal leads us to believe one thing only to cancel or negate it in the very last paragraph of the chapter. It is hard to know how to interpret these deceptions and corrections, especially since they are almost always mixed in with a lot of truth telling by Neal about himself. The chapter title indicates that it is to be a "partial recapitulation" of what we know about Neal before the actual conclusion, not of the life, but of what we have been told about this life in the novel. The recapitulation begins with a return to the antinomian philosophy with which the novel begins and which dominates most of part 1. The point of this recapitulation, as we soon find out, is to indicate that Neal deliberately chose his antinomian philosophy and lived in accordance with it. He was the way he was because he chose to be that way. He was not a victim of fate or bad luck or anything else external to him, but acted throughout in accordance with his own carefully worked-out conception of purpose. As he says, he maintained the "integrity of his character" throughout, often at great inconvenience to himself. The "integrity" of this antinomian character requires that he "put Genevieve from me, not because our relationship was faulty, but because I had to put some dear thing from me" (198–99). We can only interpret this curious and disturbing remark as an example of the sadomasochistic, self-destructive, self-punishing motivation that is at the center of the antinomian philosophy and hence at the center of Neal's character.

A few pages after this remark, Neal gives us a catalog or recapitulation of his actions that, he says, show that all of his antinomian life he "chose unerringly" in such a way as to promote his own loss and failure; his list of such choices and actions includes the Florence-Anthony relationship, the return of Florence in part 2, the driving away of Genevieve in part 3, and the abandonment by Alter Ego, also in part 3. He says of himself that he is "a man whose purpose never wavered" (202). His justification for his mode of living is that "through living under difficulty, one learns the mode of thinking, feeling, and acting best suited to cope with difficulty" (202). This, of course, is a somewhat specious justification for many of Neal's negative, often cruel actions and cynical comments on the actions of others. He cannot justify or excuse his treatment of Genevieve by reducing it to, or explaining it in terms of, a *theory,* and especially a theory that benefits only Neal and his clearly perverse view of human nature. It is right after this attempt to justify his antinomian philosophy and the actions that derive from it that we come upon his account of an action that is completely opposite to the antinomian Neal we have seen thus far and for only the second time in the novel (the first is when Florence reveals his name to us) exploits the pun in his name in such a way that we immediately say to ourselves: Yes, Neal has finally come to knowledge of his evil ways and destructive philosophy and has changed, has learned the lesson of his proud, self-serving, arrogant ways and understood that humility, love, charity, and the ability to empathize and sympathize with humankind in general will be his salvation, as it was King Lear's. This scene occurs on pages 203–6. It is a great scene, clearly reminiscent of act 3 of *King Lear* and of scenes in *The Rime of the Ancient Mariner.* Neal is, as he was in the previous chapter, speaking of himself in the third person. He says, of John Neal, that having been reduced to himself alone he turns to God, who, in the past had only served him as an oath (204). As in *Lear,* he speaks of the two storms that are raging, one in his "lone man's brain" and one outside. The next morning, after the storm subsides, he walks down to a small lake and there sees nine pure white cranes. After the fury of the storm, he interprets the cranes as "white gentleness" and realizes that "a sign has been vouchsafed him." At this point, "he knelt, while love poured from him, or poured into him from all outward things—and to his vast astonishment, he heard words of prayer issuing like missiles from his lips. For a manner of understanding, unsought for, had blossomed within him" (205).

We want to say of this extraordinary scene that though we are later told that it did not occur (208), it should have occurred and that if it is not part of the reality of Neal's life, it should be. It is at least symbolically true. We may note here the contrast between the deliberate purposeful actions, rationally determined, of his earlier life and the spontaneous, unsought-for actions of this scene. The contrast between head and heart, intelligence and love, self and other, self-serving and other-serving is very pronounced in this scene. It is like what was found in the letters to his mistress in the previous chapter where, if he is not able to get out of himself, at least he is able to understand that he needs to get out of himself and admit to his reliance upon another—that is, admit to the power of love.

This great scene of spontaneous regeneration brought about by Neal's obeying the punning imperative in his name and kneeling to someone other than himself (which has been the sole focus of his life except during periods of his relationship with Genevieve) is canceled in the last paragraph of the chapter. There we discover that it is what he wished might have or should have happened. But it has not happened yet. "Thus documented, John Neal loved all mankind and prayed? On the contrary, he went to no hilltop, he shouted against no storm, he invited neither friends nor demons to ride Valkyrie-like. But sitting in his room, in this inexorable city, he said, rather: 'Watch the mind, as you would eye a mean dog. Wait. Die as a mangled wasp dies.' He constructed for himself a story, picturing himself as gentle, and imagining Genevieve as a woman who had deserted him (which was not difficult to imagine, for he had called her so often in his thoughts, that she seemed cruel in refusing to answer). But the sanction of no vast mythology was permitted him" (208). As at the end of the previous chapter, he must still arrive at and acknowledge the truth without subterfuges. And that is what he finally does in the last chapter of the novel, having glimpsed bits and pieces of the truth up to this point.

Purgation and Redemption of John Neal

It would be exceedingly hard at this point to argue that the "jottings" of "Testamentum Meum" are those of a mad man. John Neal never seems saner. He has abandoned or purged away his antinomian self and is down to a few basic truths and a clear understanding of what he has done in the past and what he must do now. The last three chapters of the novel are really a continuous process of coming to knowledge of purgation and of preparation for redemption—not in the religious sense, but in the purely secular sense, which has always been Burke's primary concern.

First of all, we should note that the final chapter of the novel represents a break in the characteristic form of the novel because it does not consist of unsent letters to either Anthony or Neal's mistress, but of Neal's testament, which is presented to us in the form of "jottings"—or short notes on a variety of topics that collectively make up his final testament, not his last will and testament, but either (or both) a covenant with himself or an affirmation of his beliefs and convictions at the end of the long, painful journey of purgation and self-discovery he has chronicled for us in the novel.

Let us just look at the first five jottings and note that they are literally jottings, not fragments, not the discordant and disoriented fragmentary remarks and observations of someone who is lapsing into madness (209). The absence of an initial capital in most of them seems insignificant. Syntactically, everything is under perfect control here. All have a particular relevance to the life of Neal as we know it. He has thought about God fairly often, and the reduction of God to a mouse is not so strange in a man who has gradually lost his own power in the course of the novel. The second jotting is directly related to the first and to his earlier rejection of faith as an easy solution to his problems and hence as a form of solace. What he needs now is true power within and a form of power that is not going to be destructive, the way his earlier antinomian power was. The third jotting about Alter Ego makes perfect sense in this novel so filled with symbolic abandonments and the scapegoat principle. The fourth jotting refers to Prometheus. Neal has substituted himself for Prometheus and is thinking about two things: that he is no Prometheus (not a god with a god's power) and that his own punishment for what he did do was bad enough, but not in a class with what Prometheus did. Also, he is thinking that what he did benefited nobody; in fact, most of what he did was destructive in some way. But he is suffering and from this suffering will come knowledge. The fifth jotting lists different ways of solving or responding to problems: By going mad, by traveling to escape them, by taking drugs, by faith, by suicide. All have figured in the novel in some way and most have been discussed by Neal. He has tried some of them and been tempted by others.

If we go on through the rest of these jottings, we find them all quite coherent and all either referring back to something in Neal's earlier life or to his present condition (such as his suffering—the vulture gnawing his liver—or his guilt—the eye watching him) or to future possibilities (his pledge of fidelity to Genevieve, were she to return; his affirmation that he will rise again; his final pledge of silence that he may listen to the torrent and learn from it). Many of the jottings acknowledge his awareness of his past errors and sins, as well as his failings, especially with regard to Genevieve. Pain, guilt, remorse, a sense of powerlessness (the metaphorical bull on pages 211–12), his sense that he is still "fettered by lack of purpose," his awareness that he has been a victim of his own attitudes, his need for new knowledge, new ways of seeing things (become bat blind, that he might have bat vision; learning how to hear the cells of his body speaking): all of these are rendered by different jottings, but most of all, I think the jottings, collectively, give us a sense of a Neal, now more affirmative than negative, as a "battered survivor" who realizes that, finally, "some thing has been changed to meet my needs. And if night falls without this new thing's becoming apparent, then the event was a letter written at a distance and started on its way but not yet delivered; or a decision reached by some one who has still to act upon it; or if the relief is to come wholly from within me, the process is even now at work, but has revealed its presence before revealing its nature" (210–11).

We may not know exactly what it is Neal is moving toward; we know much more precisely what it is he is moving *away from* and we know that by the end of the novel, he also knows very precisely what he has been, what he no longer wishes to be; he also knows that the past cannot be undone or redone, but that the self may change, may get out from under or overcome or purge out what has oppressed it and move toward something better. At one point in the testament, Neal, in a passage that Burke is fond of quoting in his later comments on the novel, says: "Though you, in learning, brought trouble upon yourself, let no man discredit your discoveries by pointing to your troubles. Nor must you turn against your bitterness. The sword of discovery goes before the couch of laughter. One sneers by the modifying of a snarl; one smiles by the modifying of a sneer. You should have lived twice, and smiled the second time" (217). This is a passage we may, first of all, read as a description of what has happened to Neal and of how, finally, he learns to modify his antinomian sneers into a smile. Or, we may read it as prophetic of what will happen to him in the hypothetical future of this novel. We can certainly read it, as Burke says, as "the enigmatic inception of [his] devout belief that the best possible of worlds would have the Comic Muse for its tutelary deity" (viii). The Comic Muse has reigned over all of Burke's criticism since he first developed a systematic view of comic criticism in *Attitudes toward History.*

John Neal and Genevieve

Burke has said of writing *Towards a Better Life* that it was a "job of orientation" and that writing it marked a turning point in his life (*Letters* 193). He also said that he "relied upon" the declamations to "burn away certain very uncomfortable parts of me" (*Letters* 195). The uncomfortable parts are clearly embodied in the character of John Neal up to that point in the novel where his coming to knowledge and purgation begin. And the job of orientation—a directional term, like the title of the novel—would certainly manifest itself in the transformation that occurs in Neal during the last three chapters of the novel. What Burke never talks about in all of his many comments on this novel is the role of Genevieve in the transformation of Neal. Burke has said, however (though I can't really remember whether it was just in a conversation or whether it is written down somewhere), that if we but knew how to read the secret code of the novel we would realize that it was all about his relationship with Libbie. Without trying to pry into Burke's personal life, and certainly without the benefit of some factual knowledge about his relationship with Libbie during the period when his first marriage was breaking up, we can still apply this remark to a reading of the novel—as I have tried to do—by examining as closely as possible the relationship between John Neal (Burke's fictional figure for himself) and Genevieve, whom I assume is in some ways his fictional figure for Libbie. We should not be too simpleminded in these matters: Just as Neal is not Burke, so Genevieve is not Libbie. However, in reading the novel as Burke's symbolic action, his fictional ritual of rebirth, resurgence, and transcendence, which, as he argues at length in the title essay of *The Philosophy of Literary Form,* most certainly "*does* something significant" for the author. We are quite justified in exploring the Neal-Genevieve relationship further.

This relationship is presented to us in the following stages: Before Florence, when Genevieve is still quite young and very pliable; after Neal has lost Florence, largely as a result of his own actions, and before he marries his anonymous wife; after Neal regains and then rejects

Florence and leaves his wife, children, and settled life in the village and persuades Genevieve to leave her husband. All of his times with Genevieve are described as happy times and Neal is always grateful to her for rescuing and restoring him. Nothing bad is ever said about Genevieve; in fact, nobody but Neal ever says anything about her. The final stage occurs after Neal has driven Genevieve from him. Only then does he come to understand her true worth and the extent to which she was able to make his life generative. Her effect in absentia is probably more important or significant for him than the three times they were together. Driving her away is the act that finally begins to change Neal and force him toward self-knowledge—that is, knowledge of his antinomian character and the cynicism and cruelty, the manipulation and destructiveness, the sadomasochism of which it (he) was capable. When Neal, late in the novel, admonishes himself to watch the mind as you would "a mean dog" he is certainly referring to his own antinomian mind that, hackles up, was always ready to bite almost anyone or anything. He speaks a number of times of the corrosive acids of the mind. The antinomian mind is one that is not restrained or checked by humanizing traits—by irony and humor, by love, by sympathy and generosity. It is a jealous, destructive mind, suspecting always some ulterior motive. Whatever Genevieve is, she is certainly not a *mind* character and never once, even under the worst of circumstances, acts in accordance with an antinomian motive. She is positive, constructive, generative, restorative, life-saving, sustaining; her sweetness is able to lift John Neal from the entanglements he has gotten himself into (214). She has apparently loved John Neal from the very beginning, in spite of his character. Whatever it is Neal needs to move toward a better life is apparently to be found in Genevieve in the sense that once Neal understands that he must first be unformed before he can be reformed, he also understands that his reformation must move him internally in the direction of Genevieve's values. That is what he means when he says that he must make himself worthy of her love even though it is quite clear she is gone forever. In doing this, he would make himself worthy of more than Genevieve, because he would have changed himself, fundamentally, by reorienting himself toward a whole set of values opposite to what he began with in the novel.

Alter Ego, who enters Neal's life just as he drives Genevieve out of it, does to Neal what John Neal has always done to others: uses him, manipulates him, and then abandons him. Alter Ego is not so much

Neal's other self as he is a mirror self, only worse, a kind of projection of what Neal will become if he goes on as he has been going. But he doesn't, and from this point on to the end of the novel, our whole attitude toward Neal changes from rejection to partial acceptance as Burke moves him through his coming to knowledge, purgation, and partial redemption—that is, prepares him for his ritual of rebirth.

Rejecting and Accepting John Neal

Burke's theory of symbolic action is a triangulated theory, involving, first, the author-text relationship, which I have been exploring, and then the text-reader relationship. Its uniqueness as a functional theory of literature lies in its argument that what the text does for the author it also does for the reader. In both cases, the text's primary function is cathartic, or, as Burke would have it in *The Philosophy of Literary Form,* purgative-redemptive. Burke's insistence on keeping the author-text relationship in a primary position was an attempt to humanize literary criticism by insisting that a literary text was not just an aesthetic object and that reading it was not just an aesthetic experience. According to Burke's theory, every text is a piece of symbolic autobiography, and if we ask ourselves what the text might have been doing for the author we are going to find out a lot about the text as a symbolic structure (or structure of symbols) and we will better understand what the text is doing for us or why we have identified with it so strongly. Consider *Towards a Better Life* in these terms. John Neal is certainly a repellent, nasty character who arouses in us a kind of morbid fascination for someone as negative, cynical, and self-destructive as he is. Although we may admire his cleverness and his way with words, especially as it manifests itself in his many aphorisms, he is a character whom we reject even as we examine our reasons for rejecting him. The opposite can be said of Genevieve, even though she is hardly developed as a character but mostly just represents a set of positive values. Toward Florence, we tend to feel nothing, though we do pity her in part 2 for having fallen on hard times and being so cruelly rejected by Neal in her time of need. Anthony is generally a negative character, a lesser Neal, but so little developed that we do not really get involved with him. It is really only Neal who engages us deeply because we want to try to understand why we dislike, even fear, him so much, recognizing in him traits that are present in our own characters or in those who are close to us. Our rejection of Neal, which has vacillated somewhat each time he is rejoined by Genevieve, is most complete at the end of the first three chapters of part 3. In rejecting Neal, we reject what he has come to represent. It is at this precise point that Burke begins to change Neal and our attitude toward him begins to change from rejection to partial acceptance. This change carries with it or includes the fundamental conception of character that is so central to this novel and to Burke's reasons for writing it (and to all of his later thought about humans, the human condition, and the importance of the comic attitude—even if events themselves are tragic). Even someone like John Neal can change, not by fiat or some leap of faith, but as a result of coming to knowledge, especially self-knowledge, of moving from error to, or toward, truth, as Neal certainly does in the last three chapters of the novel, largely because of Genevieve. In following this change in Neal and in realizing how our attitude toward him changes as a result of it, we can't help but apply the title of the novel to this process, since it is both a directional and a process title, and ask ourselves: *from* what *to* or *toward* what and *by means* of what sort of a *transformation*. The *from* part is not hard to answer: the novel has dealt with it very specifically in depicting what Neal was like before the change. The *to* or *toward what* is not so easy to answer. The *transformation* part is not so hard to answer since we know it has to involve purging from the mind (the self) whatever it was that caused Neal to have such a negative and destructive mind-set through much of the novel. What will come to replace it? A radically different mind-set, to be sure, and one that will combine the poetic attitude of *Permanence and Change* with the comic attitude of *Attitudes toward History.* Perhaps we can't really say much more than what John Neal says to himself at the end of one of his jottings: "You should have lived twice, and smiled the second time" (218). What Neal's life and the novel do is leave certain negative and destructive weapons of the mind *behind* so that Burke, John Neal, and the reader may move toward a better life. In the novel, that life is not defined in any way; it is only hinted at in the character of Genevieve and in Neal's realization in the last part of the novel that if/when he is worthy of the love of such a woman as Genevieve, then in a relationship with such a woman as Genevieve he could achieve a better life. This is an extremely limited view and a highly romantic one. Love is essential to it. The better life is conceived of in highly individual and personal terms and in terms no larger or more inclusive than a male-female relationship. In fact, the title really only applies to one individual, John Neal, and what he must do to move himself toward a better life. In a sense, society does not really exist in this novel and no larger social goals of the kind that one finds in *Permanence and Change, Attitudes toward History,* and every other book by Burke are ever spelled out. The closest one comes to such an ideal is in the scene, later negated, where John Neal kneels in a spontaneous act of universal love and achieves a Whitmanian unity between the within and the without with love flowing both out of and into him. But at the end, it is Neal alone who is going to listen to the torrent and wait for directions. It will only be a beginning, but that is all that is really required in a reorienting—a start in the right direction.

Burke's Later Interpretations of the Novel

By way of conclusion, let us remember some points from the beginning of the essay. This is a novel begun in the heady days before the crash of 1929 and the Great Depression, when one could perhaps afford the luxury of simply writing well; it was completed after the Great Depression was well underway, in 1931, when perhaps someone like John Neal, even as a fictional character, as a device for writing well, was a luxury one could no longer afford and represented a point of view that would be anathema to someone who was just beginning his career as a social and cultural critic. We should remember, also, that the author of this novel was in the process—always painful and traumatic—of bringing a marriage of more than ten years, which had produced three daughters and a settled life in rural New Jersey, to an end and had begun a relationship with his wife's sister that was to lead to a second marriage, two sons, and a much longer settled life (down the road from where he had lived with his first wife and their three daughters). Both the nation, then, and the personal life of the author were going through painful crises. So also was his career, which he had begun as a fiction writer, literary critic, and editor, but which would now, and for the rest of his life, be devoted to social and cultural criticism, or criticism with a much larger scope. Burke would go on writing literary criticism, but no more fiction until "The Anaesthetic Revelation of Herone Liddell" in 1957. His ambition to become an American Flaubert died with this novel. Even if it had not died with the writing of this novel, the reception of it would most certainly have helped to, and maybe in fact did, kill it off.

Burke had high hopes for the novel. The critics received it in more or less stoney silence, or, as Burke ironically put it, in a way that reminded one of trying to hear a feather land at the bottom of the Grand Canyon.

Burke has made many remarks about this novel that encourage us to read it personally; that is, to apply his own theory of symbolic action, as he developed it in *The Philosophy of Literary Form,* to a reading of this novel, if only experimentally, to discover what kind of a reading or interpretation it might yield. He has said that the novel names his number. We have to conclude from this remark that he means that John Neal and what happens to him names his number. He has also said that the novel is in some way all about his relationship with Libbie. If we apply that remark to the novel, we must certainly examine the character of Genevieve and her relationship with Neal in detail. Doing this would also encourage us to examine the kinds of things Burke says of his relationship with Libbie, both before and after her death, in his letters to Cowley. Some of the phrases he uses to describe this relationship appear almost word for word in the novel in what Neal says of his relationship with Genevieve. Burke has also said that writing the novel was a job of orienting or reorienting; that he settled scores; that he was able to work off some of his depression; that reading the novel many years after he wrote it, in 1965 when the second edition was published by the University of California Press, he realized that it was a ritual of rebirth and was much more hopeful at the end than he realized or even "intended" way back in 1931. As late as 1984, in the afterword to the third edition of *Attitudes toward History,* Burke says that he now sees *Towards a Better Life* as "a ritualistic transformation of the author from the vestiges of the 'autistic' in childhood, through the ambiguous moody ordeals of adolescence to what (for better or worse) became the attempt at a 'comic frame of acceptance' that this book *Attitudes toward History* plumps for" (390).

We should note also Burke's comments on the novel in "The Thinking of the Body" (LASA 338–39), in which he also affirms his changed later reading of the novel as ending on an affirmative image of rebirth. In this same comment, Burke also says some interesting things about the Ark cluster that figures in the novel in a number of explicit and implicit ways. Also, inveterate punster and lover of joycing that he is, Burke points out that *towards* can readily be read as "tord" (which we hear as "turd"), thus complicating somewhat our interpretation of the title, if only in a comic way. The Ark cluster is much more interesting because if, as Burke says, the final words of John Neal really belong to this cluster (being in a secure place while a storm rages outside) then his later interpretation of the ending is surely correct. When Neal is remembering his happiest times with Genevieve, he compares their room in the city to an Ark that kept them safe and happy while the storms of the city raged outside. And just before Neal has his imagined experience of universal love, he is in an Arklike place (a hut on a mountain) while a storm is raging outside. The Ark is never anything but a positive image in the novel and is invariably identified with love and happiness. The point of all this is that whatever Burke intended or thought he intended when he was writing the novel, the imagery—and Burke insists that images cannot lie—certainly seems to suggest that the later, more positive reading of the ending of the novel is the "correct" one. Briefly, Burke says, his later interpretation of the novel is that of a "tale foretelling a transformation from the novel's grotesquely tragic narrative to my later concern with criticism as a theory of 'comedy' " (LASA 339).

Conclusion: The Ark Cluster

I have had no interest here in trying to offer a definitive reading of the novel. If anything, this has been a rather Burkean exploration of the novel using all, or much of, what there is to use and being especially careful to examine in great detail what is actually there, in the text, to use. The most interesting result of taking this Burkean approach to his own novel has been the extent to which it shifts the focus of the interpretation to the Neal-Genevieve relationship as a key to the understanding of both the antinomian character of Neal and the changes that occur in him in part 3. This is especially interesting because Burke, in his many comments on the novel, seldom mentions Genevieve and never examines the relationship in any detail—even in his long "Stress, Its Seeking" essay on the novel. And other commentators have become so fascinated with the morbidities of John Neal's character that they tend to forget or overlook Genevieve. Yet one of Neal's last jottings is "stop and examine dark alleys, as Genevieve may be there" (217). Not only can this jotting be interpreted symbolically, but it comes right after the "*resurgam*" jotting, thus linking Genevieve to that motive and promise and to the title of the novel.

There are clearly two basic ways in which one can read *Towards a Better Life*. Burke's own earlier interpretation of the novel would suggest that John Neal was a true symbolic scapegoat who is loaded up with all of Burke's worst sins and vices and is then dispatched into the desert to die. In fact, Neal may have functioned in this way for Burke way back in 1931. It would certainly give a certain finality to the novel because John Neal would in fact then disintegrate at the end of the novel and lapse into catatonic silence, presumably having been driven mad by his own mind and actions. But Burke's later interpretation of the novel is much more affirmative and we might have to dismiss or discount it as a cheerful or more hopeful comic invention of an older mind if the evidence of the novel did not strongly support it. This interpretation makes the novel transitional rather than terminal because in the more recent interpretations, John Neal is not driven out into the desert to die, is not dispatched into madness and silence at the end, but is saved by knowledge, induced by guilt and suffering and a capacity to change. This is especially obvious if one looks at the Ark cluster Burke identifies and describes in "The Thinking of the Body" essay and remembers what Burke has to say about image clusters in *Attitudes toward History* and, especially, in *The Philosophy of Literary Form.* Certain terms and images jump out at you in a novel, even if they are only used two or three times. *Corrosive* as a term describing Neal's mind is one of them. Ark is another. Ark appears three times in the novel, twice explicitly and once, according to Burke, implicitly. All the uses of the term *Ark* derive from Burke's memory of a painting by a Chinese peasant in which the Ark appears "snugly enclosed, while rain fell all around it in furious cascades" (LASA 338–39). In the biblical story of Noah and the Ark, it is the Ark that literally saves humankind and all living creatures from death by drowning by providing them with a safe haven during the forty days and nights of the great rainstorm. The Ark first appears in the novel in a passage in the letter of January 19 Neal writes to his mistress. It concerns his fond memories of Genevieve: "He remembered how they had crept together, with the city roaring about them like a monster; how he had felt the warmth of her while she slept, as though they alone were spared from a cataclysm, as though all mankind, torn by madness, were fleeing from danger, while they lay safely in sweet segregation, enclosed in the Ark of their four walls" (183–84). This passage is so loaded symbolically that one hesitates to begin unpacking it. But let me just say, here, that the passage makes a profound statement about the relationship between the self and what is outside the self and places an extraordinary positive value upon love (the relationship between John Neal and

Genevieve) and a negative, almost paranoic value upon what is going on outside the four walls and apart from the sanctuary and Ark of the relationship. Perhaps it is best to examine it in conjunction with the second explicit Ark passage, which occurs in the next chapter of the novel, toward the end of Neal's "Recapitulation," in a remarkable scene he later tells us never occurred. Again, the Ark figures in one of those illustrative hypothetical passages where Neal speaks of himself in the third person. At this point in the novel, he has driven everybody away from him and is in considerable distress. He turns to prayer, but under rather unusual circumstances. He "had left the city, had gone to a little hut on a hilltop, and was living there alone. . . . A stifling August twilight had been converted, by sudden clouds, into a blackness without direction. A storm of vast proportions had let loose against the hut, which shook, for it was a little Ark, and outside was such a chaos as beat upon the Ark" (203–4). He rides out the storm in his Ark, and the next morning he has his remarkable experience of spontaneous universal love—which we are told a few pages later never happened. Whether it happened or not, the Ark imagery is quite clear and quite consistent with the earlier, heavily symbolic use of the Ark. The last Ark image occurs in the last line of the novel where John Neal is again alone. It is linked to the other two Ark images in the cluster by the "torrents" beating and pounding down outside the Ark. No specific Ark is mentioned in the last line of the novel—"Henceforth silence, that the torrent may be heard descending in all its fulness" (219)—but we can surely assume here that Neal is going to ride out this storm, as he did in the hut and in his room, in the safety of some Ark that will enable him to survive. There is thus a promise in this last line, as Burke suggests, that Neal will survive this storm also to "rise again," as he had promised in an earlier jotting.

The first Ark image describes one kind of Ark. We might call it the Ark of love because it really describes the ways in which the love relationship with Genevieve—the fact that she is there with him in the room—provides Neal with the security and certainty he needs to survive the madness and chaos of life in the city. The second Ark image is different. We might just call it the Ark of shelter, part of the poetics of inside space as Bachelard explains these matters in "The House and the Universe" and "The Dialectics of Outside and Inside" in *The Poetics of Space*. First a room and then a hut function symbolically as Arks. In the final Ark image we have neither room nor hut, but only the self as Ark, which must become its own secure shelter against the storms raging outside of it if it is to survive. In the three Ark images we go from romantic love, as we understand it, because of the relationship between Genevieve and Neal, to the triumph of sanity over madness, in a great cleansing action, followed by universal love (where the barriers between inside and outside break down and no Ark is needed), to self-love, where, ceasing to hate itself—for Neal is a great hater of himself through much of the novel—the self can acquire the knowledge and strength needed to become its own Ark.

The Ark cluster makes clear the extent to which the relationship between the self and brute "reality"—whatever is outside the self, whether in city or country—is an adversarial one, which makes it necessary for everyone to find or have an Ark of some kind. This same cluster also makes clear the extent to which the self can be in an adversarial relationship with itself, as Neal most certainly is, and so can be threatened both from without and within. The self must become its own Ark. The Ark is always part of the imagery of survival. Arks make continued life possible, both in the biblical story and elsewhere; and in this novel, they make the possibility of a better life possible. Genevieve is an Ark for John Neal. At the end of the novel, we do not really know exactly what Neal's Ark will be. We know that Libbie was an Ark for Kenneth Burke and that she probably had quite a lot to do with saving Burke from himself. Anyone who has visited Burke's place in Andover knows that it and the house Burke and Libbie lived in there were certainly Arks, sanctuaries, not just in the thirties but for all the years after that. We know that Burke devoted most of his books after *Towards a Better Life* to what we might call Ark research. *Permanence and Change* was a book he put together to keep himself from falling apart. The comic frame and comic criticism are a defense against, a way of dealing with, the tragic realities of life. The motto of *A Grammar of Motives* certainly belongs to the Ark cluster. Writing in February of 1991 it, and Burke's work in general, have never seemed more relevant. For all these years now, since *Towards a Better Life,* he has been trying to teach us (as he did John Neal) by one means or another, how to keep from destroying ourselves, how to find, or construct, Arks that will protect us and enable us to survive.

Notes

This essay was originally written in the winter of 1991 just because I wanted to work out a reading of this novel that satisfied me and wanted to apply Burke's theory of symbolic action to his own fiction. It has not seemed useful to clutter up this long essay with a lot of footnotes. All references to and quotations from Burke's novel are to the second edition published by the University of California Press in 1966. All other references to and quotations from other Burke books are also to the University of California Press editions. Some parenthetical citations are given using standard abbreviations for the titles of Burke's works, e.g., RM, CP.

1. The main sources for Burke's comments on his novel are the following: conversations between Burke and the author; letters from Burke to the author; *The Selected Correspondence of Kenneth Burke and Malcolm Cowley,* ed. Paul Jay (New York: Viking, 1988) (there is also a University of California Press edition, which is referred to in the text as *Letters*); prefaces to the first and second editions of the novel; preface to *The Complete White Oxen;* afterword to the third edition of *Attitudes toward History;* "On Stress, Its Seeking," which is Burke's long essay on the novel, published in *Why Man Takes Chances,* ed. Samuel Z. Klausner (New York: Anchor Books, 1970); "The Thinking of the Body," in *Language as Symbolic Action,* 338–39; and no doubt in some other places that I have missed or can't find. The main critical discussions of the novel are in the relevant reviews and essays collected in *Critical Responses to Kenneth Burke, 1924–1966,* ed. William H. Rueckert (Minneapolis: University of Minnesota Press, 1969), especially the essay by Denis Donoghue, "When in Rome, Do as the Greeks"; Armin Paul Frank, *Kenneth Burke* (New York: Twayne, 1969); an unpublished essay on the novel by Tim Crusius, "Meaning and Significance in Kenneth Burke's *Towards a Better Life,*" which I first read in 1979; Barry Maxwell's talk on the novel at the 1990 Modern Language Association meeting in Chicago as well as letters from Barry Maxwell to the author; also letters from and discussions with other Burkeans over the years, as well as comments by some students of mine here at Geneseo who were much taken with the novel.

I have drawn on whatever I knew or could remember of whatever I have read or heard about the novel over the years—which is, now, a lot of years. I first wrote about the novel in a brief review of the second edition when it was published in 1966. However, I have been thinking about this novel, and rereading it, for many years. I finally decided to write about it to bring it—or my thoughts about it—to rest, which I think I have done in this essay. I do not think of my reading as definitive, but it has enabled me to answer a lot of questions I have always had about the novel and its central character and hence it has given me a way to think about the novel that pleases me.

My intentions here should not be misunderstood. I have never wanted to mess around in Burke's personal life, though I know quite a lot about it. I have used some of what I know of his personal life in my analysis of the novel, but the primary emphasis is always on the novel itself, on the place of the novel in Burke's development, and on the relationship of the novel to some of Burke's other books. Eventually, someone will write a biography of Burke—but probably not until he is dead. Only then could one mess around with the relationship between his life and this work with any assurance—especially his relationships with his first and second wives.

Finally, this essay had its origin in my longtime desire to apply Burke's theory of symbolic action as he explains it in the title essay of *The Philosophy of Literary Form* and, briefly, at different places, in *Attitudes toward History,* to some of his own works—especially his prose fiction and poetry. I did some of this in "Kenneth Burke's Encounters with Walt Whitman," and was tempted to do it with his *Collected Poems*. Tim Crusius has written brilliantly about the poems and their relationship to Burke's other works (see his "Kenneth Burke on His 'Morbid Selph': *The Collected Poems* as Comedy," *CEA Critic* 43 [May 1981]: 18–32); he has also analyzed the stories in *The White Oxen* most illuminatingly in yet another unpublished essay, so I left these two texts alone and decided to concentrate on the novel. Had the essay not gotten so long, I might well have added a section on Burke's last fiction, "The Anaesthetic Revelation of Herone Liddell," which Burke himself says is a kind of sequel to the novel and was clearly written out of the same kind of stressful situation he discusses in his essay on the novel. In fact, I started to write that section, as an epilogue to the essay, but abandoned it out of kindness to the reader.

Part 3

Logology, Ecology, and Technology

Chapter 7

. . .

Logology and the Rhetoric of Ecology

Our subject—a rather large one—is Kenneth Burke, one of the great Word-Men of our time. The general topic is his rhetoric and logology, both most appropriate concerns for this annual post-Christmas orgy of word processing. My specific topic is intended to take us away from language (as an exclusive concern) because I intend to look at the relationships between rhetoric, logology, and ecology in Burke. I am not trying to be perverse in adding this apparently alien ecological third to the language-centered rhetoric/logology pair. I don't think Burke would find it strange that I wish to concern myself with both language and its nonverbal ground or that I wish to speculate on the constructive and destructive relationships that do in fact exist between rhetoric, the principles of logology, logologic, and logocentricity and the principles of ecology, ecologic, and ecosystems.

As a way into this topic I want to establish some working relationships between my three principal terms (rhetoric, logology, and ecology), more or less as I think Burke might attempt such distinctions. Rhetoric, as Burke and others have defined it, is persuasive speech. More exactly, Burke says that rhetoric consists of persuasion by means of identifications, which, of course, does not limit it to speech, since identifications can be affected by symbolic means other than speech or language. By persuasion, Burke (and others) mean persuasion from and to a particular set of attitudes, beliefs, values, or actions. To keep this topic manageable, I intend to focus on the verbal dimensions of rhetoric. I will not make any attempt here to recapitulate either the rather complicated conceptual framework of Burke's *Rhetoric of Motives* or the enormously complex and involved thesis of his *Rhetoric of Religion*. However, both books argue that the rhetorical (that is, persuasive) motive is intrinsic to language and symbolic action, regardless of the specific end or purpose to which language is being used. This, I think, is an essential point to remember about rhetoric. Anyone familiar with Burke's development knows that from the "Lexicon Rhetorica" to "The Rhetoric of Hitler's *Battle*" through *The Rhetoric of Religion* and beyond, a concern with rhetoric, rhetorical motives, and, especially, the ends to which the ingenuities and resources of verbal rhetoric can be put has been central to everything that Burke has thought about and done with language, literature, symbolic action, culture, and the drama of human relations. Burke has been meditating on the rhetorical resources intrinsic to language and symbolic action for more than forty years now. We can but touch upon the ironies and profundities of the results here.

Logology is a term that does not appear in Burke's published work until *The Rhetoric of Religion* (1961). The main difference between rhetoric and logology is that rhetoric is an essentially neutral term with a long history (at least as far back as Aristotle's *Rhetoric,* always one of Burke's favorite resource books), and that *logology* is a term and discipline whose history begins with Burke. He coined or minted this term, with all of its derivatives: *logologer, logolese, logocentric, logomachy, logomania, logological,* and so forth. *Logology* is the study of words, or, as Burke sometimes says, words about words. It is the study of the timeless forms and principles of language, and would thus include rhetoric, in its verbal dimension, as well as grammar and poetics. It is Burke's most inclusive term for what he does with language and must always be understood in relation to dramatism—another term and discipline of Burkean coinage.

Logology cannot really be understood or practiced apart from logolese (its terminological screen), logologic (the timeless logic of language, which must manifest itself in all acts of language or verbal symbolic acts), and the entelechial motive, which, for Burke, the logologer, is the master motive intrinsic to all symbolic action and the key to the understanding of humans the symbol-using animals. All of this is readily available to the student of Burke in his rich and brilliant book *The Rhetoric of Religion,* in the major theoretical essays collected in *Language as*

Symbolic Action, and in the many as yet uncollected logological studies Burke has done since 1966. The basic operative principles of logology are available to anyone who will take the trouble—which is considerable—to work his or her way through *The Rhetoric of Religion* and the analogies Burke develops there between logology and theology. Though there are many resemblances, the principles one finds in *The Rhetoric of Religion* are not the same as those that can be found in either *A Grammar of Motives* or *A Rhetoric of Motives.* Retrospectively, the principles of logology would be common to both of these books, and for this reason the title of *The Rhetoric of Religion* is somewhat misleading unless one remembers that the subtitle is *Studies in Logology.* The rhetoric of religion is Burke's representative anecdote for establishing the logological principles that are, subsequently, to become his main operative principles for the study of language, symbolic action, and humans the symbol-using animals. He chose the rhetoric of religion, he says, because it is the most perfect, the most thorough example of rhetoric that he could find. His reasons for making it his model are not doctrinal at all, then, and one must not view this book as a piece of Christian apologetics.

Again, I am not going to recapitulate these logological principles—the timeless forms and principles of language—here; but since it is in them, and in the whole nature of Burke's logological endeavor that one finds the justification for triangulating rhetoric, logology, and ecology, I will have to discuss some of the main logological principles.

Rhetoric is grounded in logology (or logologic); logology is grounded in the speechless human body, which in turn has its grounding in the pre- and nonverbal realm of nature. Humans add language, and with it, the negative, to nature, and thus provide themselves with the means by which they can alter, manipulate, transform, and transcend (or attempt to transcend) their origins. One of the most fundamental of all logological principles is that, given words, humans will always drive and strive toward the generation of the WORD; or, put a little differently, beginning with nature and words (humans are the symbol-using *animals*), humans will always strive to ascend, via language, and driven by the entelechial, beyonding motive intrinsic to language, toward some form of supernature that is always beyond both nature and language. This is the movement from words to the WORD, or from the empirical to the meta-empirical realm. Once having arrived at the WORD, the human tendency is to descend with the WORD and infuse it into nature; or, one might say, to persuade nature with it. The counterpart to rhetoric in our material, empirical dealings with nature is technology, which, Burke says, is made possible by symbolicity. It is by means of technology that we coerce, manipulate, persuade, transform, and try to "improve" nature.

What does all of this have to do with ecology? Well, considerable. Ecology is the study of the relationships between organisms and their environments, and humans, because of their capacity for symbolic action, have a unique ability to alter radically their natural environment and, in fact, add a whole other human environment to the natural one. Humans can quite literally invent and add "unnatural" elements to the natural environment, which is something no other species can do. This capacity, according to Burke, derives from man's logocentricity.

The central concern of ecology is with ecosystems and, in the largest and most inclusive sense, with the biosphere or ecosphere as one vast interrelated and interdependent ecosystem. Ecology, like logology, is empirically grounded at every possible point and deals with the timeless (or is it time-bound) forms and principles of nature and ecosystems. Just as there are logological principles, so there are ecological principles that manifest themselves in all ecosystems and in all relationships between organisms and their environments.

How are ecology and logology related? Well, in a number of rather interesting ways. First of all, it is humans' capacity for symbolic action that makes it possible for them to study, master, manipulate, transform, and destroy ecosystems. This is just a way of saying that logology and ecology are related in a number of malign and benign ways. In some fundamental way, it seems that the principles of logology and ecology (that is, the entelechies of each) are at odds with each other, for logology, logologic, and logocentricity, if unchecked by large eco-ethical concerns, and allowed to drive entelechially toward the perfection and completion of themselves in the symbolic realm, seem destined to destroy, or perhaps just deny, ecology, ecologic, and the natural world. The book of Revelation gives us such a symbolic vision of the natural world coming to an end, of massive exobiologic action, of words all being absorbed into the WORD, and of humans the symbol-using *animals* ceasing to exist. The priorities in this vision are perfectly clear.

From a more realistic and empirical vantage point, though, ecologic and logologic still would seem to be at odds with each other. Unlike a purely verbal system, an ecosystem cannot be made to conform completely to logologic, and the primary ecological concern cannot be the internal consistency of a set of terms. An ecosystem is not just a set of terms and can never be treated as if it were one. This is nowhere better illustrated than in the inability of the systems analysts to adequately model a complex ecosystem and program a computer so that it accurately reflects the ecosystem. Stress an ecosystem with too much logologic or logocentricity or logomania and you will destroy or impair the system, with disastrous consequences.

Rhetoric can manipulate the logological principles in any way it likes, to any ends. History confirms this. Every MLA I ever attended confirms this. Rhetoric has no morality, and this is the central point we must remember about it. Rhetoric serves Hitler, Stalin, advertising, Kennedy, Nixon, General Motors, Iran, and Christianity with absolute indifference and neutrality. But ecosystems stand in a different relationship to logologic and logological principles. No amount of logological manipulation or rhetorical exhortation will alter the logic of an ecosystem, even though both may lead to the destruction or the incurable sickness of one. Even if there were no terms to describe them—as there were not before humans and language developed—ecosystems would still exist, and the forms and principles of ecology, as well as the ecologic that is so essential to life on earth, would still exist. The point to be made and stressed here is that there is a fundamental difference between a purely verbal system—say a novel, a poem, an elaborate rhetorical construct, a philosophical system, a critical system, or a theology—and a natural system. Natural systems are the subject of ecology. Verbal systems are the subject of logology. The question to be addressed here is how to maintain the integrity and health of both systems. Since neither can now be denied, we have to use language or some other symbol system (as in math, physics, and chemistry) to describe and enable us to conceptualize and think about these natural systems. They are not subject to logologic in the same way that a purely verbal system would be, though, as recent experiments have shown, it is quite possible that the logics of the two systems may have some amazing similarities.

Human history—especially the recently highly technologized history—has been characterized by massive intrusions of logologic into ecologic and ecosystems and by equally massive economic and political rhetorical campaigns designed to justify these intrusions. Ecologists have countered with an equally powerful, persuasive, and, to some of us, terrifying ecological rhetoric designed to force a modification of these intrusions that will allow the ecosphere time to reestablish, and then maintain, its biospheric health and stability. Some have regarded this as a purely rhetorical struggle, as if it were a political campaign; historians have often regarded it as merely another example of millennial doomsdayism, with the accompanying rhetoric and hysteria. Politicians have taken it seriously when it suited them. Economists have had trouble with it in relation to gross national product projections. Developing nations have tended to ignore it on the grounds that it is not compatible with their national destinies. Burke, like the ecologists, has always taken this evidence of the logological disruption of healthy ecosystems with deadly but ironic seriousness.

In the triangulation of logology, ecology, and rhetoric we have an interesting and significant confrontation between two necessities—the logological and the ecological—and an endlessly resourceful variable—the rhetorical. Burke has always recognized both necessities, however much some may think that he thinks (or thought) that language was the only reality. A man, who by choice, in northern New Jersey, uses an outhouse year round into the sixties and has no running water in his house does not believe that nature is unreal or that the ecological necessities can be made to give way to the logological ones. Burke has recognized, studied, feared, and practiced the power of verbal rhetoric from the beginning. From *The White Oxen* on, one can hardly think of a book or major essay by Burke that is not powerfully, relentlessly, passionately rhetorical and persuasive. Few people have believed in the power of language more thoroughly than Burke. He is always bent on changing people's minds by means of the written and spoken word, and though he is in a class with Henry Adams as an ironist, he still believes, somewhere in there, that he can persuade people to act differently.

I seem to be wandering away from the topic, but I don't think so. If we are to understand Burke properly—perhaps from the very beginning of his critical work and not just in terms of what he is doing now in the Helhaven satire and in his latest work on nonsymbolic motion and symbolic action (that is, nature and humans/language)—we must recognize the extent to which all of Burke's work has been an "anatomy of purpose" in which he has held steady to his attempts to find a generative nondestructive human purpose that would make it possible for logology and ecology to lie down together for more than an orgasmic night or two in some strange motel. The enormous powers of rhetoric and logology must be in the service of the "right" human purpose and we must learn to recognize when they are not. Think of how much of Burke's work has been devoted to both these endeavors, beginning with *Permanence and Change*. That he has been so little known abroad is one of the sad ironies of his career, for his mission has been truly global. I don't want to attempt to say what Burke's "final" vision will be, but it will certainly be ecologically oriented. Burke's most passionate recent rhetoric has been the rhetoric of ecology, grounded in the most profound kind of logological knowledge. It is rhetoric tinged, as always, by this master logologician, with irony and paradox.

Why all this irony?—which as Burke says, is a gift of language, a capacity for negative perception.

The logologer knows that humans the symbol-using animals are driven by the genius of symbolicity and symbol-using toward the perfection of this capacity. That is its (and their) entelechy. This is what Burke means when he says we are "rotten with perfection." Symbol-using is self-persuading. That is part of its logologic. It is the rhetoric of logology. "Language divides us into fragments" even as we yearn for wholeness. As symbol-using perfects itself, it separates from the animal out of which it arose; it transcends its biological environment and creates a new symbolic environment or ground in accordance with logological principles. It acquires a rhetorical radiance and becomes increasingly persuasive for other symbol-users as well. Symbol-using begins to transform the animal out of which it came in accordance with the logological principles it has discovered. It begins to transform the common ground it shares with other animals and organisms. It begins to seem as if the perfection of itself requires the total transformation of the other, but it is cursed (or blessed) with double vision and is bound in a hundred thousand ways to the animal body and natural world it so readily and compulsively (naturally) tries to transcend.

Burke the ecologist takes over. He knows that symbol-using is grounded in the human body and that symbol-using animals are grounded in an environment that is largely nonsymbolic and part of an enormously complex ecosystem upon which, as living organisms among hundreds of thousands of others, they are completely dependent for life. Humans cannot live by words alone. Burke knows that if we continue to tinker with and manipulate this larger other environment in the same way that we tinker, naturally, with our symbols and symbol-using capacity, under the delusion that the two are the same and we have the same freedom with and power over both, then there is going to be deep, irreversible, terrible trouble. Logologic must give way to ecologic at certain points, though we do not know, yet, exactly how or where. The two must learn to live together or perish together, and the burden is upon the logologers and symbol-users. Burke knows that our compulsion to perfect ourselves as symbol-users will surely destroy us, and our home, if it is not purified, checked, and modified in some way in accordance with the ecological necessities. Burke the ecologist and Burke the logologer both know this. Burke the ecologist knows this *because* he is a logologer. He knows that this is a part of the ironic, paradoxical, and perhaps tragic human condition. Humans, with the help of their symbol-using capacity, will free themselves from disease and then die of overpopulation and starvation. Humans will forget they are animals and cease to perceive and respond to the biological rhythms and impulses in their gene code that keep them and all the other nonsymbol-using animals alive. Humans will forget their ancestors, lose the significance of their history, and ignore the warnings of the poets, ecologists, and logologers. Humans as in Burke's Helhaven satire, driven to it by their symbolic genius for the beyond, will foul their home, take exobiologic flight, and perish, finally, on alien ground.

Enter Burke the rhetorician. He knows that we must save ourselves from ourselves, for what could save symbol-using animals from their self-destructive entelechy but specialists in symbol-using who have developed the capacity to see around the corner of symbols into a reality purely and simply extra- and presymbolic. The rhetoricians must use the enormous powers and resources of symbol-using, of logologic, to fight against the destructive powers of logocentricity become logomania. This will be the gift of irony, the way to turn this symbolic resource (the ability to have negative perceptions, to project what is not yet there) to constructive ends. The rhetorician must be poet, logologer, and ecologist. NO: logologers must become rhetoricians who are both poets and ecologists or else they will be left with nothing but the ironic perception of the logologer—which is that humans are rotten with perfection and will pollute everything they touch. Rhetoric and logology are not enough.

We must not forget, in the logomania of this convention or in the course of our enchantment and absorption with Burke's rhetoric and logology, that he is also an ecologist.

Note

This essay was originally written for a session on Burke at the 1980 meeting of the Modern Language Association in Houston and was read for me by Mike Stugrin, who organized the meeting.

Chapter 8

. . .

Poetry, Logology, Technology, Admonology: Kenneth Burke in 1981—from Counter-statement to Counter-nature

A headnote to his summer 1978 article in *Critical Inquiry* entitled "(Nonsymbolic) Motion (Symbolic) Action" says that "Kenneth Burke is now developing the implications of the position stated in the present essay. He is also editing his 'Symbolic of Motives,' a work designed to complement his *Grammar of Motives* and *Rhetoric of Motives*" (810). That was three years ago, more or less. So far as we know, Burke is still "editing" his "Symbolic of Motives," but he has pretty much developed or ramified the position he lays out in this splendid essay. In fact, that position began to take shape as early as 1971 in Burke's wonderful Helhaven satire; and the most recent and complete statement of the position that I know of appears in a 1981 article entitled "Variations on 'Providence.' "

Burke's "Symbolic of Motives" was to have been the third volume in his projected dramatistic tetralogy of motives. More exactly, it was to have been his poetics, and appeared in a draft entitled "Poetics, Dramatistically Considered" in the later fifties, which he circulated among his students at the Indiana School of Letters. By the early sixties, the "Symbolic" was essentially finished and most of it was published as essays. Had Burke wished, it could easily have been published as a book between *The Rhetoric of Religion* (1961) and *Language as Symbolic Action* (1966). Instead, edited and sometimes abridged pieces of it were published in *Language as Symbolic Action* where they became demonstrations of logology rather than the third major systematic ramification of dramatism. This distinction is crucial, as is the fact that the "Symbolic" has really been finished, or should I say in progress, for almost thirty years. Had it been published when it came to term, as was Burke's usual practice, it would probably have taken its place next to Frye's *Anatomy* as one of the major formative works of literary criticism of its time. But that was not to be.

Some parts of the "Symbolic" are well known. There is the remarkable Keats essay; the brilliant essay on *Othello* in which Burke works out and applies his dramatistic theories of imitation and tragedy; there is the equally brilliant "Fact, Inference, and Proof in the Analysis of Literary Symbolism," in which Burke defines and applies the formidable dramatistic methodology; and there are the essays in part 2 of *Language as Symbolic Action*—in particular "Form and Persecution in the Oresteia," the two essays on Goethe's *Faust,* and the Roethke essay. Both the *Oresteia* and the first of the *Faust* essays were abridged for *Language as Symbolic Action* by having their dramatistic conceptual frameworks removed. The first *Faust* essay, for example, was originally part of a long, illuminating essay on the language of poetry dramatistically considered; and the *Oresteia* piece was the first of Burke's many essays for the "Symbolic" on tragedy, catharsis, and persecutional form. The Roethke essay —a stunning study of symbolism and poetic imagery—is unchanged.

Though parts of the "Symbolic" are well known and frequently used, the "Symbolic" as a whole is not, and even such notable critics of Burke as Wayne Booth, Fredric Jameson, and Geoffrey Hartman write about Burke's literary theories as if the "Symbolic" did not exist. In fact, most students of Burke jump over the fifties, going from the *Grammar* and *A Rhetoric of Motives* (1951) right to *The Rhetoric of Religion* (1961) or *Language as Symbolic Action* (1966), ignoring one of the most fertile and productive periods in Burke's remarkable career. Hundreds of pages of truly vintage dramatistic Burke remain largely unread and unused; and the "Symbolic," which is more or less complete and available to anyone who wants to take the trouble to reconstruct it from Armin Paul Frank's definitive bibliography, remains almost unknown.

Why has Burke chosen to have a major completed work of his both known and unknown in this way; why has he chosen to leave his dramatistic system incomplete, and suppress the most masterful and complete work of literary criticism he ever wrote, since he knows, as well as the rest of us, that we live by books, not by articles hidden away in journals? I do not have the answer to this question, and I'm not sure Burke does. After ten intense years of writing it and thirty years of tinkering with it, even Burke's capacity to see around corners and maintain a perspective by incongruity might well be impaired. A version of the "Symbolic" Burke proposed in 1978 bears little resemblance to the "Symbolic" as he wrote it between 1950 and the early sixties, but consists of yet another omnibus grab-bag collection of essays written over a forty-year period and would resemble, as a book, *The Philosophy of Literary Form* and *Language as Symbolic Action*. Such a collection of twenty-nine or more essays and reviews would still not provide anyone with access to Burke's systematic poetics and would not remove the hiatus in his development and in dramatism as a system. I'm not questioning Burke's right to do this; it is after all *his poetics:* I'm merely noting, as he has taught us to, an eccentricity in his development, a break in his form, and speculating, or should I say, prophesying, after the fact.

When Burke might have been completing and publishing his "Symbolic," he was distracted into logology and wrote and published *The Rhetoric of Religion*. This dazzling book would have been enough to distract anybody from anything once the conception of it had occurred. So far as we are concerned here the importance of it lies in the fact that it provided Burke with a terministic screen, a nomenclature and a methodology that displaced dramatism and replaced poetry with theology as the perfection and culmination of language. As much as he loves poetry, Burke probably loves theology more. We should have known he could never resist the Word/words, Logos/logology pairings. A patient study of Burke's work since *The Rhetoric of Religion* would reveal the gradual disappearance of the dramatistic cluster of terms and their replacement by an elaborate logological cluster of terms. Unless I am mistaken, neither dramatism nor any of its many variants appears in Burke's latest work. This does not mean that he has abandoned the central energizing concepts of dramatism; it means that he has absorbed them into what he considers to be an even larger, more inclusive system and terminology.

Let me beat away at some paradoxes here for a moment before moving on. *The Rhetoric of Religion* is the ultimate dramatistic text. Two of the most complete and definitive statements of what dramatism is are contained in the last two chapters of that book: "The First Three Chapters of *Genesis*" and "Epilogue: Prologue in Heaven." *The Rhetoric of Religion* could even be considered Burke's ethics and the fourth volume of the projected tetralogy. But dramatism is essentially a closed and closing system, and just as it begins to close in on him who made it, he, being a master of irony and dialectics, and never one to get trapped if he could help it, escapes into logology. Logology is the perfect Burkean construct and invention. We might say that it is his entelechy. It is comic, ironic, endlessly resourceful, can be applied to any verbal text, and, by analogical extension, to all forms of symbol-using. It is not bound by the tetralogical strictures of dramatism but remains always an open system. All of Burke's work in progress, especially the work of the last ten years, has been part of this final, ultimate, logological endeavor.

Here are some recent statements by Burke about his logological enterprise: Burke's ultimate, final, basic logological definition of humans is that we are "bodies that learn language." This dualistic definition is developed into a much more inclusive dualism involving nature (bodies, nonsymbolic motion, speechlessness) and language (symbol systems in general, symbolic action, technology, and what Burke calls "counter-nature," which is a product of language, symbolism, and technology). The mission of logology is basically educational and admonitory; it reminds one a lot of the early mission of dramatism, as Burke stated it in his *Grammar of Motives*. Irony, which has always been so central to Burke, is among the most basic insights of logology. Here, for example, is one of Burke's latest mission statements. It comes at the end of "Variations on 'Providence' " and is the thirteenth and last proposition in the last ironically entitled section of that essay: "Counter-Nature: Fulfillment *via* Technology." It is a closure of closures. I quote most of it because it tells us so much about where Burke is at these days.

> It is the claim of logology that, for an *ad interim* design, our cultural task is to build a tentatively Providential body of speculations around the specific question: Just what is involved motivationally in the possible likelihood that the realm of counter-nature produced by symbol-guided (hence man-made) technology is a kind of culmination, a fulfillment of specifically human self-engrossments, conceived as an ironic version (a burlesque?) of the "egotistical sublime," the mirror image of a spirit in this case materialized. Why ironic? Because any instrument has a nature of its own beyond its nature as an instrument designed for a given purpose—and therein lies the vast new realm of counter-nature and its unintended by products, to be studied with regard to its possible relations and disrelations to the natural order, including the nature of our species.

We are a long way from the "Symbolic" here with its assertion that humans are poets and poetry is the perfection of language and a long way from the central metaphors of dramatism. Yet have we not come here to still another attempt on Burke's part to devise an inclusive scheme that will help us save us from ourselves? Who can forget the resonant closure of *A Rhetoric of Motives* or the admonitory tone of *A Grammar of Motives?* And did Burke not begin, as critic, with *Counter-Statement* and its elaborate thesis about the nature and function of poetry and criticism as necessary cultural counter-statements? And was not all the work of the middle thirties motivated by a strong counter-stating sociocultural drive to establish poetry and the creative imagination as alternatives to scientism and determinism?

But there is a difference. Burke's final vision is one of the ultimate ironic human comedy. Basic to this vision is the term that dominates all his work since 1978: counter-nature. Before he came up with that term, Burke conceived, wrote, and commented on a satire he entitled *Helhaven,* in which the priests of high technology, having polluted the earth to the point where it has become uninhabitable, migrate to the moon where they build themselves a completely counter-natural environment called Helhaven, which they advertise as the highest fulfillment or perfection of human possibilities. Therein lies the basic irony of counter-nature: that in perfecting himself by means of his technological genius, man will destroy his essential dualism and grounding in nature, under the delusion that he has transcended to a higher level of being. Whitman's dream, Burke says, has become our nightmare. What can we do about it? Well, we can treat it with the counter-statements of logology, the science of admonology. What does logology tell us: well, it tells us, with appropriate irony, that we will achieve our fulfillment as human beings (bodies that learn language) *via* technology, though this fulfillment may take the form of a counter-natural *Helhaven.*

Now I ask you: if you had had such an apocalyptic vision, would you, could you, go on fiddling around with poetics?

Note

This essay was originally written for a session on Burke at the 1981 meeting of the Modern Language Association in New York City.

Chapter 9

• • •

Kenneth Burke's Encounters with Walt Whitman

Our project here is to examine the relationship between Kenneth Burke (a twentieth-century American critic and sometime poet) and Walt Whitman (a nineteenth-century American poet and sometime critic). This is not going to be an "influence" study, nor is it going to deal with the "anxieties of influence" in the usual sense of this phrase. The justification for this project is that both Burke and Whitman are major American writers from different centuries; that both were specifically concerned with America, with what it means to be an American writer, with democracy, and with capitalism; that Burke wrote a fair amount about Whitman as well as a number of explicitly Whitmanian poems; and that it is always useful and illuminating to bring great American writers from different centuries together. Coincidentally, both were self-taught, highly idealistic, remarkable Word-Men, and they shared New Jersey as their adopted home.

1—First Serious Encounters

Burke first wrote about Whitman in *Attitudes toward History* (1937) in the opening section of that book entitled "Acceptance and Rejection." The section deals with "frames of acceptance" and discusses, briefly, William James, Walt Whitman, and Ralph Waldo Emerson. Whitman is discussed as the "poetic replica of James" and is used to illustrate what Burke means by pluralism and "frame of acceptance." The Whitman that Burke draws upon is basically the "Song of the Open Road" Whitman. Burke's treatment of Whitman here is somewhat superficial and contains nothing substantive about Whitman or his poetry. Whitman, like James and Emerson, is mostly used to get this book underway and to provide ready concrete examples of "acceptance" as an attitude toward history. If Burke had made any significant contact with Whitman by 1937, it is not obvious in this brief treatment of him.[1]

The same can be said for the two brief references to Whitman in *The Philosophy of Literary Form* (1941).[2] One of these references is worth noting, though, because in it Burke identifies an idea in Whitman he will later use in his twentieth-century "attack" on Whitman's nineteenth-century vision: Burke points out that Whitman constantly justified the destruction of our seemingly limitless natural resources in the name of progress, which, of course, is perfectly true. To the best of my knowledge, Whitman is never mentioned in either *A Grammar of Motives* (1945) or *A Rhetoric of Motives* (1950)—presumably because Burke had not yet read Whitman in any serious way.

Burke's first serious encounter with Walt Whitman is in his long essay "Policy Made Personal: Whitman's Verse and Prose-Salient Traits" in *Leaves of Grass One Hundred Years After* (1955).[3] When Burke wrote this essay he had finished the first two volumes of his projected tetralogy of *Motives* (the *Grammar* and *Rhetoric*) and was working on his poetics (or as he was to call it, his "Symbolic of Motives"). The essay on Whitman is conceived and written within the context of Burke's dramatistic poetics. I point this out because what Burke tries to do with Whitman is determined by his need (or desire) to work out his own poetics, and the emphasis in the essay is equally divided between service to Whitman and service to the poetics. This has always been Burke's way of doing things, and we could say of this essay what Burke said of his own great essay on *Othello*—that it was an essay to illustrate a method and a poetics.[4] It is important to note here before turning to the essay itself that the emphasis in this essay is upon the relationship between Whitman's prose and poetry rather than upon his vision and that many of the things Burke does in the essay are the result of his desire to illustrate one of the basic premises of his poetics—which is that all great literary works are symbolic acts for the author and have a private psychological dimension that can only be gotten at by a careful analysis of the image clusters in the writer's work. When poets make policies (say, Whitman's vision of America) personal they translate them into concrete imagistic terms, drawing their images from the human body, the natural body, and the body politic. But, lest I get lost in Burke's rather complex dramatistic poetics, let me turn to the essay itself and work directly from it.

The essay is divided into Burke's characteristic three-part (plus some kind of an epilogue) structure. Burke often refers to this structure as a trilogy plus a satyr play. In part 1 of the essay ("Vistas"), Burke uses "Democratic Vistas" as his text for establishing Whitman's "policy," or vision. He does not use any other prose text, though the 1855 "Preface" would seem like a natural. In part 2 ("Leaves"), Burke uses *Leaves of Grass* (rather selectively but very effectively) to show what happens when the policy is made personal in the poetry. Burke does not analyze individual poems but selects passages from all through *Leaves of Grass* to establish and discuss some salient image clusters and dramatistic coordinates. In part 3 ("Lilacs"), he takes the evidence from 1 and 2 and applies it in a sustained analysis of "When Lilacs Last in the Dooryard Bloom'd." In other words, in his characteristic fashion, he selects a representative text (a synecdoche) and subjects it to intensive analysis to read the whole. This is certainly the best part of the essay and yields a reading of this great poem any Whitmanian can learn from. In the epilogue, Burke creates a "Whitman Medley" for us by assembling the first lines of fifty-five Whitman poems into eight stanzas under the title "First O Songs for a Prelude," which is the first line of the first poem in *Drum-Taps*. This creates a deliberately comic and playful event as a way of closure to this long and intensely serious essay.

Burke has certainly engaged Whitman here in a most significant way. All the rest of his serious encounters will derive from this one, though it will be many years before they occur and they will take very different forms from the basically literary critical encounter of this essay.

It is not a scholarly essay. Though Burke is scholarly and learned, he is not a scholar in the usual sense and relies upon his own genius most of the time, just as he tends to pursue his own interests no matter what he is writing about. He says in his prefatory note to the essay that a better subtitle would be "On Interrelations among Key Terms in Whitman's Language," and that would in fact describe the main thrust of the essay. Burke is not interested here in the complex history of *Leaves of Grass,* nor even in the fact that he is writing in the twentieth century about a great nineteenth-century text. That interest comes later in his encounters with Whitman. He is interested in the relationship between prose and poetry, in different kinds of symbolic (verbal) actions, in how ideas (a vision) get embodied in images in poetry. The texts are treated as finished verbal structures that provide one with irrefutable empirical evidence for analysis. Since everything is by the same author, it is all interrelated and coherent. The critic's task is to locate that coherence and try to determine what is really being said. The poems are both private acts and public statements. Burke wants to know what Whitman really meant, what his policy really was. He—Burke—does not want to act on this policy; he just wants to learn what it is and document it. Later, in his encounters with Whitman, he will be much more interested in action and will have a much stronger personal reaction to Whitman's vision and poetry. But here he is much more interested in examining the texts and in establishing the interrelationships between the key terms in these texts.

Burke's interest here is abstract and clinical. He does not care—or less likely, did not know—that he is dealing with a statement of policy that was written after most of the poetry he discusses as an example of how this policy gets personalized. For Burke the texts exist in a kind of timeless realm of verbal interrelationships, and so the policy could easily have been personalized in poetry before it was codified in prose. It is not so much the before and after that Burke is interested in; what interests him are the different modes of verbal discourse and the fact that the poetry has a psychological fullness and truthfulness that is lacking in the prose. We have to remember that Burke believes that poetry is part of our equipment for living and that it functions covertly for the poet in important and beneficial ways. (This will later prove to be very important when we examine Burke's own long, highly personal, and important Whitmanian poem "Eye Crossing—From Brooklyn to Manhattan"[5]—a poem written when his second wife, Libbie, was dying of incurable, progressive muscle failure.) Here, in part 2 of the essay, of course, he is interested in discovering how Whitman personalized his own private self and democratic policy after the terrible war and the assassination of President Lincoln. Consider the following passages from the essay, which demonstrate how abstractly or theoretically Burke deals with the situation of the poem and the poetic strategies Whitman devised to deal with it:

> Imagine, then, a situation of this sort: A poet has worked out a scheme for identifying his art with the ideal of a democratic "em-

pire" that he thinks of as a matrix, an All-Mother, a principle of unity bestowing its sanctions upon a strong love of man for man, an "adhesiveness" generally "spiritual," but also made concrete in imagery of "athletic" physical attachment. Quite as God is conceived as both efficient cause and final cause, so this poet's unitary principle is identified with both a source from which he was "unfolded" (the material origins "out of" which his art derived) and an end toward which he "ever-tended" (death, that will receive him by "enfolding" him, thus completing the state of "manifold ensemble" through which he had continually "passed," by repeatedly "coming" and "departing"). A beloved democratic hero has died—and the lyric commemoration of this tragic death will be the occasion of the poem.

How then would he proceed, within the regular bounds of his methods, and terminology to endow this occasion with the personal and impersonal dimensions that give it scope and resonance: (For a good poem will be not just one strand, but the interweaving of strands.)

Note, first, that the poem involves several situations. There is the commemorated situation of the commemorating poet, among a set of sensory perceptions that he associates, for us, with the hero's death. There is the national scene that he can review, after the fashion of his catalogues, when charting the journey of the coffin (and when radiating into another details loosely connected with this). Near the end, a national scene that had preceded the hero's death will be recalled (the time of civil war, or intestine strife, that had accounted historically for the tragic sacrifice). And in the offering, "over-arching" all, there is the notion of an ultimate scene (life, death, eternity, and a possibility of interrelationships in terms of which immediate sensory images can seem to take on an element of the marvelous, or transcendent, through standing for correspondences beyond their nature as sheerly physical objects). The reader shifts back and forth spontaneously, almost unawares, among these different scenes, with their different orders of motivation, the interpenetration of which adds subtlety and variety to the poem's easy simplicity. ("Policy Made Personal" 101)

I have not made any attempt to summarize what Burke says about Whitman's *Vistas, Leaves,* and "Lilacs"; it is always best to encounter Burke firsthand so you can follow his complex arguments step by step and experience his massive assemblage of concrete detail from the texts he is dealing with. The full force of his concluding "Whitman Medley" can only be felt by experiencing the huge infusion of Whitman that results when this marvelous entitler and master of opening lines assembles fifty-five glorious first lines of Whitman. My point here is that Burke's encounter with Whitman was serious and profound, though primarily critical and theoretical rather than deeply personal. As a critic, Burke has an amazing essentializing mind, and even when he is pursuing his own theoretical interests (as he most certainly was in this piece), he always tells us wonderfully illuminating things about the texts he is considering. What he says about the maternal cluster in Whitman is not so far-fetched as it at first seems; and the reading of "Lilacs"—the one sustained reading of a whole text in the essay—is brilliant. His justification of the homo-/heteroerotic imagery and activity in Whitman (it is made necessary by the democratic policy itself) makes a lot of sense when we contemplate as he does the relationship between politics and sexuality (political, social, and sexual wooing are a major theme in his *A Rhetoric of Motives*).

There is only a brief mention of Whitman in *The Rhetoric of Religion* (1961). It is in a subsection of a long essay on "The First Three Chapters of *Genesis,*" which in part is concerned with the circular nature of images as opposed to the rectilinear nature of plots and arguments. The subsection is entitled " 'sensory' and 'mythic' images." The maternal image cluster Burke worked up in the 1955 essay is used to illustrate what "mythic" images are and what constitutes circularity. I quote the whole reference to Whitman: "Such [mythic] terms reveal their circularity by the ease with which they shade into other terms. Consider, for instance, how in Whitman such terms as night, mother, death, voyaging, democracy, prophecy, 'blades of grass' and 'songs of myself' cyclically coalesce" (RR 254).[6] There is not much to be said about this encounter with Whitman: it is in the back room of Burke's mind and is really the reuse of old material.

The same cannot be said for most of the references to Whitman in *Language as Symbolic Action* (1966). There are six references to Whitman in this long book, and five of them are worth thinking about because they are obviously the result of Burke having thought about Whitman as more than simply the illustration of some point or other. The first two significant references to Whitman come in an essay on Emerson entitled "I, Eye, Ay—Concerning Emerson's Early Essay on 'Nature' and the Machinery of Transcendence." The first passage is as follows:

> All told, however, at their extremes there is a notable difference between tragic catharsis and dialectical transcendence—and the Emerson essay serves as a delightful illustration of this difference. To be sure, the essay is a bit innocuous; but it is delightfully so. It has a kind of exaltation, thanks in large part to Emerson's profuse mixing of his ideas with ingratiating imagery. And we can readily understand why he was so enthusiastic about Whitman, before a more quizzical look at Whitman's poetic evangelism led him to see that it was beckoning "Come hither" to much more than a highly respectable vendor of uplift such as Emerson had bargained for. Both approached the conflicts of the century in terms that allowed for a joyous transcendental translation. To apply in a twisted way (and thereby twisting a twist) Rimbaud's demand for a poetry based on the "reasoned derangement of the senses," we might say that Emerson was as idealistically able as Whitman to look upon traveling salesmen and see a band of angels. (LASA 189)[7]

Everything Burke says in this essay about the dialectic of transcendence could be applied to Whitman, and it is surprising that he did not work more references to Whitman into the essay. But let's examine the two specific references: the first one is about the essential and important similarities and differences between Emerson and Whitman. Burke states this difference very nicely, very wittily in a way that is quite similar to Lawrence Buell's more serious statement of it in his wonderful book *Literary Transcendentalism.*[8] As Buell points out, Whitman went far beyond Emerson in his openness and acceptance of the heroic possibilities of the self, and this allowed him to "indulge and express the chaos of experience that Emerson came to fear" (330). Burke's statement of the major difference between Emerson and Whitman is probably more important than his witty and ironic comment about being able to "look upon traveling salesmen and see a band of angels." I'm not sure Whitman ever did that: when he looked at traveling salesmen he tended to see traveling salesmen, just as, during the Civil War, when he looked at corpses he saw corpses; if he wanted to see angels, he went space traveling, as in section 33 of "Song of Myself." The dialectics of transcendence in Whitman were not just a matter of optical illusion or delusion, as Burke was to discover.

Burke's next reference to Whitman comes a few pages later (192) and identifies very explicitly his ambivalent response to both Emerson and

Whitman. It also epitomizes, I think, the essential twentieth-century post–World War II response to both of these writers:

> So, if one feels that Emerson's essay is not tough-minded enough (and I'd be the last to assert that it is, for all my love of it), I'd contend that such a judgment is not enough to dismiss it.
>
> If only like loving a pleasant dream, love him for his idealistic upsurge. For *it reads well.* It is medicine. Even in those days, I feel sure, both he and Whitman suspected that they might be whistling in the dark. But they loved the gesture (if whistling is a gesture)—and it is an appealing gesture, albeit a gesture much more plausible then than now. Emerson's scheme for transcendence (like Whitman's variant) was propounded before his fellow townsmen had lost their sense of a happy, predestined future. There was not yet any crying need to turn, rather, and begin hoarding relics of the ancestral past, like an unregenerate Southerner's attic, with its trunk-load of Confederate money. (LASA 192)

In this passage, we are clearly far beyond the somewhat superficial encounter Burke had with both Emerson and Whitman in 1937. When Burke says that Emerson's essay—and by implication, Whitman's poetry—is not tough-minded enough, he means that it does not give us realistic equipment for living in our own time. It might have been good medicine then, but certainly not now. We may love Emerson and Whitman (and love has certainly been one of the most fundamental recurrent responses to the poetry of Whitman, in his time as in our own) but we can no longer believe them, and we are reduced to a kind of purely aesthetic response to both. Knowing that both are like pleasant dreams, we should enjoy them for what they are: we should enjoy the "idealistic upsurge" we get from reading Whitman; and we should enjoy the style. Whitman certainly "reads well" and, yes, it is good medicine, perhaps like an upper, or, since Burke always liked to call the alky he drank "medicine," perhaps reading Emerson and Whitman these days is like having some good drinks. But neither Emerson nor Whitman can be dismissed (or retained) quite so easily. I doubt that either one thought he was whistling in the dark. Both had considerable experience of the dark side of life: Whitman had his family, the war, his stroke. Whitman never tried to whistle away the war, as any careful reading of *Drum-Taps, Specimen Days,* and other post–Civil War prose will reveal.

As Burke is fond of saying, it is more complicated than that and he knows it (if only because Whitman's poetry is so deeply, so profoundly political). His later encounters with Whitman confirm just how well he knew it. Burke himself is full of "idealistic upsurges"; his works have passages of splendid idealistic upsurge that rival Whitman and Emerson. They read well. They are good medicine. For all of his irony, Burke is an incurable idealist and is strongly drawn to the likes of Emerson and Whitman. Trying to reconcile idealism (Whitman) to twentieth-century realities is one of the ambiguities of our time. Here, Whitman and Emerson are not being treated just as writers and dealt with in highly abstract and theoretical terms: they have been absorbed and have become part of the mind's attempt to understand, confront, and cope with the realities of one's own time. This is clearly the most serious way in which one can read books. All the rest of Burke's encounters with Whitman will be of this kind.

The next reference to Whitman comes in an essay on "Kubla Khan" and is apparently a passing reference to the prevalence of death and paeans to death in Whitman's poetry. Like many of Burke's passing references, there's more to this one than first meets the eye. The reference to Whitman is preceded by the following remarks: "inasmuch as no living poet has experienced death, I take it for granted that, when a poet speaks of death, he is necessarily talking about something else, something witnessed from without, whereas [the] poem is wholly from within" (LASA 209). Reading this passage one immediately thinks of Emily Dickinson's many poems about death, including her own death—such as "I Felt a Funeral in My Brain." And naturally, in this context, one thinks about Whitman's continual concern with death—from the very beginning (1855) to the very end. Of Whitman's many "paeans" to death, Burke says they "indicate how Death becomes rather like the ultimate maternal repository from which the forms of conscious life emerge" (LASA 209–10). This is clearly suggestive without being conclusive, as so many of Burke's remarks on poets are, and we can only determine its real value by applying it at more length to the poems. The remark takes us back to the 1955 essay and Burke's encounter with Whitman as a poet and to the terminological interrelationships he finds in the poems; and, of course, it takes us deep into the whole complex matter of poetic symbolism in Whitman.

The next reference to Whitman is in Burke's wonderful tribute to his friend and fellow poet William Carlos Williams, who was also one of the contributors to the 1955 volume of essays on Whitman. The relationship between Whitman and Williams as American poets and poets of democracy—that is, poets in the American grain—is a large topic, which we cannot explore here, but that is what Burke is concerned with. He points out that though both Whitman and Williams were body poets for whom touching was an essential action, Williams's experiences as a doctor "led him to a kind of democracy quite unlike Whitman's, despite the obvious influence of Whitman upon him" (LASA 284). Yes, but it would take a rather careful analysis of *Paterson* to show exactly how and why this is true. The general point, I think, would be that twentieth-century democracy is not the same as nineteenth-century democracy, even though Whitman would certainly have loved Williams's "Sunday in the Park" and almost everything else about *Paterson*. As usual, here, when thinking about Whitman, Burke is thinking in Now and Then terms, not just to isolate the differences, but to assess the relevance. The other remark he makes about the difference between Whitman and Williams is as follows: "In any case, the political editorializing in Whitman's come-one-come-all attitude had lost its meaning, other than as a pleasant sentiment, in proportion as Congress erected legal barriers to the flow of immigrants by a quota system" (LASA 284). As in other and earlier references to Whitman, Burke is here concerned with the ways in which poets and texts become historical anachronisms and gradually lose some of their meaning as the context of situation (scene) in which they were enacted changes. His response here is not to Whitman the poet but to the enduring relevance of the poetry—or lack of it.

The final reference to Whitman in *Language as Symbolic Action* comes in Burke's long essay "A Dramatistic View of the Origins of Language." The nature of the essay guarantees that Whitman is going to be used again for illustrative purposes. Much of this essay is about the negative, which Burke says humans introduced into the world with language. Whitman's life-long, or career-long, attempt to negate the negative—certainly one of the major dialectical actions of his poetry—makes him a natural for Burke in this essay. Unfortunately, only a single paragraph is devoted to one of Whitman's most strenuous attempts to negate the negative: "Song of the Open Road." I quote the whole paragraph while expressing regrets that this great specialist in the negative did not write more here about this ingenious and joyful yea-sayer—especially section 13 of this ecstatic affirmative poem.

> What of Whitman's "Song of the Open Road"? Historically, it preceded traffic conditions as we now know them in the era of the automobile. But the principle of the completely regulated road was already present, in Whitman's time, owing to the fact that the railroad was then the culminative form of travel. Though wrecks were comparatively plentiful, while both safety devices and traffic regulations were comparatively rudimentary, the whole "logic" of railroading was in the direction of more highly developed negatives, as with the elaborate signals and controls on a much-traveled sector of a modern first-class system. So Whitman had had the experience of the regulated range; and he could in imagination combine this with the ideal of free ranging. The combining of such opposites could be celebrated in a "song" of the "open" road, proclaiming a yea that arose from the mounting tangle of nays. Was it medicine, or hysteria? In any case, it could fuse, or confuse, the obsolescent with the future (LASA 472).

2—Whitmanian Poems

I move now to Burke's Whitmanian poems. Burke has been writing poems for most of his adult life (since 1915), but more profusely in his later years (since 1954). Though Burke has written all kinds of poems, two of his more recent long poems are directly indebted to Whitman and are about him. It is these two poems that I want to take up as further examples of Burke's encounter with Walt Whitman. The first of these poems is "Tossing on Floodtides of Sinkership, a Diaristic Fragment" (CP 277–93), a poem that assumes the reader's familiarity with Whitman's "Song of the Open Road," from which it quotes and upon which it depends for many of its ironic effects.[9] The date of this poem is probably 1966–67. Without being too categorical, one could call it a poem of the sixties. It is strongly influenced by the politics of those years, by the environmental movement, and by the Vietnam War. In some very useful prefatory prose remarks about this and other later poems, Burke says that the poem was written in the "run down, post-Whitman era" (CP 216) and that it is concerned, in part, with the poet's relationship to his machines (especially as represented by the Vietnam War), and his self (including his vocation as poet and critic). To these we can add: travel, nature, and the American continent, especially the western part of it.

The poem is in five parts. Parts 1, 2, and 4 are based upon a transcontinental trip Burke and his wife made by car from Andover, New Jersey, to the Northwest. This is what gives the poem its subtitle, since the poem is quite literally composed of fragments of a diary. Part 3 of the poem is a Whitmanlike catalogue of other cross-country trips (eight, in all, all by car, we are told). Part 5 is completely different from the rest of the poem and is an account of Burke walking the country roads around his house in Andover, New Jersey. Throughout parts 1, 2, and 4 Burke is trying to decide what he will lecture about when he gets to the West Coast (in other words, Whitmanlike, what is he going to tell his audience); more specifically, he is trying to decide what he will tell them about America, which, of course, he is seeing firsthand on his trip. The automobile is developed into one of the major symbols of the poem, along with travel in general and the road or superhighway (the ultimate open-closed road). Other major symbols are the great natural monuments Burke and his wife visit on their various trips, some of which have survived the assaults of humans and technology and some of which have not. Niagara Falls—which Burke calls a "pure sewer"—is the prime example of what humans and technology have done to nature and to the great "limitless" American continent Walt wrote so ecstatically about.

The automobile is developed as the symbol of personalized or individualized technological power; and the national monuments—Zion, Yellowstone, the Grand Tetons, the Big Horns, Grand Canyon, Glacier Lake—come to stand for the overwhelming power and grandeur of nature. What we have done to our own country (destroyed and polluted it) is seen in relation to (not in contrast with) what we were then doing in Vietnam. If, Burke says, that is the American Dream (Walt's dream), then who could possibly want it anymore? All during the trip Burke is trying to decide what has happened to Walt's dream as he expressed it in the grand lines of "Song of the Open Road" (from which Burke quotes the lines beginning "forever alive, forever forward"), and what he can possibly tell his audience out west (surely Walt's favorite direction, and the direction of Burke's trip) about what he has seen on this trip—the ravages of technology, the perils of overpopulation, the immorality of American imperialism, the power of technology to pollute. How can he talk to them about his ironic, rundown, post-Whitmanian perception of and response to Whitman's assertion that if people will just join him on the open road, he can assure them (as he does) that they will "go toward the best, toward something great." Nobody, Burke suggests, can sing Whitman's songs in the twentieth century (as Allen Ginsberg would like to, though he knows that he really can't). Certainly no one, unless one is just indulging in political or poetic rhetoric, or perhaps talking about space travel, can cast the last six sections of "Song of Myself" into twentieth-century terms and mean it, as Whitman most certainly did (in spite of Burke's assertion in this very poem that "Whitman [was] whistling in the dark" [CP 280]).

Burke repeatedly asks himself what "message" he can take west with him. Not Walt's, that's certain—and that's clearly part of the problem. Burke can't free himself from the responsibilities of being an American (as so many of the rest of us lovers of Whitman can't, though we might like to). Thinking about what we have done to our own country and what we were then doing to Vietnam, Burke hopes that "history proves unjust,"

> Lest our great country suffer desolation
> proportionate to that
> now done by the squandering of our enormous treasure
> upon the naked back of peasants.
> Great God our Law-Word, let history prove unjust . . .
> Babylonian Towers everywhere
> Temples to a Trinity
> of science, finance, and war.
> Cook them with napalm in the name of freedom
> tear up their way of life
> herd them
> let their girls get work as whores
> then tell yourselves how you can buy those people off
> once you have loaded them with U.S. gadgets,
> gifts from the technologic Christmas tree. (CP 290–91)

At the end of this section of the poem, Burke decides, in his characteristic ironic fashion, that

> Only this I can say in full authority:
> "To be safe in striking at the powerful
> make sure your blows are powerless." (CP 292)

Then immediately—first line of section 5—he negates so negative a conclusion and offers us one of his characteristic Whitmanlike upsurging closures, in which he appeals to another one of Whitman's major sources of appeal, which is the kind of life that is available to the self. The last section of the poem moves completely away from machines (cars), technology, politics, imperialism, the Vietnam War, pollution (even the spray at Niagara Falls is polluted), national destiny, and the justness of history and moves to the I, the self in a direct relationship with nature.

The first word of section 5 is *No,* which refers back to the last three lines of section 4 and rejects them. He can speak with authority about some other things and tell his audience something more affirmative, more Whitmanian (though Burke does not put it in these terms). He describes a nighttime walk he took on the country roads around his house in Andover in the spring. He decides that

> All seasons have their season
> only if
> each after its fashion . . . only if
> all seasons lead toward spring. (CP 292)

We have to conclude that Burke is not whistling in the dark here any more than Whitman was and that his deeply American belief in the possibility of always being able to begin again is as authentic as Whitman's profound commitment to this same belief, a belief that probably found its most complex expression in Whitman's responses—in *Drum-Taps* and elsewhere—to the Civil War and the assassination of Lincoln. Burke goes on in section 5 to write about our inescapable awareness of our own unique selfhood—which is brought on by hearing the frogs—and of our equally inescapable awareness while walking in nature of how "every eachness merges into allness." One could hardly ask for a more perfect Whitmanian set of perceptions. Finally, he ends the poem with an upsurging image that is repeated (in kind, not exactly) hundreds of times in his poetry and criticism:

> seeing every sunset/from every angle/at every instant,
> and all the while
> seeing every sunrise. (CP 293)

We can note, coincidentally, that this image joining beginnings and endings (or endings and beginnings) and ecstasy appears everywhere in Whitman but especially in "Song of Myself," "Song of the Open Road," "Passage to India," and *Whispers of Heavenly Death.*

What of the title of this poem: "Tossing on Floodtides of Sinkership, a Diaristic Fragment"? Burke was always a great entitler, so we should pay some attention to this one. *Sinkership* is certainly a punword for the various kinds of sinking dealt with in the poem—the self sinking in a floodtide of grief and shame at the imperialism of its country, the ship of state sinking in a floodtide of misdirected actions and misconceptions of national destiny. It is the poet, Burke, who is obviously tossing on the floodtides of sinkership—that is, who is caught in the historical storm and in danger of sinking; it is also, I think, America—Whitman's beloved America—that is caught in the historical storm and is tossing on floodtides of sinkership. *Sinkership* surely refers to the policies that make for sinking, the opposite of a term like *statesmanship*. The poet is tossing on floodtides of sinkership he can experience, recognize, acknowledge, analyze, understand, lament but do little about beyond telling people about "them." Technology is going to fulfill its destiny (humans' entelechy is technology, Burke has written) and no poet or critic or single human being is going to turn it back or keep it, or the human genius for it, from fulfilling itself. The first four sections of the poem are about this. This poem is a diaristic fragment because it is but a part of a much larger, more comprehensive record Burke has kept. This record would be all of Burke's criticism and poetry and all of the other masses of material he has written and collected on these same subjects.

Finally, the fifth section of the poem is Burke's dialectical other voice asserting that even if he is tossing on floodtides of sinkership, there's still nature, the self, the self's experiences of both nature and itself, the self's awareness that it is part of a larger whole that is perhaps beyond sinkership, the possibility of new beginnings and the diurnal reaffirmation of sunsets, sunrises, and the pleasures of sensory experience. This dialectical other, yea-saying voice does not make the powerfully negative things go away; it simply affirms other possibilities against them. It is not a transcendent voice; that is, it does not function the way Burke says the dialectics of transcendence function in Emerson and Whitman because it does not resolve and transcend the conflict. We might say that it is an unresolved conflict, a doubleness one simply has to live with. This is a crucial difference between Burke and Whitman, and I will return to it later.

We come now to one of Burke's longest, most complex, and most personal poems—"Eye Crossing—From Brooklyn to Manhattan."[10] It is quite different from "Tossing on Floodtides of Sinkership" and represents an entirely different kind of encounter with Walt Whitman. Since

Burke—ever the reflexive, self-analytic writer—has provided us with an account of the circumstances under which the poem was written and has written a commentary on the poem, we will begin there. The commentary on the poem is entitled "An Eye-Poem for the Ear (with Prose Introduction, Glosses, and After-Words)." Remembering the title of Burke's essay on Emerson—"I, Eye, Ay—Concerning Emerson's Early Essay on 'Nature' and the Machinery of Transcendence"—we can't help but read the first part of the title of the poem as pun-laden, giving us all kinds of clues as to the symbolic action of the poem: I crossing, Eye crossing, and Ay (yea, yes) crossing. That Burke would surround this poem and interlard it with his own critical action is perfect, for it tells us what kind of poem we have here, or it tells us how much the critical and poetic modes interact in Burke, everywhere, to reconfirm the both/and attitude that has been part of his equipment for thinking and living from the very beginning. And finally, the three eyes (I, Ay) are fitting for such a Whitmanian poem, for he was a great poet of all three just as Burke is (the eye for the senses, the I for the self, and the ay for the powerful if always ironic affirmations that have always been part of Burke's criticism and poetry).

The poem was written in the winter of 1968–69 while Burke was living in a hotel apartment in Brooklyn overlooking the New York harbor and the skyscrapers of lower Manhattan. He lived on the same street where Hart Crane lived when he was conceiving and writing parts of *The Bridge;* and, of course, below the apartment was the river Walt Whitman had crossed by ferry so many times before and after writing "Crossing Brooklyn Ferry." Marianne Moore, to whom the poem is dedicated, was a longtime resident of Brooklyn, a former fellow worker with Burke on *The Dial,* and a poet he much admired. In his dedication to her he says her poems are "kindly verses" that "give us exceptionally many twists and turns to rejoice about in a lean season" (DLC 288). It is a lean season because Burke's second wife, Libbie, was dying of progressive failure of the muscle system, a horrible affliction that first immobilizes, then affects speech (the tongue muscle), and finally kills when the tongue and all the other muscles necessary to sustain life fail. All the while, the brain remains clear as the victim becomes more and more helpless. The poem was written while his wife was in the last stages of this illness, and the commentary was written (probably in 1972) after she died. The commentary acknowledges this deeply personal dimension of the poem and comments on it as is appropriate in the glosses.

However, Burke's wife is never explicitly named or mentioned in the poem, nor is the nature of her illness. If it were not for the commentary we would not know that "eye crossing" (instead of crossing physically by ferry or bridge) is an oblique reference to Burke's sympathetic reaction to his wife's immobility; and, of course, we would not know that the many references to "we" in the poem are to Burke and his wife looking—eye crossing—to Manhattan.

I will combine my analysis with a summary of the poem. It is in seventeen Whitmanlike sections with one section—"Confrontation at Bohacks (an Interlude)"—carrying a title. The poem is 491 lines long and has numerous references to Walt Whitman and Hart Crane throughout, as well as individual sections (15 and 16) devoted specifically to Walt and "Crossing Brooklyn Ferry" and Hart and *The Bridge*. Burke, of course, knew Hart Crane in New York during the twenties. And we, as readers, know of the centrality of death in the life and works of all three poets. The poem is written in the first person and is centrally concerned with the actions of this lyric I. Even if we did not know about Libbie Burke, we would still respond to this poem as a deeply personal one because of what Burke tells us about his self and actions in the course of the poem.

The poem begins with imagery of stress and testing (passing punwise between Charybdylla and Scyllybdis), acknowledgment of old age (Burke is seventy-one), and considerations of the preferability of oblivion to an afterlife. There is also a brief acknowledgment of the scene. Section 2 introduces more strife and tribulation into the poem in the form of a long accusatory letter from a friend who has gone sour. Burke refers to himself as "Hypochondriasis"—a person who makes his peace with his condition (illness) by studying the symptoms and learning how to "appreciate" them. That of course is what he is doing in this poem, the condition being the illness of his wife and her suffering as well as his impending loss of her. This is the personal brute reality with which the poem deals. Section 3, after acknowledging the title (and hence Burke's symbolic and his wife's actual immobility), and bringing "Walt" (never "Whitman" in this poem) and "Hart" (never "Crane" in this poem) into the poem, finally gives us a series of images that characterize his condition: "I think of Pandora's box uncorked / while I was trying to untie / Laocoön's hydra-headed Gordian knot, / entangled in a maze of Daedalus, / plus modern traffic jam cum blackout" (DLC 230–31). In these opening sections, Burke keeps exhorting himself to begin, to begin again, to begin yet again because of the difficulty and pain of the subject. In all the early sections, he is *inside* looking out, or inside his head. Section 4 is a detailed description of what he sees from their apartment—which, of course, is the great frantic city, a place he describes symbolically as having "a restlessness unending, back and forth / (glimpses of a drive or drivenness, / from somewhere underneath the roots of reason)." Because he is looking west from his apartment and often sees the sunrise (or east) reflected in the windows of the skyscrapers, this leads him in section 5 to thoughts of East versus West and the world conflict. We could call this a kind of globalization of the conflict, stress, and tension in Burke's personal life, a movement that is very common in Whitman, but usually to different ends.

In section 6 he goes outside for the first time and ends his inside immobility; however, he is also alone since his wife can't go with him, as she would have done in the past. In going outside, on his way to the supermarket, he says he meets the hoards of people "face to face" (and the dog droppings "face to feces"). This reminds him of "The Waltman" who saw things "face to face" and of his own need to confront his own situation face to face, as Walt always assured us he did. Section 7 is the "Confrontation at Bohacks (an Interlude)." Bohacks is the supermarket. The "confrontation" is more stress and conflict because it turns out to be a semicomical altercation between two crazed shoppers anxious to get through the same checkout line Burke is in. The "interlude" is a comic one, though Burke tells us in the gloss that he regards supermarkets as "the flowering of a civilization in decay," and so the interlude is more serious at the symbolic level than we realize. More important, perhaps, the episode, like most everything in the poem, really happened and, like the accusatory letter from a friend, is all part of the stress-conflict-apprehension cluster that dominates the poem.

In section 7 Burke is again outside, alone, walking, looking at "Walt's Madhatter" and "north to Hart's graceful bridge." He's walking alone at night (just as he was in section 5 of "Tossing") because he's somewhat tanked (full of "alky") and that makes him restless and a bit frenetic. Section 9 is a flashback to when Burke was younger, living in Newark with his father and mother. We can only read this somewhat out-of-place flashback as purely symbolic. It's about how two tugboats cooperate to push and tow the barges first on the Hudson, then on the river they can see from their window. The tugs clearly are Burke and his wife in their intensely cooperative life together. Looking at them, he is thinking what life will be like when he is the only tug. In section 10 Burke is outside again, alone, in a bar, at night, having a drink or two. Even without the long gloss that explains the symbolism of the episode, we recognize this sad scene as an image of what life will be like when Libbie is gone. In earlier days, Libbie would have gone with him to the bar, just as she would have gone with him on his walks and to the supermarket. Hence, every outside episode in this poem is charged with loss and sadness, with the apprehension that fills Burke at the sure prospect of his lonely future. Section 11 is the last outside section of the poem; Burke is walking back from the bar, picking his way among the dog droppings when he meets a "dolled up Jog-Jog" accompanied by her police dog. This episode has no gloss and we can only assume that it has vague sexual as well as obvious apprehensive implications.

All the rest of the poem is inside, looking out or deeply inward—"words see but within," Burke says in section 13. Burke is trying to work his way out of the "Profusion of confusion" brought on by his wife's condition and the reality of her coming death and loss. "Problems pile up, like the buildings," he tells us in section 12. In 13 he is looking at and meditating upon the city. It is here that the public part of the poem is most explicit: What are we to make of our cities? How can we understand (and live with) technology? What of progress? These are all great Whitmanian themes. But it is also here that the public and the private dimensions of the poem come together and that the theme of transcendence enters the poem. The buildings of Manhattan are described as tombstones, mausoleums, powerhouses of death and decay. Obviously Burke is seeing the city through the screen of his own loss. And he sees city building as analogous to poetry writing: "(My own words tangle like our entangled way, / of hoping to stave off destruction / by piling up magic mountains of destructiveness." If we did not know about Burke's wife, we would turn to section 13 for the central concern of the poem, which of course would not be Burke's personal loss, but his critical and ironic response to the great achievements of his own time and country and to the poems and themes of Walt and Hart. There is a stunning quotation from Remy de Gourmont in section 13 that makes one think about the poems of Burke's two predecessors in a new way: "Intelligence is an accident, genius is a catastrophe." I think these lines can really only be interpreted (and applied to the poem) in one way: Burke is certainly a genius, as Walt and Hart were; genius burdens you with knowledge few others have; "the fruits of intelligence and genius . . .

are visibly beset by sinister 'side effects.'" Knowledge, as in the case of Oedipus, is often persecutional. Also, the author of this stunning statement was, in Burke's terms, both an "Olympian" (that is, a genius) and a leper—for real—so that all of his knowledge was burdened.

Here, I think, it is useful to think about Whitman and the way in which, for the most part (remembering the two crises in "Song of Myself" where Walt is betrayed by his own genius for touch and empathy), his extraordinary capacity for experience and knowledge were not a burden to him. Whitman had a lot of experience of death, and he never tried to wash death in the heavenly baths of Christianity. Burke has always seen and known more than the rest of us and tried to keep his genius for knowing from becoming a catastrophe. He says that de Gourmont always seemed "in his writings" to "so lightly" transcend his misfortune. This is certainly what Walt seemed to do with equal lightness and what Hart tried to do but could never quite accomplish. The ups and downs, the manic swings of Hart in *The Bridge,* testify to the heroic attempts and failures of this ecstatic poet to do it all with words. Burke, also, would not be able to do it quite so lightly as Walt apparently could and as de Gourmont seemed to be able. Poetry may help, but it was certainly not going to enable Burke to transcend the loss of his beloved wife.

Section 14 is the most purely political part of the poem and follows directly from 13. From the city and technology Burke goes directly to Whitman's great theme: the manifest destiny of America, America as the future of the nations of the world. Here, as in "Tossing on Floodtides of Sinkership," Burke takes up the theme of the responsibilities of being an American and what America, the nation, is actually doing to itself and the world at large. He does not like what he sees (genius is a catastrophe with its burden of knowledge), and he hopes he is wrong. The political, like the other public parts of the poem, can also be seen in relation to the private because in all three Burke perceives and tries to "cope" with historical necessities: that is, the life cycle of his wife, of technology, and of his nation. One curse of genius is the ability to see to the end of the line, a trait that Whitman used with quite different results from Burke. The end that Walt's genius saw was not "the pyramidal piles of empire-building hierarchal stylized dung remains" or the pestilential city Burke envisions in section 13.

Let us move on to section 15, which is Walt's section, and examine what Burke says about what Walt saw and recorded in "Crossing

Brooklyn Ferry." Section 15 is a kind of brief (forty-one quotation-filled lines) analysis of and commentary on "the Waltman's testimony" from Burke's personal and public twentieth-century perspective. The personal perspective is what we get in the earlier parts of the poem, but 15 is mostly concerned with the public significance of "Crossing Brooklyn Ferry"—the attitude toward history Burke finds expressed in it, and especially the attitude toward America. The poem goes around between Walt (the promissory), Hart (the nostalgic), and Burke (the apprehensive). Walt clearly believes; Hart would like to believe, but can't really and tries to recreate belief with metaphor and self-hypnotic lyric ecstasy; Burke is apprehensive: he can't write away his personal loss and he can't believe Walt anymore and he won't do what Hart did.

Burke's treatment of Walt's poem acknowledges and discredits it and him at the same time. It's stuck in ambivalence. Burke correctly shows how dependent Walt is on the eye (seeing, eye crossing, as opposed to doing, ferry crossing) and how he too must deal in appearances. He points out the great irony of Walt's certainty that future generations would be "crossing and recrossing / on the ferry which no longer runs." He focuses on section 6, where Walt catalogues "his vices / as though basking on a comfortable beach" and writes of Walt's "tricks" of "ideal democratic promiscuity" and "ideal man-love." He says that Walt was "blindly bland to the promotion racket stirring already all about him" and that Walt "bathed in the waters" without reference to their "imminent defiling" (which seems a bit excessive: who in 1856 could possibly even imagine the massive pollution of the twentieth century?). And finally, he says of Walt's testimony, "He sang as though it were all his— / a continent to give away for kicks. / And such criss-crossings made him feel pretty damn good." Then Burke ends section 15 with a wonderfully ironic and still ambivalent interlacing of echoes from the last section of "Crossing Brooklyn Ferry":

> Flow on, filthy river,
> ebbing with flood-tide, and with ebb-tide flooding.
> Stand up, you feelingless Erections,
> Fly on, O Flight, be it to fly or flee.
>
> Thrive, cancerous cities.
> Load the once lovely streams with the clogged filter of your filth.
> "Expand,"
> even to the moon and beyond yet.

> "There is perfection in you" in the sense
> that even empire-plunder can't corrupt entirely. (DLC 244)

Walt's section is followed by Hart's section (16), the penultimate one of the poem. The overall movement is from Walt to Hart to Burke (the "apprehensive whosis"). This is both a historical movement and a movement through attitudes from the promissory (looking forward) to the nostalgic (looking back) to the apprehensive (looking right at it). Hart's section, like Walt's, is built of quotations (here from *The Bridge*) plus commentary. Like Walt's section, it acknowledges and discredits at the same time, showing that Hart tried, by the "logic of metaphor," to "span whole decades of division." At the end of Hart's section, Burke returns to himself (the primary locus of the poem) as the "apprehensive whosis" who is still talking of *crossing* on a river when humans have crossed space and circled the moon; he returns to Manhattan as seen from Brooklyn, where it appears as a set of signs (that is, as real and symbolic) spelling out the genius of technology, and, for the first time since the beginning of the poem, he returns to the accusatory letter from the friend gone sour.

The final brief section of the poem backs away from the heavy public issues of the previous three sections and returns to the sensory and the personal—inside looking out rather than completely inside the head and deep in the world of words (poetry). The section opens with a classic city image: gridlock, the traffic congestion when crossing into the city in the A.M. and leaving it in the P.M. Since Burke says that "Many's the driver that crosses cursing," one has to wonder if this whole passage is not symbolic, referring to the agonizingly slow crossing over of his wife Libbie. Gridlock is also a wonderful image for the near paralysis and immobility Burke refers to early in the poem and in his introduction. The next few lines refer again to the city seen from the apartment at sunset and nightfall and are pure examples of eye crossing. The poem ends with more pure eye-crossing images as Burke looks first west to the lights in the harbor and then right to the "towerings of Lower Manhattan." But these quite lovely sensory images and perceptions are not allowed to remain pure: are the lights just lights and "pure of human filth"? And Burke's last response to the city is that it is a "catastrophe." This drives us back to the quotation from de Gourmont that "intelligence is an accident, genius is a catastrophe." The city represents the genius of technology and is a catastrophe in that sense. Burke surely recognizes himself as a genius, and much of the poem has been about the catastrophe of what he knows. The situation he is in is personally catastrophic, beyond the reach of words and knowledge, a brute ironic fact of his existence. Neither the promissory nor the nostalgic nor Hart's logic of metaphor nor Walt's tricks will make it go away or enable him to transcend it. No attempt is ever made in the poem to transcend it. Walt's way and Hart's way are both acknowledged and rejected. We have to understand that both Walt and Hart have been responded to in profoundly personal (private) and public ways.

What has not been rejected is the action of making poetry out of catastrophe, which is certainly what both Walt and Hart also did. As Burke has pointed out elsewhere, when Hart could no longer make poetry out of the catastrophes of his life, he killed himself. As readers of Whitman know, Walt was always able to make poetry out of catastrophe—both his own and that of his nation. Burke has written brilliantly about how Walt did this in "When Lilacs Last in the Dooryard Bloom'd." Burke has done this in "Eye Crossing—from Brooklyn to Manhattan," but instead of ending on the promissory he ends with apprehension and resembles William Carlos Williams (just as this poem, in its form, resembles the Williams we encounter in *Paterson*). Knowledge leads to an apprehensiveness that cannot be transcended: it can only be mixed with irony, as in the closing lines of section 15 quoted above. Burke's poem is very accurately entitled, since all that is really available to him is eye crossing and words. Burke does not exhort us with verbs, as Walt does in section 9 of his testimony (flow on, frolic, cross, stand up, throb, sound out, live, play, consider, fly on, receive, diverge, come on, flaunt, burn, thrive, expand, keep): he presents us with images of stress and frustration (the traffic) and with problematic images of "Walt's Madhatter"—the city as a vast accumulation and producer of a monument to human filth that, ablaze with light, looks like a catastrophe (a huge fire) and "doubtless . . . is" a historical one.

3—Helhaven Satire

Burke's encounters here with the Waltman, as with the Hartman, have been complex and profound. It is not easy to reject Walt: he's so loveable and reassuring and poetically ravishing that one always wants to believe him and believe in what he says, but. . . . It is this *but* that will occupy us as we consider Burke's final two encounters with Whitman in his Helhaven satire (1971, 1972, 1974)[11] and in his bicentennial lecture, "Towards Looking Back" (1976).[12]

It is inevitable that Burke would be attracted to satire. The kind of knowledge that is the basis of great satire—like Swift's *Gulliver's Travels*—is the curse of genius. Satire provides a way of using this knowledge that keeps it—the knowledge—from becoming too destructive because in a satire the knowledge can be used to both destructive and constructive (or apparently corrective) ends when the satire is universal rather than purely topical. The theme of Burke's satire—technological pollution and rationality as human beings' tragic destiny—is certainly universal and global in nature, and more so every year as more and more developing nations "modernize" in imitation of the advanced industrialized nations of the world and so contribute to the destruction of the resources that make modernization possible. In Burke's terms, we could say that more and more nations imitate the history and development of the America Whitman celebrated, with more and more disastrous results. This, in fact, is the theme of Burke's satire: that Walt's dream has become our nightmare, but that hypertechnologism will still try to redeem this dream with more technology.

Burke first wrote up his Helhaven satire in 1971 in an essay entitled "Towards Helhaven: Three Stages of a Vision." The subject of the satire is "technological pollution," or, in Burke's neat ironic phrase, the proposition that "man's entelechy is technology," and that in the second half of the twentieth century the great creative genius of technology has become destructive on such a massive scale that it threatens to destroy the very planet it helped to civilize. Burke's first version of his satire is relatively brief (fourteen pages) and essentially sums up a number of ideas that had been present in his work from the thirties on. Technology and its attendant bureaucracies and problems (especially pollution) have been major concerns of Burke's since *A Grammar of Motives* (1945). What is new is the satiric Helhaven idea in which the elite of humankind, having polluted the planet earth with their technology, use this very technology to migrate to the moon and create a second home there, leaving the polluted earth behind, along with the millions (billions?) who could not afford to migrate.

Whitman does not figure in this version of Helhaven, nor in the incidental uses of it in *Dramatism and Development* (1972), but he is the central figure in the second, much longer, and more elaborate version of the satire Burke published in 1974 in an essay entitled "Why Satire, with a Plan for Writing One." The whole of the earlier essay is incorporated into the later, longer one. There, the object of the satire is still "technological pollution" but to that object (or subject) Burke has now added Whitman and his vision, specifically Whitman's ecstatic, affirmative vision of the future as he expressed it in these lines from "Song of the Open Road": "I know not where they go, / But I know that they go toward the best—toward something great." It is the ironic fulfillment of this prophecy in the twentieth century that is the object of Burke's seriocomic anti-Whitmanian satire. Here is how Burke puts it:

> The [satire] involves certain implications in such poems of Whitman's as "The Song of Occupation," "The Song of the Open Road," "The Song of the Broad-Axe," and "O Pioneers." But they are to be seen satirically in the light of subsequent developments. Considered thus, they are reducible to a proposition of this sort: Since they are celebrating almost an orgy of construction, and since there is no construction without destruction, it is now clear that those poems were joyously ushering in the very era of care-free destruction now nearing its care-worn culmination in environmental problems due to technologically caused pollution. Whitman's poems of that sort were in effect (or at least for purposes of satire they could be viewed as) utterances by a great prophetic bard of real estate promotion. Of course there is more to Whitman than that, and I am among those who have said so. But for reasons that will become apparent my project needs him badly, in the role I have assigned him. And now that all the territory within our borders has become the transformation of nature into real estate of one kind or another, we need but ask ourselves how, by putting satire in place of his easy idealism, we can reclaim and thus enjoy once more the accents of the exultantly promissory. (MQR 13:315)

Naturally, there is more to Burke's satire than this somewhat ironic use of Whitman would seem to indicate, especially the heavily ironic final sentence. The central idea of Burke's satire has to do with the relationship between rationality and technology and the way in which "rationality attained its material counterpart in the rationalized procedures of the machine," and in this way ceases to be an "*ideal of the few*" and becomes instead "*a problem of the many.*" "Materialize an ideal and you get a problem, including the ultimate ironic fact that an excess of rationality as so defined adds up to a new level of irrationality"

(MQR 13:319). What is being satirized here is a tragic perception of the human condition, or the fact that humanity's major asset is going to be the basis of its destruction. It is like the curse of tourism and fame: the very things that bring the tourists bring what will eventually destroy or degrade the place; and fame (either of a place or a person) is such a liability in these days of media hype that many are destroyed by what they seek. Burke, of course, is contemplating this irony or paradox on a global scale, and his satire works "on the assumption that, by carrying such speculations to the end of the line, one keeps the admonitions alive." "In this way," Burke says, "satire would enable us to contemplate a situation to which we might otherwise close our minds, by self-deception, or by dissipation" (MQR 13:321).

Much of "Why Satire" is concerned with developing specifically Burkean ideas that are very important to an understanding of Burke's later work on language and technology, but are not particularly pertinent here in the discussion of Burke's final encounters with Whitman. This same is true of the details of Burke's delightful satire about building a culture bubble on the moon to which the masters of technology can migrate once they have polluted the earth with their technology, leaving all the rubble behind. It is the idea behind the satire, rather than the details of it, that must concern us here, for that is precisely where Burke's encounter with and use of Whitman comes in.

We need to remember that the basic plan for the satire was well worked out some years before Whitman was inserted to become part of it, as well as one of the objects of the satire. Here is the way Burke introduces Whitman into his satire and justifies the use of him. It is technology he is satirizing, and he says that the

> task of the satirist is to set up a fiction whereby our difficulties can be treated in accents of the promissory. Whitman in his accents of gladness, had given us the clue:
>
> . . . I know not where they go,
> But I know that they go toward the best—toward
> something great.
>
> The satirist's quasi-solution would track that down, not just leaving it *en route* as with Whitman's words, but the the end of the line.
>
> There are further tangles, still to be considered. But for the moment let us be content with what opens up before us: a post-Whitman,

> neo-Whitman vision carrying the ambiguities of construction and destruction into areas of pioneering and colonization unthinkable to the technology of Whitman's times. Thus was born the project of *Helhaven,* a scientifically designed culture bubble on the moon, and also involving a high degree of technical organization, whereas Walt was but content to loaf and invite his soul. (MQR 13:315–16)

Whitman, in other words, is made a spokesman for a historical development he did not cause, but which he ecstatically affirmed in many of his poems as part of the manifest destiny of the United States, whose destiny, he said, would show the way for the rest of the world. It is the ironic fulfillment of these historical prophecies, and Walt's prophecies themselves, that become the objects of Burke's satire: the somewhat naively affirmative *attitude* toward technological development and the positive future that is found in Whitman's poetry (according to Burke). This attitude is not unique to Whitman, but Whitman has been chosen to represent it, and it is for this reason that Burke says he "badly needed" Whitman for his project and so added him to the Helhaven satire.

Whitman is next mentioned in the essay some pages later when we are told that The Master—the leader who formulated the Helhaven projects and who writes the two mock Whitman poems at the end—had begun "as a disciple of Whitman and had got into dire trouble until he found a way out" (MQR 13:322). The way out was to take the strong promissory accents of Whitman's poetry and transfer them to the Helhaven project, using it as the "something great" Whitman affirmed as our goal. One of the ironies here, of course, is that only the few, rather than the many Whitman was addressing in "Song of the Open Road," can ever go to Helhaven, and further, Helhaven—by its very name—is not the "something great" Whitman promised in his poem.

Whitman is mentioned (used) again a few pages later—again in relation to The Master, the "generating spirit of the whole [Helhaven] enterprise." This time we are told that The Master had "begun as a Whitmanite, elated in poetically cataloguing the revolutionary environmental changes that the predatory European invaders had visited upon this continent. When it gradually dawned upon him, if you could call it a dawn! (Where did we hear that before?), that Walt's dream was becoming a nightmare, he was desolate." The Master needed a way to affirm that "Whitman's promises [were] as good as ever" (MQR 13:326). This he did, of course, in the Helhaven project whereby "the *ills* of technology could be left to soil the Earth, the *virtues* of technology could raise transcendentally elsewhere" (in the culture bubble on the moon).

There are two other passing references to Whitman and The Master I want to quote before turning to the two mock-Whitman, burlesquing "Effusions" of The Master with which Burke ends the essay. Recapitulating the steps by which The Master arrived at his "final solution," Burke says that it was "the growing evidence that pollution [manifested] the fatal costs of technology [that] had first caused The Master, the Personalist Supreme, to lose his faith in the Whitmanite ideal of conquering a continent by Ecstatic, headlong, anti-conservationist upheaval" (MQR 13:329). I leave this without comment as an example of how Burke is using Whitman here. As to this use of Whitman, Burke admits that Whitman, if he were still among us, might with some justice "object to discussing certain poems of his in terms of vatic real estate promotion" (MQR 13:330).

And now we move to what Burke calls "Apocalyptic Affirmation (Effusions of The Master)." These "effusions," he says, while they were "obviously written under the influence of *his* Master, Walt Whitman, even to the extent of outright borrowings and sometimes transforming lines from *Leaves of Grass,* they were conceived in the light of subsequent developments which Walt's ecstatic salesmanship, with all its stress upon the future, could not foresee" (MQR 13:331). These unforeseen developments and problems Burke describes as follows: the technological enterprise, with its "rationality of technics," has "so greatly progressed (now) that, everywhere you turn, it raises problems (thus in effect transforming our greatest hope for salvation of mankind, rationality, into major incentives making for cults of the irrational)" (MQR 13:331). (This, by the way, very succinctly states the most serious theme of the satire, a theme that Burke will return to in more detail in his bicentennial lecture.) Now, briefly, back to Whitman before going on to the "effusions" in which The Master "transformed Walt's over-idealistically easy-going promises for all into a more realistically apocalyptic Vision of Division" (MQR 13:332). Referring back to the "unforeseen development" in technology, Burke says that Whitman hit upon a "gladsome way of helping out" with this problem, and again quotes a line from his "favorite" Whitman poem, "Song of the Open Road": "it is provided in the essence of things that from any fruition of success, no matter what, shall come forth something to make a greater struggle necessary." The Master, he says, took this line and went on from there. Which brings us to the two "effusions."

Burke is a master of irony and comedy, especially in his poetry. We see both of these traits in the first of the effusions, which, Burke tells us, "stresses the exhilaration of the Vision's promise (for the Chosen)" (MQR 13:333). It is entitled "'O Lesson Opportune' (The Master's Call)." It is too long (eighty-seven lines) to quote the whole of it, but I will quote a few lines so one can get the flavor of them:

> O Sons of Sons of Sons etc. of Pioneers,
> have you your super pistol and your super sharp-edged axes?
> Singing the Song of Occupations, are you?
> You—and the one-time natives' land is now your native land.
>
> O Sons etc., even the desert you have now redeemed
> even there you have transformed nature into real estate.
> Already I say to you what later I will say to you.
> Hitch your new kind of covered wagon to among the stars.
> (MQR 13:333)

And so forth throughout, mixing bits of lines from Whitman in ironic contexts, altering lines slightly for comic, ironic, and satiric purposes, and in general taking the promises of Whitman and fulfilling them with ironic and historically true later developments, usually having to do with the displacement of the Indians, the destruction of natural resources, and the conversion of wilderness into real estate. The poem moves steadily toward its ironic conclusions, which is the call to the chosen few to follow The Master, who speaks in the promissory accents of Whitman in "Song of the Open Road": "towards home in (hail! Heaven!) in Helhaven, home!" (MQR 13:335). Burke is at his comic, ironic, satiric best in the first of the effusions. The tonal balance between outrage and laughter is well maintained; he has caught the promissory accents of Whitman very well, imitated his style very accurately, and quoted wonderful lines from the different poems that are mixed in with later historical facts in a kind of crazy, often hilarious appropriateness.

The second effusion is not so successful. It is certainly not very Whitmanian, until the very end, and is somewhat overly obvious. It is entitled "'Far, Far off the Daybreak Call' (Night Thoughts of The Master)," and is an ironic celebration by The Master of the rubble, filth, and massive pollution that is left behind when the chosen few go "Onwards, Outwards, and UP!" to Helhaven. In fact, the poem expresses the loathing on the part of The Master for what is left behind (the Masses, the massive pollution) and has no counterpart anywhere in Whitman. However, it does have a central place in the satire and is a most appropriate conclusion to it as the Chosen Few celebrate their escape from the earth they polluted and their arrival in Helhaven, where they may contemplate from afar the mess they left behind.[13]

The most obvious contrast to the way in which Burke has used Whitman here is to be found in Allen Ginsberg who, I think, expresses a reaction many of us have to Whitman, which is nostalgia for the "lost America of love," nostalgia for the lost promises and hopefulness, for the broken promises of history, nostalgia for the closing of the open road, especially the open ontological road that had such a powerful effect on Lawrence, for the closing of the frontier, and nostalgia for the lost sense of unity (of the self, between selves, between self and nation, self and cosmos, life and death) that pervades Whitman's poems and gives them much of their power. This sense of nostalgia is much more obvious in Burke's two Whitmanian poems, so it isn't that he has not experienced it reading Whitman, but that he has suppressed it here in the interest of his satire. Burke himself has expressed considerable nostalgia for what we have lost to history (beginning in the thirties) and has written many powerful exhortations to us, full of the promissory accents of Whitman, to not lose sight of and to keep moving steadily toward the better life. We should keep in mind, when thinking about Burke's Helhaven satire, what he said about satire in general, way back in *Attitudes toward History:* "THAT THE SATIRIST *attacks in others* the weaknesses and temptations that are really *within himself*" (MQR 13:317).

4—Walt Whitman and Henry Adams

Burke's last encounter with Whitman occurs in his dense and complex bicentennial lecture, "Towards Looking Back" (1976). As is most appropriate for a bicentennial lecture, "Towards Looking Back" is concerned with how we, as twentieth-century Americans, conceive of America and of ourselves as Americans as compared and contrasted with how Henry Adams and Walt Whitman conceived of America and themselves as Americans. There are some references to other earlier writers, but the bulk of the essay, after the preliminaries, is concerned with *The Education of Henry Adams* and *Leaves of Grass*. The preliminaries are important because they introduce the components of the discussion: the wilderness, the Indians, the "civilizing" domesticating process, technology, and democracy; America as a nation, how American writers conceive of themselves and their work in relation to their country; and, finally, America and the world, or the national and global.

As usual in a really good Burke essay, there is a lot going on here, but basically what Burke is concerned with is America, technology, and history. It was superior technology that enabled Americans to domesticate (despoil) the wilderness and destroy the Indians and their way of life. America and American democracy are not really separable from technology. Whitman put his faith in all three and, according to Burke, it was in "Walt Whitman, Celebrant" that "the half-responsive, half-adversary 'Americanism' that grew out of the 'wilderness' and its despoliation . . . reached its poetic fulfillment in Whitman's way of being nationalistically infused by the spirit of Emerson's moralistically pragmatic transcendentalism" (JGE 28:175). It is Whitman who has given us "a truly 'American' song, even in the strictly political sense" (JGE 28:179). "Whitman's . . . stylistics of promissory assertion put the stress not upon the contrast between rival ways of life on this continent (the white man's and the red man's) but upon a contrast between the vestiges of European feudalism and the boisterous development of bourgeois democracy *pari passu* with the expansion of white settlements" (JGE 28:179). Without trying to summarize Burke's rather complicated presentation of Whitman, we can move to his conclusion, which is that Whitman's "entire life and work" can be seen as "a kind of national conclusion" which comes to a head in Whitman's "gospel of Democratic brotherhood, which will first unite the nation and then the world ('all nations, and all humanity')."

Fifty years later, Henry Adams saw things differently, moving from a global scheme based on politics to a global scheme based on technology (the dynamo) and technological innovation. As Burke points out, Adams was not so much concerned with what it meant to be an American but with "what it is to be what comes next" (JGE 28:175). Put somewhat differently, Adams perceived that history and technology were moving us toward transnationalism and that identity could no longer be worked out in purely national or even political terms. Though Burke does not put it this way, he implies that Adams clearly saw that

Whitman's song was becoming an anachronism—that is, largely rhetorical, or "sheerly symbolic exercising" (JGE 28:186).

Burke's conclusion is entirely concerned with technology and the fact that we can no longer be solely or primarily concerned with what it means to be an American because now, seventy years after Adams, "all mankind collectively confronts a platitudinously inescapable situation, emerging with the qualitative step from the quantitative technological multiplicity of Whitman's day to that of Henry Adams', and now dreadfully obvious in the Era of the Atomic Pile, along with assists from chemical and bacteriological advances in weaponry and the likelihood that applied science (Adams' Dynamo) will soon have 'perfected' the potentialities of harnessing even the weather for genocidal purposes (JGE 28:187). Here is the final paragraph of the essay in which Burke again takes up the "Bicentennial implications of the step from Whitman on democratic brotherhood to Adams on the later developments of technology":

> The essential "rationality" of our inventions is what raises much of the trouble. For mankind is in trouble indeed when the great accomplishments of human rationality raise more problems than can go well with Whitmanlike accents of the promissory. In technology, we confront an objective fulfillment, since it is so rational in its essence; yet its very rationality is but a caricature of human reasonableness. When the implementations of rationality multiply our problems, we are conflicting with rationality itself. I would call such vexations the universal puzzle with which the Dynamo now Bicentennially confronts us. (JGE 28:189)

The opposition between Adams and Whitman is deeply symbolic for Burke because the same two voices have argued inside his head for most of his publishing life. The "promissory" voice of Whitman is everywhere in his books and especially in his persistent belief in the power of knowledge and the value of criticism. However, the ironic rational voice of Adams keeps whispering, or sometimes shouts to him that knowledge is powerless and the self is helpless against the relentless compulsion of rationality to perfect itself in technology, even if this technology can destroy all the life that created it. This is the "universal puzzle" only rationality itself can identify, understand, and try to solve. If in fact it does solve it, it will be in part because of Whitman's persistent "promissory" voice. Eliminate Whitman's promissory voice and you have only cynicism, extreme misanthropy, debunking, and despair—none of which have ever been characteristic of Burke's work.

In some ways, Burke's encounter with Whitman in this essay is the most profound and most appropriate one he has had because Whitman—our greatest poet, our first great poet, our national poet—really does represent and express precisely what Burke says he does in *Leaves of Grass*. No thoughtful American reader of Whitman in the last half of the twentieth century can read Whitman and fail to ask the political and historical questions that Burke does. Ontological questions having to do with Whitman's idea of the self are quite another matter, as D. H. Lawrence correctly pointed out many years ago; Burke has never been much interested in these and has never really addressed them, which is one reason he seldom mentions "Song of Myself," *Children of Adam*, and other such poems. Even Burke's frequent use of "Song of the Open Road" shifts the emphasis from ontological to political, historical, and even ecological matters. Burke's encounter with and use of Whitman here is much different from his use of him in the Helhaven satire, though he makes many of the same points in both essays. There is no attempt to satirize or burlesque Whitman here, no attempt to discredit Whitman's authentic voice, nor to suggest that he may have been whistling in the dark. If, more than a hundred years later, we can no longer believe in the America Whitman celebrated in the same way he did, his songs, his *Leaves* are not necessarily vitiated. If Burke, himself something of a celebrator (though always ironic—in the great modern mode), can't be the "celebrant" Walt Whitman was, he can, as he does here, recognize celebration as one of the essential human "offices," and he can lament (another essential human office), as many of the rest of us do, our inability (not our failure) to celebrate our country and its future the way Walt did.[14] The bomb, one of the great achievements of rationality and technology, one of the great creations of human genius, keeps exploding in our brains, and the celebratory in us suffers some from radiation sickness.

5—Conclusion

What can we say, then, of Kenneth Burke's encounters with Walt Whitman? To summarize the obvious, we can say that these encounters took a lot of different forms, from the initially superficial to the intensely critical-theoretical to the monothematic (Whitman, technology, and the promise of America) to the deeply personal and poetic to the satiric and finally to the personal/national—which is to say, Whitman becomes absorbed into the deepest concerns of Burke's later (post-1966) work with language, rationality, and technology. To state another somewhat obvious point, we can say, as we could probably say of any genius, that Burke's encounters with Whitman changed as his interests changed over the years and that he always used Whitman to his own ends, subordinating Whitman, using him to support his (Burke's) own ideas and development. This is probably most obvious in the Helhaven satire.

Although I said at the beginning that I was not going to discuss influences, it does seem clear that "Song of the Open Road" has had a long and powerful influence on Burke, not just as a model poem (in "Tossing on Floodtides of Sinkership," "Eye Crossing," and other poems), but as an essential American text, one that gives us a way to think about America and being American, as do *The Great Gatsby, In the American Grain,* and *Absalom, Absalom!* We can say also, thinking of just what Whitman texts Burke actually refers to and uses, that he either did not really know a lot of Whitman or was only interested in what met his immediate needs at a given point in time. Even in "Policy Made Personal," where he seems to be ranging over a lot of Whitman poems, he is really only ranging over a lot of Whitman lines, looking for different kinds of images, as if he were working out of a concordance and working out a thesis about how poetic images function.

In other words, we do not go to Burke for a reading of Whitman (though there are a lot of interesting hints and clues as to what Whitman is about in "Policy Made Personal"); we do not go to Burke for knowledge about the making of *Leaves of Grass* from the 1855 edition on or for a detailed reading of any poem except "When Lilacs Last in the Dooryard Bloom'd." Burke really does subordinate most texts to his own interests or theories, and he seldom analyzes whole poetic texts, but rather fixes on some element in them that will serve his immediate needs. Most of the whole literary texts Burke has analyzed—often with great, if highly specialized, brilliance—are novels or plays. But even there, one tends to take a theory or a methodology away from Burke's reading, rather than a usable specific reading. With a few exceptions, then, these encounters with Whitman tend to tell us more about Burke than they do about Whitman except insofar as Whitman still represents a powerful and persuasive attitude toward America and the American dream. If it were not so powerful and persuasive, Burke would not spend so much time trying to qualify it, even as he begins to succumb to it yet again, as so many of the rest of us do every time we submit ourselves to those passionate and persuasive lines and listen to Walt assuring us that it is all true because he has been there before us and checked it all out. We do so want to believe him. If nothing else, Burke's encounters with Whitman testify to the enduring power of his poetry and the deep ambivalence of the American mind.

Notes

This essay was originally published in the *Walt Whitman Quarterly Review* 6 (Fall 1988): 61–90, and appears here slightly revised. Reprinted with permission. Portions of this essay were read at the national conference on Burke at Seton Hall University in 1986. Other speakers included J. Hillis Miller, Paul Jay, Howard Nemerov, Harold Bloom, Denis Donoghue, and Ralph Ellison.

1. It is nearly ten years later before we find any further references to Whitman and any discussion of him. See Kenneth Burke, *Attitudes toward History,* 3d ed. (Berkeley: University of California Press, 1984), 3–18, in which Whitman, James, and Emerson are discussed as examples of "Frames of Acceptance." There are, in fact, other passing references to Whitman in *Attitudes toward History,* some of which do anticipate Burke's later encounters with Walt Whitman, especially his response to "Song of the Open Road." These references are as follows: 33, 52, 91, 208, 261, 322. It is probably not important to try to determine when Burke first read Walt Whitman since this essay is solely concerned with his encounters with Whitman in print, and especially with his serious encounters. For the record, I note here that Burke first refers to Whitman in a passing way in print in the "Musical Chronicles" he wrote for *The Dial* in the late twenties. See *The Dial* 86 (1929). For a discussion of these "Musical Chronicles," see Denise M. Bostdorff and Phillip K. Tompkins, "Musical Form and Rhetorical Form: Kenneth Burke's *Dial* Reviews as Counterpart to *Counter-Statement,*" *Pretext* 6 (Fall-Winter 1985): 235–52. In the early thirties Burke wrote but never published a monograph entitled "Auscultation, Creation, and Revision" or "The Rout of Esthetes" or "Literature, Marxism, and Beyond." I did not see a copy of this unpublished manuscript until long after I had completed this essay. I was surprised to find many substantive references to Whitman in the essay, which could indicate that Burke read and absorbed Whitman somewhat earlier than I give him credit for doing here. For a discussion of this manuscript, see Timothy Crusius, "Kenneth Burke's *Auscultation:* A 'De-struction' of Marxist Dialectic and Rhetoric," *Rhetorica* 6 (Autumn 1988): 355–79.

2. Kenneth Burke, *The Philosophy of Literary Form,* 3d ed. (Berkeley: University of California Press, 1967), 118, 316.

3. *Leaves of Grass One Hundred Years After,* ed. Milton Hindus (Stanford: Stanford University Press, 1955). Burke's long essay is on pp. 74–108. Other essays in the book are by William Carlos Williams, Richard Chase, Leslie Fiedler, David Daiches, and J. Middleton Murry.

4. Kenneth Burke, "*Othello:* An Essay to Illustrate a Method," *Hudson Review* 4 (1951): 165–203.

5. This poem originally appeared in *The Nation,* 2 June 1969, 700–704.

6. Kenneth Burke, *The Rhetoric of Religion* (Boston: Beacon Press, 1961); hereafter abbreviated RR.

7. Kenneth Burke, *Language as Symbolic Action* (Berkeley: University of California Press, 1966); hereafter abbreviated LASA.

8. Lawrence Buell, *Literary Transcendentalism: Style and Vision in the American Renaissance* (Ithaca: Cornell University Press, 1973), 328–30.

9. Kenneth Burke, *Collected Poems, 1915–1967* (Berkeley: University of California Press, 1968); hereafter abbreviated CP.

10. This poem exists in two versions. The first and shorter version is identified in note 5. The second and longer version appears under the title "An Eye-Poem for the Ear (with Prose Introduction, Glosses, and After-Words)" in *Directions in Literary Criticism: Contemporary Approaches to Literature,* ed. Stanley Weintraub and Philip Young (University Park: Pennsylvania State University Press, 1973), 228–51; hereafter abbreviated DLC. All my comments are based upon and refer to the second, longer version of the poem and have drawn heavily upon Burke's commentary upon his own poem. Burke has always been a great self-commentator, which is an indication of the highly reflexive nature of his genius and of his compulsion to always make sure he has set the record straight. The occasion for this commentary on his own poem is as follows: A longtime friend and admirer of Burke's—Henry Sams, the former chair of the English Department at Penn State—had given Burke's poem to his graduate seminar, without telling them who wrote it, and asked them to comment on the poem. Burke's own commentary is a response to their commentary. All of this creates a very curious situation because the poem is deeply personal and arises out of the situation I have described.

11. Burke's Helhaven satire was published as follows: "Towards Helhaven: Three Stages of a Vision," *Sewanee Review* 79 (1971): 11–25. This is the shorter version of the satire and makes no use of Whitman. The central ideas of this satire had been on Burke's mind for some time and are related to his thinking about technology—a subject that has preoccupied him for the last twenty years. Pieces of this satire also appear in *Dramatism and Development* (1972), the published version of the Heinz Werner Lectures Burke gave in 1971 at Clark University. The longer version of the satire was published as "Why Satire, with a Plan for Writing One," in *Michigan*

Quarterly Review 13 (Winter 1974): 307–37; hereafter abbreviated MQR 13. It is in this version that Whitman appears, and my discussion is mostly based on it.

12. Kenneth Burke, "Towards Looking Back," *Journal of General Education* 28 (Fall 1976): 167–89; hereafter abbreviated JGE 28. This is the published version of the Joseph Warren Beach Memorial Lecture Burke gave at the University of Michigan in April 1976.

13. It is difficult to do justice to these two mock-Whitman poems without quoting them at length. The first and most successful of the two—" 'O Less Opportune' (The Master's Call)"—works especially well because of the historical, almost dramatic ironies that operate throughout to cancel or work against the ecstatic affirmations of Whitman's wonderful lines and because of the skillful mixing in of twentieth-century facts amongst the Whitman phrases and lines. Most of the lines and phrases Burke quotes are from "Pioneers! O Pioneers!" "Song of the Broad Axe," and "Song of the Open Road." Burke's second poem is much less successful as a mock-Whitman poem but quite successful as a conclusion to the satire. There are few Whitman lines in this poem because it is really an anti-Whitman poem, rejecting what Whitman spent so many lines and poems accepting: namely, the masses. The poem is written by an elitist—The Master—and rejects what is left behind on earth when the elitists, having polluted the earth, depart for Helhaven. What is left behind is described in often rather coarse images of a kind one would never find in Whitman. The poem is only Whitmanian at the end when Burke quotes some lines from "As Adam Early in the Morning" and uses the ecstatic (but mocked) rhetoric of *Children of Adam* and perhaps "Passage to India" to celebrate (ironically) the ascent of the elite to the culture bubble on the moon, the Helhaven of the title, the new antihome of the technologists. Anyone who has gotten this far in this essay should go to the library and read these two poems if he or she wants a good sense of how Burke has encountered and used Whitman here.

14. See Burke's essay "Appendix: The Seven Offices," in *Attitudes toward History,* 353, 375.

Part 4

Other, Earlier Essays

Chapter 10

. . .

Not/But: The Rhetoric of John F. Kennedy's Inaugural Address

When Professor Griffin asked me to come here and apply Burke to the text of a speech, I said yes, thinking, of course, that my knowledge of Burke would be sufficient. But I was soon engaged in a wild and ignorant search for a text. Professor Griffin kindly ended that difficulty over the phone by selecting President Kennedy's inaugural address.[1] This speech provided me with what, in my line of work, should have been an ideal situation: a verbal document for the trained mind to work on. However, it did not take me long to realize that the text, though verbal, and in this respect like poems, novels, and plays, was different in fundamental ways from the verbal acts I have studied and taught for many years. Furthermore, I soon discovered that the analysis of speeches is a separate, highly sophisticated discipline, with its own theoretical and methodological traditions and current problems—and that I knew nothing about such matters. These discoveries left me in a rather desperate situation, because I had no way of knowing what the nature and level of my own discourse should be: neither from experience nor from reading have I any knowledge of what is routinely and profitably done with the text of a speech.

To avoid demoralization and, as Burke would have one do, to develop a strategy to encompass this situation, I adopted a kind of Burkean perspective by incongruity and approached the inaugural address as if it were a literary text—which, of course, it is not. I brought my own tools to this job of work; they are primarily those of a literary critic, and many of them were either made or redesigned in Burke's factory. The analysis that follows is essentially Burkean—though I must admit that I can now no longer always tell the difference between what is purely Burke's and what I have modified to suit my own needs.

In relation to the literary works I read and teach, this text seems to me almost embarrassingly simple; but of course, as a verbal act addressed to millions of people, it would have to be. I go through it then, not to explicate it, but to characterize it in a Burkean manner and to locate and discuss what I take to be the chief sources of persuasive power intrinsic to it. I would oppose such an analysis to one that concerned itself with the speech as delivered, as live rhetoric made resonant and radiant by the traditional and ceremonial occasion and charged, as all of his speeches were, even though he was a very mechanical speaker, by what Burke would call Kennedy-magic.

President Kennedy was a very skillful rhetorician. His skill can be seen in the style of this speech, which is deliberately archaic—that is, high imitative—because he set out to concoct a ceremonial, semibiblical style he thought would be appropriate and effective. After the fact, the New Frontier presented to us in the manner of someone like Hooker is anachronistic; at the time it seemed very moving. From a literary critic's point of view, President Kennedy was no stylist at all: he had no sense of metaphor, but only the knowledge that he ought to use metaphors. His are all stale, frequently inaccurate, and sometimes inappropriate. Nor did he have any real gift for terms or phrase-making; in both matters he was given to clichés and textbook verbal play. His two chief syntactical resources are antithesis and parallel construction, especially in combination. He was given to the excessive use of exact parallels—that is, ones with a balance so perfect they seem to have been written in time with a metronome. And the tick tock of his not/buts is relentless. Yet, herein lies one of the sources of power in this speech. President Kennedy knew that the secret of advertising is repetition and he put it to the service of high and moving ideals. And if, in good Burkean manner, one picks up and follows these stylistic tics—here the not/but rhetoric of antithesis that dominates the speech—one can discover all kinds of things about the inwardness of any verbal work. I propose to chart President Kennedy's use of the not/but construction and to show how it is not only the salient feature of the style but more important the key to the rhetoric, dialectic, and ethics of his speech. At the same time, I will chart the developmental or progressive form of the speech, the negative and positive clusters of identifications, and the major transformational moments.

The speech begins with the negation of a party victory, or all those competitive and divisive forces at work in the bitter campaign and close election, and moves to the celebration of freedom, or all those things that made the election possible and now reunite the two parties. The speech thus begins by reaffirming what Burke has described as the essence of democracy: the institutionalizing of the dialectic process in a political structure that gives full opportunity for the use of competition to cooperative ends. The opening and recurrent movement is from division to merger, from party strife to united effort, from war to peace. There are the major dialectical opposites in the speech as a whole; and it is to the end of canceling or purifying the negative war cluster and affirming the positive peace cluster that all the rhetoric of antithesis is used. In the rest of the introduction, he relates present to past, shows how nuclear power has altered the world and established the threat of ultimate war, identifies the ideological differences that divide the world, and states flatly by decree to all nations the extent to which his generation and his nation are united and will fight to the death for freedom. By the end of the introduction, then, all the major terms have been introduced, the poles of the conflict have been set, and the characteristic movement from war to peace has been established. What remains to be accomplished in the rest of the speech is the major transformation, which is the conversion of division into merger, of war into peace. This is done by calling for the divided and warring powers to unite in a peaceful war against human beings' common enemies: tyranny, poverty, disease, and war.

In Burke's terms, this major dialectical transformation is brought about by negating the negative, by saying not/but to the Ultimate No. This is accomplished in three steps in the main body of the talk, which consists of the pledges, the requests, and trumpet-call sections. The five pledges are routine and among the most platitudinous and metaphorically garbled paragraphs in the speech. Their chief rhetorical and dialectical function is to establish the ground for peaceful war against the common enemies; it is for this reason that the last pledge is to the United Nations. The next two sections are rhetorical and dialectical marvels: there are more not/buts here than in any other section of the speech; there are so many, in fact, that one thinks surely so profound an antithesis can never be resolved; and yet it is here that the antithesis is dialectically transformed into a synthesis and it is this transformation, I think, that accounts for such power as the speech has. In Burke's terms, the movement from pledges to friends' requests to enemies is a movement from covenant to prayer, from "there shall be" to "may there be." What President Kennedy does here is establish the antagonism, the division—the requests are all addressed to *the* adversary—and then, in a long series of not/buts, negate the negatively charged terms, canceling them, as it were, with the double negatives, in order to transform them to positives. At the end of this second, or request, section, after the vision of the new order—"a new world of law, where the strong are just and the weak secure and the peace preserved"—President Kennedy goes into what for my purposes is a wonderful rhetorical maneuver: he uses four negatives in a row—not, nor, nor, nor—all applied to time, in an incremental sequence designed to negate time as a factor and dignify the task he has just set by the difficulty and duration of it. He ends by saying, "But let us begin."

In the third, or trumpet-call, section of the main body of the speech President Kennedy now comes home from abroad: he has set the task, which in Burke's wonderful phrase is the purification of war; he has set the time, which is now; he has set the duration of the task, which is lifelong; and in the curious mixture of magic and prayer which he used throughout, he has decreed and requested a beginning. Now, in terms that are essentially religious, and using the rhetoric of service at which he was so expert, President Kennedy will ascribe the task to the American people by presenting it as a special summons to answer the call of national and historical destiny.

A great many fearful and normally negative things are now transformed and presented as positive values by being linked to the call to service in the international army that is to march against the common enemies of humankind. Death, sacrifice, bearing burdens, enduring tribulation, and long struggle are all dignified by being subsumed under, or being necessary to, the unifying historic effort to assure a more fruitful life for all humankind.

The next step is a form of special pleading and is a variation on the call to service idea introduced earlier. The sequence goes from one generation specially selected for a unique and dangerous role in history to President Kennedy's use of himself as a rhetorical device by being the first to offer himself to negating even the possibility of anyone's not being ready to answer this call from history. One could certainly call this President Kennedy's use of the manifest destiny theme as a persuasive device. Rhetorically, dialectically, ethically, and stylistically considered, this is the finest paragraph in the whole speech. President Kennedy begins his speech at home and then goes abroad; once he sets the worldwide task and calls the world to service, he returns home to call his fellow Americans to service. Now, at the end of this paragraph, he will do two main things: state the requirements for this service—energy, faith, and devotion—and the rewards to be won. He does this in the famous torch passage where the three rewards are metaphorically presented as lighting one's country, one's self, and the world. Incurably Burkean, I cannot avoid the puns on light, especially the moral one about lightening one's load, after all of President Kennedy's talk about burdens; and I cannot help interpreting the powerful appeal of this call to service as in part due to the opportunities it provided for the expiation of the individual and collective guilts of a rich president, a rich people, and a rich nation. In fact, I think Burke would surely want to say that anyone who used the not/but construction as obsessively as President Kennedy, who was so adept at transforming negatives to positives, and was, finally, so messianic about the call to service, would have to be concerned with guilt and perhaps be himself guilt-ridden and that one major source of appeal in his rhetoric would be found in the extent to which he offered people an opportunity to cancel their own guilt by enlistment in a vast social enterprise for the redemption of the world from war, disease, poverty, and tyranny.

The resonance of the concluding three paragraphs—the ask not/but section—certainly derives more from the power of this call to service than it does from the mechanical style and textbook verbal play found there and throughout the speech. This conclusion is in three steps; in the first two steps the not/but antithesis is used for the last times. In the first step, President Kennedy negates the whole idea of the handout, which had been used to beat him and his party to death during the campaign; in its place he now reaffirms the ideal of service, which, by now, has really assumed the magnitude of a holy mission to redeem the world from all its ills. The second is a repetition of the movement from America to the world: it is a call to everyone to join in the peaceful war against the common enemies. The third step and final paragraph of the speech echoes the ask not/but form of the previous two, but the negative has been eliminated and the conclusion consists of a series of reverberating, merging affirmations. The major antitheses have all been dialectically transformed into one grand ethical synthesis; war has been purified of its destructive elements; the burden has been made light. And the peaceful army, with all the energy and collective force of a warring one, but bent now upon constructive ends, awaits its leader. He appears and makes himself a part of that army in the sequence from citizens of America to citizens of the world to "ask of us here the same high standards of strength and sacrifice which we ask of you." All three are now united under the call to service and the heroic virtues that have been identified with it. The whole last paragraph is in the collective voice—our, us, we—and completes the process of merger begun in the opening sentence. In keeping with the selfless ethical ideals of service, all members of this peaceful army are to disavow any claim to personal material reward, all are to throw themselves upon the mercy of history for final judgment of their deeds, and all are to act out of patriotic and humanitarian motives. The final steps are first to make an ultimate identification by asking God's help and blessing and then to identify the call to service with God's work and, finally, in keeping with the high moral rhetoric of service used throughout, to shift the purgative burden of doing God's work to the members of the peaceful army.

Notes

This essay was originally written for a meeting on Burke in Chicago in 1965 arranged by Lee Griffin of Northwestern University, one of the pioneers of Burke studies in speech and theater.

1. For the text of the speech see the Appendix.

Chapter 11

. . .

Kenneth Burke and the Geneva School

I begin with two functional—rather than modest—qualifications. The first has to do with what I say about Burke. In accordance with the precepts of the Geneva School[1]—the group of French literary critics that included George Poulet and Marcel Raymond—I long ago entered and tried to apprehend the structure of Burke's interior space.[2] But the critical self takes its own vision to and from this task and refracts another person's space through the eyes of an alien mind. The optics of criticism must always be a science of partial distortion. One brings back what one can, but especially what seems most useful to the current life of the self in its space of words. If what follows is not pure Burke, it is at least very Burkean.[3]

The second qualification has to do with my knowledge of modern French literary theory—which is really rather minimal—and the way I will use what I do know in the interests of cross-cultural exchange. My focus here is Burke, rather than the development of modern theory in France. My aim is simply to read Burke from the vantage point of a certain moment in French literary criticism, namely the phenomenological criticism of Poulet, Raymond, Jean-Pierre Richard, Jean Strarobinski, and others that flourished in the fifties and sixties and influenced, among others, the early work of J. Hillis Miller and Geoffrey Hartman. In the midsixties it was still possible to see this as the defining model of the new French literary theory. Barthes himself at one point characterized the Geneva School that way.[4] Thereafter, of course, French literary theory went in other directions, retaining from the Geneva critics their focus on the systematicity of language but abandoning their belief that language is mediated by and organized within the self.

The Geneva School itself represented a radical break with the past. As Barthes pointed out, the differences between the old criticism (which was asymbolic, monistic, and tied to an antique correspondence theory) and the newer criticism (which was symbolic, pluralistic, and derived from a much larger language theory) are considerable. My task will be to explore some connections between Burke and this strand of post-war French criticism, thereby simultaneously establishing their common ground and clarifying Burke's enterprise. Certain working assumptions are shared both by Burke and the Geneva School, and I will state these before going on to Burke himself.

In addition to the fundamental recurring assumption that there is—or should be—an old and a newer criticism, the other most important assumptions are that there is no longer any such thing as purely literary criticism because there is no longer any such thing as a purely literary work. As Roland Barthes put it, there are no longer poets or novelists; there is only writing. What we deal with now are words, verbal actions, verbal structures; and what we practice is verbal analysis. The old rational categories have been broken down; the space of literature has been redefined; the whole nature of criticism has changed. The idea of genre, for example, except perhaps as it has been reconceived in psychological terms by Northrop Frye, is not really operational anymore. The old generic distinctions have been abandoned by the writers themselves because language and form have been reconceived as phenomena of the self. Until structuralism abandoned the subject, then, much of the newer criticism was language centered, form (but not necessarily text) centered, symbolic, pluralistic, psychologically oriented, and concerned in some way with the relation of language and imagination to vision and system-building. One can sum it up by saying that literature was reconceived as a creative action of the self and that criticism became obsessively concerned with the poetics of vision.[5]

2

For Kenneth Burke, everything begins with language.[6] Literature is an act of language, or, more precisely, it is a symbolic and functional verbal action of the self in a hierarchic scene. A completed literary work is a structure of words with at least three other structural and symbolic centers. In addition to language, there is literature, the self, and the hierarchic scene. I won't even attempt to discuss the specific verbal forms, about which Burke has written at least four million words over the last forty years, but will take them up later in a synoptic way. The literary forms as such are those specific conventional forms that are unique to literature rather than common to verbal discourse as a whole. Generalized, they become the inherited forms within and against which all writers work. Generalized still further, they become the hypothetical structures Frye[7] speaks of or the virtual structures Susanne Langer speaks of.[8] At the highest level of generalization, the literary and verbal forms tend to merge at the point where creation and abstraction meet.

The self is always psychosomatic for Burke and has language in its genes; this makes language a phenomenon of the self and, because of Burke's view of the relation of action to being, it makes the self a structural presence in all verbal discourse. Like Bachelard, Burke believes that the self polarizes words in accordance with its own interior space to create a poetics of the self. Language is a coercive agency the self uses to control and transform both the self and the Other. All verbal structures derive from the self.

The hierarchy, to turn to the fourth structural and symbolic center, is a general principle of ordering that begins with nature and the preverbal and runs upward to humans and language to all the language-caused things humans have added to nature and then beyond to the supernatural and the metaverbal. Otherwise put, hierarchies run from genesis to apocalypse. A hierarchy as an abstract form represents the extreme polarization and range of possibilities open to the self.

I mention all of this partly to indicate that Burke, like Frye, Cassirer, and Langer, is a systematic thinker who works within a completely thought-out vision of reality. Within Burke's language-centered system literary works, which he regards as paradigmatic verbal actions, have a central position. They are, as in Frye, verbal multicosms,[9] and they require a highly developed systematic methodology that will enable the critic to journey over, into, through, and beyond them.

3

A literary work is a unique structure of words with an outer and an inner form.[10] Analysis begins with the outer form and moves over the verbal surface seeking entrances. For analytic purposes, the surface is initially viewed as flat and nonsymbolic, so that the purely verbal or terminological relationships—the so-called raw evidence—can be discovered and studied. Even though one's inherited language is a public grammar and the existing literary forms are conventional and hence social, both are always recast from a deep inwardness in accordance with the grammar of the private self to create a unique poetics of the self. It is the objective structure of this grammar that one tries to discover by regarding the work initially as flat verbal space. As a structure of verbal facts the literary work is empirically knowable and describable and can be the object of exhaustive scientific study. Within these limits, Burke believes in a science of literature. The unique structural components of any verbal work provide the basis for inferences about—really entrances into—the work; these inferences enable one to move through the body or outer form into the inner form of the work and toward the inwardness one is seeking. All complex verbal works are finally completely symbolic and resonate from a deep inwardness.

A systematic analysis for Burke is always a strenuous action of the seeking self; it begins when the reader moves from passive reception to an active entrance into the verbal work. The direction of an analysis for Burke is the reverse of the creative process and moves from without to within. Criticism is a journey inward toward the forms—or perhaps the transforms[11]—at the center of the verbal multicosm. These forms are the structural and symbolic centers mentioned earlier—that is, language, literature, the self, and hierarchy—as they begin to merge at the higher levels of unity language makes possible. The absolute center of a verbal multicosm is ultimately transformational, a wondrous empty form—as Barthes describes it—which is both one and many, still and moving, full and empty. When one arrives at the true inwardness of a complex verbal structure, one is at the still point of the turning words, at the paradigm of form itself.[12]

Systematic methodology, one of Burke's greatest achievements, provides one with the necessaries for all critical journeys. As must be quite clear by now, this journey is back and forth between nature, the self, language, and society; or, in simpler terms, it is back and forth between language and the self. According to Burke's own transformational grammar, the forms of language and the forms of the self are the forms of literature are the forms of hierarchy. Methodology is necessary because these forms at the still point of the turning words are generative and regenerative. The critical journey is purgative and redemptive in Burke as it is in Frye. It is a secularized verbal journey to total vision, to apocalypse, to pure identity, to the possibility of absolute freedom. At the end of the analytic journey the seeking self is released into the ultimate order of words, into the pure poetics of vision.[13]

4

Over the last forty years Burke has compiled, invented, and adapted a methodological terminology for the analysis of verbal action and the self that is really an instrumental and perceptual wonder. During this same forty years, after a succession of attempts, Burke has also succeeded in perfecting a brilliantly simple four-part methodology for the analysis of all verbal action, which is as close to vision as method can ever be. I will conclude with a discussion of this methodology, its relation to the four structural and symbolic centers discussed earlier, and the language theory that supports it.[14]

Burke's four-part methodology—which he calls indexing—is designed to permit one to locate, describe, analyze, and interpret the four kinds of structure one finds in verbal works. These are structures of identifications, or what goes with what; structures of opposition and polarization, or what versus what; structures of progression, or what follows what; and structures of transformation, or what becomes what. Identification is the central concept in the methodology as it is in Burke as a whole. It is psycholinguistic and runs all the way from simple phonetic and imagistic linkings to such complex verbal linkings as the Trinity and the kind of total verbal identifications that pertain at Frye's anagogic and apocalyptic levels. Identifications are a matter of repetitions and variations, of terminological clusters, of verbal equations, of image, simile, metaphor, symbol, and archetype, and of what Burke calls substance clusters or masses of related detail drawn from the full hierarchic range. Behind all verbal identification lies the psychological principle of identification, which sees the conscious and unconscious actions of the self as the controlling factors in the selection and arrangement of all detail in a verbal work. This is a root principle of identification, of Burke, and surely of the Geneva School of criticism.

Like the world in which it lives, the self is polarized and generates opposed clusters of identifications to embody and symbolize its own doubleness, its divided world, and its hierarchic vision. This polarization of detail by the self always tends toward the extremes of negative and positive poles, toward what must be rejected and what can be accepted by the self. Schematically, it is reducible to such opposites as good and evil, heaven and hell, peace and war. It is mainly the addition of the principle of opposition to the principle of identification.

With almost no exceptions, verbal works progress in a time continuum that begins with the first word and ends with the last. This is an absolutely fixed internal linear order and delimits the structural boundaries of a particular verbal system. To read a verbal work properly and discover its progressive structures one must enter it at the point where its verbal time begins and follow its movements to the point where its verbal time stops and one is released. Just as all identifications and oppositions, however remote, are significant and symbolic, so also are all movements. The three-dimensional space of a work unfolds and is revealed in a time continuum; the clusters of identifications and the opposed clusters constitute a kind of lateral and vertical structure that can only develop in the course of the irreversible linear progression. This movement is always symbolic because the order of the words dances some movement in the life of the self. Burke is probably one of the greatest structural critics to have written in our time. He has seen with astounding thoroughness that every kind of structural progression in a verbal work derives a symbolic content from its origins in the life of the creating self and from the functional action of language for the self.

Identifications have to do with identity, with unified selfhood; oppositions have to do with otherness, with alienation, with antagonisms within and without; progressions have to do with time, flux, consciousness, and destiny; transformations, the fourth part of the methodology, have to do with dialectics, change, the will, and redemption, with the whole coercive, transformational, and creative powers of language. One can say that in Burke language makes transformations possible because of its abstracting, fiction-making properties. Myths, vision, and systems are made of words, and they do not imitate any existing reality but create a new one.[15] Transformations are brought about by the dialectical, rhetorical, and symbolic actions of language, so that it is accurate here to speak of dialectical structure, the rhetoric of rebirth, the dialectics of transformation, and the dialectics of the abyss. As usual, in Burke, there is a hierarchic schematization that includes movement upward toward "heaven" and movement downward toward "hell." These two represent, abstractly and schematically, the two extreme possibilities within any hierarchy. Whitman is our master of the dialectics of transformation upward; and as the German critic Gunter Blöcker has brilliantly pointed out, Faulkner, that great American explorer of "hell," is a master of the dialectics of the abyss.[16]

5

The connections between Burke's methodology, the four structural and symbolic centers, the functional theory of language as symbolic action, and the critics of the Geneva school can best be made here in a series of summarizing, somewhat gnomic statements:

> Language is a symbolic action of the self.
>
> Literature is an act of language by the self.
>
> Language and literature are symbolic actions which the self adds to nature and by means of which the self creates a kind of empty symbolic space in a verbal time continuum.
>
> Man lives a large part of his symbolic life in this space of words.
>
> In fact, it is now more true to say that man imitates words than to say that words imitate nature.
>
> Verbal space is essentially symbolic rather than mimetic because language is essentially abstracting rather than representational.
>
> Man is genuinely creative in his symbolic verbal life because invention is a function of words.
>
> Fiction and myth making, system and vision building are all functions of the abstractive and symbolic powers of language, which are themselves actions of the self and originate in the imagination.
>
> Nature is ordered, but all verbal works create and then exist in a new symbolic order which man adds to nature as a fifth dimension.
>
> This fifth dimension is empty symbolic space.
>
> Man can discover, he can even alter, the natural order, but man creates his verbal orders continuously out of himself in an organic

human process which follows logo-logical rather than biological laws.

Language adds freedom to the necessities of nature and offers man the choice of many symbolic parents in addition to his unchosen biologic parents.

Literature can no more be separated from man's life than language can; literature is an act of language and without language man would not even have the freedom to be.

Systematic methodology is a true necessity because it is the only way for many of us to experience the generative and regenerative function of symbolic action; systematic methodology is the critic's way toward the poetics of vision.

Vision is the release into pure being.

Somewhere in a phenomenology of the structures of language, the self, and vision everything begins.

In the commitment to this new genesis, Burke and the Geneva critics meet, and recognize each other.

Notes

This essay was originally delivered as a talk at the 1967 Modern Language Association meeting and was later published as "Kenneth Burke and Structuralism" in *Shenandoah* 21 (Autumn 1969): 19–28. I wrote the talk assuming that I would be addressing experts in literary theory; for this reason, the talk is very condensed, extremely abstract, and almost completely without examples. Having been cast in this style and form, it now seems to me impossible that it should be rewritten in another way, though I have added notes in an attempt to identify and clarify some of the many references in the text. I gave it the original title because it seemed at the time that the Geneva School was continuous with early structuralism. Clearly that was not the case; I have thus given the essay a new, narrower title that more accurately reflects its focus and have revised it extensively with the help of Cary Nelson.

1. The reference is to an article by J. Hillis Miller entitled "The Geneva School," which treats the criticism of Marcel Raymond, Albert Béguin, George Poulet, Jean Rousset, Jean-Pierre Richard, and Jean Strarobinski.

2. See *Kenneth Burke and the Drama of Human Relations* (Minneapolis: University of Minnesota Press, 1963).

3. I have not tried to do here what I did in my book on Burke: present an objective and coherent exposition of Burke's theories and practices. I have deliberately tried to combine Burke's ideas with those of others to form a new synthesis. The metaphor of space I have used throughout is not from Burke at all, but comes from my reading of Gaston Bachelard, Norman O. Brown, and J. Hillis Miller. I have also used Maurice Blanchot's *L'espace littéraire* (Paris: Gallimard, 1955).

4. See Roland Barthes, *Critique et vérité* (Paris: Editions du Seuil, 1966). I have used this marvelous essay throughout the essay. I have also drawn upon his *Sur Racine* and *Essais critiques.*

5. Most of the points made in this paragraph are drawn more or less indiscriminately from the works by Barthes cited above and from his *Elements of Semiology* (London: Jonathan Cape, 1967); from Gaston Bachelard, *The Poetics of Space* (New York: Orion Press, 1964), and *The Psychoanalysis of Fire* (Boston: Beacon Press, 1964); from Norman O. Brown, *Love's Body* (New York: Random House, 1966); from I. A. Richards, *Coleridge on Imagination* (New York: Harcourt Brace, 1935); from Northrop Frye, *Anatomy of Criticism* (Princeton: Princeton University Press, 1957); from Burke everywhere, but especially *The Rhetoric of Religion;* from J. Hillis Miller, *Poets of Reality* (Cambridge, Mass.: Harvard University Press, 1965) and from various articles in "Structuralism," *Yale French Studies* 36–37 (October 1966).

6. The exposition that follows is a radical condensation of chapters 4 and 5 of my book on Burke.

7. See Frye, *Anatomy of Criticism.*

8. See Susanne Langer, *Feeling and Form* (New York: Charles Scribner's Sons, 1953).

9. I apologize for this awkward, cacophonous term, but I have not been able to find or invent any other that does what this monster does.

10. The exposition that follows is true to Burke, even though some of the key terms are drawn from J. Hillis Miller's stunning essay on William Carlos Williams, which appears as the introduction to *William Carlos Williams: A Collection of Critical Essays,* ed. J. Hillis Miller (Englewood Cliffs, N.J.: Prentice-Hall, 1966), 1–14. Burke has worked out versions of this analytic journey with great thoroughness in such essays as "Fact, Inference, and Proof in the Analysis of Literary Symbolism," and "*Othello:* An Essay to Illustrate a Method," both of which may be found in Kenneth Burke, *Perspective by Incongruity and Terms for Order,* ed. Stanley Edgar Hyman and Barbara Karmiller (Bloomington: Indiana University Press, 1964).

11. According to those who know more about transformational linguistics than I do, I have not abused the term *transform* by using it as I do here. The whole drive of Burke's system is toward "dramatistic" equivalents of "transforms." Again, though this term is not Burke's, the idea conveyed by it is true of Burke. As I have done throughout the essay, I here borrow a term from one system (as Burke himself did all through the thirties) and use it to describe something in another system.

I mean this to be more than a mechanical device whereby one can relate one system to another. One of the lessons of doing a paper such as this one is to learn just how profound some of the similarities are between apparently different systems.

12. Long after I had finished this essay, I discovered that the phrasing of this point is almost word for word out of Frye's *Anatomy.* When I wrote the sentence, I was only conscious of working a variation on T. S. Eliot's line in "Burnt Norton."

13. The works of Burke and Frye are full of such ultimate moments, both of the kind that come at the end of a long, specific analysis and of the kind that come at the end of a long theoretical sequence. Frye and Burke—along with people such as Norman O. Brown and Gaston Bachelard—are visionaries of a very high order and their works are punctuated by these epiphanies from (into) the pure poetics of vision. One of the characteristic developments of criticism in our time is that it has become more and more visionary and is often an instrument of vision.

14. Burke has not yet published his poetics, or, as it will be called, his "Symbolic of Motives"; nor has he ever collected in one book all of the many published (and unpublished) essays that bear upon this subject. It is difficult, then, to refer to one place where this methodology may be studied. I have discussed the methodology at length in chapters 3 and 5 of my book on Burke; I will also cite here a few of the more recent essays in which the methodology can be observed and studied: the two essays cited in note 10; "The First Three Chapters of *Genesis,*" in *The Rhetoric of Religion* (Boston: Beacon Press, 1961), 172–272; "Policy Made Personal: Whitman's Verse and Prose-Salient Traits," in *Leaves of Grass One Hundred Years After,* ed. Milton Hindus (Stanford: Stanford University Press, 1955), 74–108; "Goethe's *Faust,* Part 1," in *Language as Symbolic Action* (Berkeley: University of California Press, 1966), 139–62; and "The Language of Poetry 'Dramatistically' Considered," *Chicago Review* 8 (Fall 1954): 88–102, 9 (Spring 1955): 40–72.

15. Anyone familiar with Gaston Bachelard's *The Poetics of Space* will recognize the extent to which I have drawn upon that remarkable book—here and elsewhere in this essay. One of the pleasures of writing this essay was to discover the many points of convergence between such apparently disparate thinkers as Burke, Bachelard, Frye, Barthes, Lévi-Strauss, Norman O. Brown, and J. Hillis Miller.

16. See Gunter Blöcker, "William Faulkner," in *Faulkner: A Collection of Critical Essays,* ed. Robert Penn Warren (Englewood Cliffs, N.J.: Prentice-Hall, 1966), 122–26.

Appendix

· · ·

Inaugural Address of John F. Kennedy

Vice President Johnson, Mr. Speaker, Mr. Chief Justice, President Eisenhower, Vice President Nixon, Reverend Clergy, Fellow Citizens, We observe today not a victory of party but a celebration of freedom—symbolizing an end as well as a beginning—signifying renewal as well as change. For I have sworn before you and Almighty God the same solemn oath our forebears prescribed nearly a century and three quarters ago.

The world is very different now. For man holds in his mortal hands the power to abolish all forms of human poverty and all forms of human life. And yet the same revolutionary beliefs for which our forebears fought are still at issue around the globe—the belief that the rights of man come not from the generosity of the state but from the hand of God.

We dare not forget today that we are the heirs of that first revolution. Let the word go forth from this time and place, to friend and foe alike, that the torch has been passed to a new generation of Americans—born in this century, tempered by war, disciplined by a hard and bitter peace, proud of our ancient heritage—and unwilling to witness or permit the slow undoing of those human rights to which this nation has always been committed, and to which we are committed today at home and around the world.

Let every nation know, whether it wishes us well or ill, that we shall pay any price, bear any burden, meet any hardship, support any friend, oppose any foe to assure the survival and the success of liberty.

This much we pledge—and more.

To those old allies whose cultural and spiritual origins we share, we pledge the loyalty of faithful friends. United, there is little we cannot do in a host of cooperative ventures. Divided, there is little we can do—for we dare not meet a powerful challenge at odds and split asunder.

To those new states whom we welcome to the ranks of the free, we pledge our word that one form of colonial control shall not have passed away merely to be replaced by a far more iron tyranny. We shall not always expect to find them supporting our view. But we shall always hope to find them strongly supporting their own freedom—and to remember that, in the past, those who foolishly sought power by riding the back of the tiger ended up inside.

To those people in the huts and villages of half the globe struggling to break the bonds of mass misery, we pledge our best efforts to help them help themselves, for whatever period is required—not because the communists may be doing it, not because we seek their votes, but because it is right. If a free society cannot help the many who are poor, it cannot save the few who are rich.

To our sister republics south of our border, we offer a special pledge—to convert our good words into good deeds—in a new alliance for progress—to assist free men and free governments in casting off the chains of poverty. But this peaceful revolution of hope cannot become the prey of hostile powers. Let all our neighbors know that we shall join with them to oppose aggression or subversion anywhere in the Americas. And let every other power know that this Hemisphere intends to remain the master of its own house.

To that world assembly of sovereign states, the United Nations, our last best hope in an age where the instruments of war have far outpaced the instruments of peace, we renew our pledge of support—to prevent it from becoming merely a forum for invective—to strengthen its shield of the new and the weak—and to enlarge the area in which its writ may run.

Finally, to those nations who would make themselves our adversary, we offer not a pledge but a request: that both sides begin anew the quest for peace, before the dark powers of destruction unleashed by science engulf all humanity in planned or accidental self-destruction.

We dare not tempt them with weakness. For only when our arms are sufficient beyond doubt can we be certain beyond doubt that they will never be employed.

But neither can two great and powerful groups of nations take comfort from our present course—both sides overburdened by the cost of modern weapons, both rightly alarmed by the steady spread of the deadly atom, yet both racing to alter that uncertain balance of terror that stays the hand of mankind's final war.

So let us begin anew—remembering on both sides that civility is not a sign of weakness, and sincerity is always subject to proof. *Let us never negotiate out of fear. But let us never fear to negotiate.*

Let both sides explore what problems unite us instead of belaboring those problems which divide us.

Let both sides, for the first time, formulate serious and precise proposals for the inspection and control of arms—and bring the absolute power to destroy other nations under the absolute control of all nations.

Let both sides seek to invoke the wonders of science instead of its terrors. Together let us explore the stars, conquer the deserts, eradicate disease, tap the ocean depths and encourage the arts and commerce.

Let both sides unite to heed in all corners of the earth the command of Isaiah—to "undo the heavy burdens . . . (and) let the oppressed go free."

And if a beachhead of cooperation may push back the jungle of suspicion, let both sides join in creating a new endeavor, not a new balance of power, but a new world of law, where the strong are just and the weak secure and the peace preserved.

And this will not be finished in the first one hundred days. Nor will it be finished in the first one thousand days, nor in the life of this Administration, nor even perhaps in our lifetime on this planet. But let us begin.

In your hands, my fellow citizens, more than mine, will rest the final success of failure of our course. Since this country was founded, each generation of Americans has been summoned to give testimony to its national loyalty. The graves of young Americans who answered the call to service surround the globe.

Now the trumpet summons us again—not as a call to bear arms, though arms we need—not as a call to battle, though embattled we are—but a call to bear the burden of a long twilight struggle, year in and year out, "rejoicing in hope, patient in tribulation"—a struggle against the common enemies of man: tyranny, poverty, disease and war itself.

Can we forge against these enemies a grand and global alliance, North and South, East and West, that can assure a more fruitful life for all mankind? Will you join in that historic effort?

In the long history of the world, only a few generations have been granted the role of defending freedom in its hour of maximum danger.

I do not shrink from this responsibility—I welcome it. I do not believe that any of us would exchange places with any other people or any other generation. The energy, the faith, the devotion which we bring to this endeavor will light our country and all who serve it—and the glow from that fire can truly light the world.

And so, my fellow Americans: ask not what your country can do for you—ask what you can do for your country.

My fellow citizens of the world: ask not what America will do for you, but what together we can do for the freedom of man.

Finally, whether you are citizens of America or citizens of the world, ask of us here the same high standards of strength and sacrifice which we ask of you. With a good conscience our only sure reward, with history the final judge of our deeds, let us go forth to lead the land we love, asking His blessing and His help, but knowing that here on earth God's work must truly be our own.

Index

William H. Rueckert is professor emeritus of English at the State University of New York at Geneseo. He has also taught at the University of Rochester and the University of Illinois at Urbana-Champaign. He is the author of *Kenneth Burke and the Drama of Human Relations*, *Glenway Wescott*, and the editor of *Critical Responses to Kenneth Burke, 1924–1966*. He was the first president of the Kenneth Burke Society from 1990 to 1992 and is the author of numerous essays on American criticism and culture.